FIGURATIVE POETRY IN SANSKRIT LITERATURE

FIGURATIVE POETRY IN SANSKRIT LITERATURE

KALANATH JHA, M. A., Ph. D.
Department of Sanskrit
Bhagalpur University, Bhagalpur

MOTILAL BANARSIDASS
DELHI :: VARANASI :: PATNA

Indological Publishers and Booksellers
Head Office : BUNGALOW ROAD, JAWAHARNAGAR, DELHI-7
Branches : 1. CHOWK, VARANASI (U.P.)
2. ASHOK RAJ PATH (OPP. PATNA COLLEGE),
PATNA-4 (BIHAR)

ISBN O 8426 0819 2

First Edition : Delhi, 1975
Price : MLBD ₹350.00

Printed in India

BY SHANTILAL JAIN, AT SHRI JAINENDRA PRESS BUNGALOW ROAD, JAWAHARNAGAR, DELHI-7, AND PUBLISHED BY SUNDARLAL JAIN FOR MOTILAL BANARSIDASS, BUNGALOW ROAD, JAWAHARNAGAR, DELHI-7

CONTENTS

PREFACE

'Citrakāvya' or 'Figurative poetry', in classical view, consists of the figures of speech and in the western-oriented present view taken, it is pictorial or imagist. Citrakāvya is figurative also because in the form of Bandhas etc. in Śabdacitra, it is expressed through figures or designs.

The concept of figurative poetry in Sanskrit literature, which I have moulded from scanty materials available here and there is comparatively a new one. The seed of the concept undoubtedly lies in the Dhvanyāloka of Ānandavardhana. It got some sprouting in the Locana of Abhinavagupta and Rasagaṅgādhara of Paṇḍitarāja Jagannātha, but its further development stopped. Thus the tender sapling of figurative poetry withered. On the contrary, in western literature this movement grew into a vigorous force in the shape of imagist poetry.

This work presents an attempt to put the figurative development of Sanskrit literature on the foothold of imagist poetry and should be viewed in this perspective. Again though only Arthacitra has the real imagist value and character, I have undertaken study of Śabdacitra and Ubhayacitra as well to bring to bear upon all the highways and byways of the development. Arthacitra, thus, has in its embryo the image of sense in its western parlance. Ordinarily, in our own classical view, it means only the peculiarity in meaning.

Based chiefly on the figures of similitude, in this background, Arthacitra would visualise production of image from reflection of the matter in hand in the standard of similitude. The image thus produced will emerge on the canvass of our mind. Its value will be determined by the measuring degree of its emotive character, as only the emotive images are the most natural, effective, and hence superb.

In Sanskrit rhetorics, suggestive poetry is the best but in western poetics imagist or pictorial poetry occupies this place. Naturally, the question whether suggestive poetry is imagist and vice-versa is relevant. In fact, suggestiveness and imagery are no bar to each other. Thus the assertion of Sanskrit rhetoricians that Citra variety of poetry is non-suggestive and hence of lowest order is far from truth. This poetry can often be of the highest order and this is proved beyond dispute in the present book.

Of necessity, in conformity with the principles of literature underlying the shift of value from suggestive to an imagist one, I had to redefine poetry in general and then to assess the place of figurative poetry in it. Other divisions and sub-divisions of poetry and their allied concepts have been dealt with in the new light. The chapter on the history of Citrakāvya consists, largely, of the historical development of figurative poetry based on Śabdacitra and Ubhayacitra.

For keeping the idea of Citra at par with that of image, I have drawn profusely upon the works of western critics, especially C. D. Lewis, to whom I acknowledge a debt of gratitude. Of the Indian critics of thought, Kṛṣṇa Caitanya has, perhaps, influenced me most. Also, my thanks are due to all those ancient and modern authors whose works I have profitably consulted. Here I beg pardon of the Ṛṣis of Sanskrit Rhetorics for my forthright expressions especially for the new concepts which I have introduced not out of vanity or vindication but for the convenience of accommodation.

Lastly, I must remember Dr. Satyavrata Singh, formerly University Professor & Head of the Deptt. of Sanskrit, Lucknow University, who gave me this topic, and my guru and guide Dr. B. Jha, University Professor & Head of the Deptt. of Sanskrit, Patna University, for his numerous valuable suggestions. I cannot also forget M/S Motilal Banarsidass who ultimately completed the onerous task of publication.

ABBREVIATIONS

AV	*Atharvaveda*, ed. R. C. Sharma, Muradabad, 1929.
AB	*Aitareya Brāhmaṇa*, Ānandāśrama Sanskrit Series.
AR	*Alaṅkāraratnākara* of Śobhākaramitra, ed. C.R. Devadhar, Poona, 1942.
AS	*Alaṁkārasarvasva* of Ruyyaka, ed. G.P. Dwivedī, Bombay, KMS, 1939.
V-AS	*Alaṁkārasarvasva* with *Vimarśinī* of Jayaratha.
AŚ	*Alaṅkāraśekhara* of Keśavamiśra, ed. A.R. Shāstrī, Benaras, CSS, 1927.
AK	*Amarakośa* ed. H.G. Shāstrī, CSS, 1957.
AA	*Artists on Art*, Pantheon Books, 1945.
B-DAP	E. Bullough : *Distance as an aesthetic principle*, The British Journal of Psychology, Vol. V.
B-PD	E. Bullough : *Psychical Distance* Aesthetics ed. Elizabeth M. Wilkinson, Bowes & Bowes, 1957.
B-RC	Bain : *Rhetoric and Composition* I.
B-HS	C.M. Bowra : *The Heritage of Symbolism*. Macmillan & Co. Ltd., London, 1959.
B-OC	Baudelairé : *Oeuvres Completes*, ed. by Y. G. le Dantee, Gallimard, 1951.
BP	*Bhāgvatapurāṇa*; ed. by Mūlacand Tulasīdās Telīwālā, Nirṇayasāgar, Saṁvat 1985.
BK	Bhāmaha's *Kāvyālaṁkāra*, ed. by D. N. Sharmā, Patna.
B-VP	Bhartṛhari's *Vākyapadīya* ; ed. by Subramania Iyer.

CL	*Candrāloka* of Jayadeva, CSS, 1950.
CM	*Citramīmāṁsā* of Appaya Dīkṣita, ed. by K.P. Śukla, Vāṇī Vihāra, 1965.
CMK	—with *Khaṇḍana* of Jagannātha.
C-A	Benedetto Croce : *Aesthetic*, translated by Douglas Ainelie, Vision Press, Peter Owen, London.
C-CO	Jean Cocteau : *A call to Order*, trans. Rollo H. Myers, London, 1936.
C-PP	Paul Claudel : *Positions et Propositions* Vol. I, Gallimard, 1928.
D-KB	*Kāvya Kī Bhūmikā*, Dinkar, Patna, 1958.
DL	*Dhvanyāloka* of Ānandavardhana, ed. M. Shāstrī, KSS, 1940.
L-DL	*Dhvanyāloka* with *Locana* of Abhinavagupta.
B-DL	*Dhvanyāloka* with *Bālapriyā* Comm.
D-KM	*Kuṭṭanīmata* of Dāmodaragupta, ed. by N. Caturvedī, Mitra Prakāshan Ltd., Allahabad.
EV	*Ekāvalī* of Vidyādhara, ed. K. P. Trivedī BSS, 1903.
ECAJ	*An Exposition of the Citramīmāṁsā of Appaya Dīkṣita and its Appraisal of Jagannātha's criticism* : A thesis by Dr. M. Jhā.
E-MP	T. S. Eliot : *The Music of Poetry*, Jackson, 1942.
E-FS Tr. L	S. Eisenstein : *Film Sense* (Faber), trans. Jay Leyda.
F-LLC	Flaubert : *Letter to Louise Colet*, 1853, Correspondence Vol. II.
HV	*Hayagrīvavadha*.
H-KN	*Kāvyānuśāsana* of Hemacandra, ed. R.C. Parikh Bombay, 1938.
HK	*Hindī sāhitya Mén Kāvyarūpōn ké Prayoga* by Dr. S. D. Avatare, Rajpal and Sons, Delhi, 1962.
H-CEL	Herbert Read : *Collected Essays in Literary Criticism*, Faber, 1909.

H-VM	Henri Mondor : *Vie de Mallarmé*, Gallimard, 1941.
IS	*Īśopaniṣad.* The works of Śaṅkarācārya series.
J-MS	Dr. Jung : *Modern Man in search of a soul.*
KD	*Kāvyādarśa of Daṇḍin*, ed. by B.D. Caṭṭopādhyāya, Calcutta 1803 Saka.
KD with MP	*Kāvyādarśa* with *Mālinya-Proñchanī* of Premacandra Tarkavāgīśa.
KP[1]	*Kāvyaprakāśa* of Mammaṭa, ed. M.C. Nyāyaratna, Calcutta, 1886.
KP[2]	*Kāvyaprakāśa* with *Udyota* of Nāgeśa Bhaṭṭa, edited by Sukthankar, Karṇātak Publishing House, Bombay, 1941.
KP[3]	*Kāvyaprakāśa* with *Pradīpa* of Govinda Ṭhakkura, edited by K. P. Parab, Bombay, KMS, 1891.
P-KP[3]	*Kāvyaprakāśa* with *Prabhā* of Baidyanāth Tatsat on it.
KN	*Kuvalayānanda* of Appaya Dīkṣit, ed. by Dr. B.S. Vyāsa (CSS, 1956).
R-KN	*Kuvalayānanda* with *Rasikarañjanī* of Gaṅgādhara Vājpeyin.
A-KN	*Kuvalayānanda* with *Alaṁkāracandrikā* of Baidyanāth Tatsat.
KSS	*Kāvyālaṁkārasārasaṁgraha* of Udbhaṭa, ed. by K.S.R. Shāstrī, Poona, GOS, 1931.
KSV	*Kāvyālaṁkārasūtravṛtti* of Vāmana, Vāṇīvilāsa Press, 1909.
K-AK	Kavikarṇapūra's *Alaṁkārakaustubha.*
KM	*Kāvyamīmāṁsā* of Rājaśekhara, ed. by M. Miśra Benaras, CSS, 1934.
KS	*Kumārasambhava*, ed. by N.R. Ācārya, Bombay, KMS, 1946.
KB	*Kādambarī* of Bāṇa, ed. by M.R. Kale, Bombay, 1903.
KV	*Kīcakavadha*, ed. by S.K. De, University of Dacca 1929.
KKA	*Kūṭakāvya* : Eka Adhyayana by Dr. R. Sharmā, National Publ. House, Delhi, 1963.

KK	*Kāvya aur Kalpanā* by R. K. Pāṇḍey.
KA	*Kāvya mén Abhivyañjanāvāda* by L.N. Sudhāṁśu, Bhāgalpur city.
KNPP : MKKS	Kāśī Nāgarī Pracāriṇī Patrikā 1962 : *Mahābhārata ke kucha kūṭasthala.*
K-SR	Kathleen Raine : *The symbol of the Rose*, published in the New York Times, Jan, 1952.
L-PI	C.D. Lewis : *The Poetic Image*, Jonathan Cape, London, 1947.
QAPP	Quoted, *Archetypal Patterns in Poetry* by Miss Maud Bodkin.
M-QW	Jaques, Maritan, quoted George Whalley.
M-OC	Stephane Mallarmé : *Oeuvres Complètes*, ed. by Henri Mondor and Jan Aubry. Gallimard, 1945.
M-CP	Stephane Mallarmé : *Crisis in Modern Poetry.*
M-CM	John Middleton Murry : *Countries of the Mind.*
M-W	C.E. Montague : *Words, words* published in the Bookman, April, 1929.
M-EE	J.S. Mill : *Early Essays* : *What is Poetry* ? George Boll & Sons, London, 1897.
MW-SED	Monier Williams : *Sanskrit English Dictionary.*
ML	*Mānasollāsa.*
MD	*Meghadūta* ed. by N. S. Khiste, KSS, 1931.
MB	*Mahābhārata* ed. by T.R. Krishṇācārya & T. R. Vyāsācarya, Bombay, 1907.
AP	*Ādiparvan.*
UP	*Udyoga Parvan.*
BP	*Bhīṣma Parvan.*
MK	*Muṇḍakopaniṣad* (The works of Śaṅkarācārya series).
NC	*Naiṣadhīyacarita* of Śrī Harṣa, ed. by V. S. Paṇśīkar, Bombay, KMS, 1933.
PY	*Pratāparudrīyayaśobhūṣaṇa* of Vidyānātha, ed. by K.P. Trivedī, BSS, 1909.
P-HSR	*Handbook to the study of Ṛgveda* with Sāyaṇa's preface by Peterson.

P-MB	*Mahābhāṣya* of Patañjali, ed. Bhārgava Shāstrī Jośī, Bombay, 1945.
PR	Pāñcarātra.
PM	Prescott : *The Poetic Mind.*
P-LQ	Paul Valéry : *Lettres a Quelques-uns.* Gallimard, 1952.
P-O	Paul Valéry : *Oeuvres* vol. I, ed. by Jean Hytier, Gallimard, 1957.
R-EMT	Bertrand Russel : *An Enquiry into Meaning and Truth.* George Allen & Unwin Ltd., London, 1961.
R-PLC	I. A. Richards : *The Principles of Literary Criticism,* Routledge & Kegan Paul, London, 1928.
R-SKB	Ratneshvara's comm. on *Sarasvatī-Kaṇṭhā-bharaṇa* Bhoja.
ṚV	*Ṛgveda Saṁhitā.* ed. by Max Müller, Oxford University Press, London, 1890.
RG	*Rasagaṅgādhara* of Jagannātha, ed. Durgā Pd., Bombay, 1939.
R-CNV	Ravigupta's *Candraprabhāvijayakāvya.*
RK	Rudraṭa's *Kāvyālaṁkāra,* ed. by S. Chowdhury, Vāsudeva Prakāshana, Delhi, 1965.
RV	*Raghuvaṁśa,* ed. by N. C. Vidyāratna, Calcutta.
RM	*Rasamīmāṁsā* : Rāmacandra Śukla; ed. by Viśvanāth Prasād Mishra, Kāśī Nāgarī Pracāriṇī Sabhā, Saṁvat 2017.
SD	*Sāhityadarpaṇa* of Viśvanātha, BSS, 1938.
L-SD	Sāhityadarpaṇa with *Locana* Comm.
V-SD	Sāhityadarpaṇa with *Vijñapriyā* Comm.
SKB	*Sarasvatīkaṇṭhābharaṇa* of Bhoja ed. by K.N. Sharmā & V. L. Paṇśīkar, Bombay, KMS, 1934.
SPB	*Śriṅgāraprakāśa* of Bhoja, Vol. II, Madras Govt. MSS.
ST[1]	*Sammohanatantra.*
ST[2]	*Sṛṅgāratilaka* of Rudrabhaṭṭa.
SRB	*Subhāṣitaratnabhāṇḍāgāra* ed. K.P. Parab, Bombay 1826 Śaka.

SP	*Sārṅgadharapaddhati* Vol. I (Text), ed. by K.P. Parab, BSS, XXXVII, 1888.
SM	*Sūktimuktāvali*, ed. by E. Krisṇamācārya, Baroda, GOS, 1938.
SV	*Śiśupālavadha* of Māgha, ed. Jīvānanda Vidyāsāgar, Calcutta, 1884.
SKD	*Śabdakalpadruma* compiled by Sri Rādhākānt Dev Bahādur, Motilal Banarasi Dass, 1961.
SAHṚD	*SAHṚDAYA*, Sanskrit Journal, Madras.
S-LPC	Shelley's *Literary and Philosophical Criticisms*, ed. by John Shawcross, London, 1909.
S-DP	Shelley : *A Defence of Poetry*.
S-CAP	L. A. G. Strong : *Commonsense About Poetry*, London, 1952.
SSMP	William Van O'Corner : *Sense and Sensibility in Modern Poetry*.
S-SI	Dr. Caroline Spurjeon : *Shakespeare's Imagery and what it tells us*, Cambridge Univ. Press, 1935.
VR	*Vālmiki Rāmāyaṇa*, ed. by T. T. Krishṇācārya, Bombay, 1911.
KK	*Kiṣkindhā Kāṇḍa* of Rāmāyaṇa.
UK	*Uttarakāṇḍa* of Rāmāyaṇa.
VD	*Viṣṇudharmottarapurāṇa*, ed. Dr. P. Sāh, Baroḍā, OGS, 1961.
V-KS	*Vātsyāyana Kāmasūtra*, ed. by G. D. Shastri, KSS, 1929.
VJ	*Vakroktijīvita* of Kuntaka, ed. by Dr. Nagendra, Ātmārām & Sons, Delhi, 1955.
VV	*Vṛttivārttika* of Appaya Dīkṣita.
VP	*Vācaspatyaṁ* (Lexicon).
VINS	A. A. Macdonell : *Vedic Index of Names and subjects*, vol. II.
W-SME	A. N. Whitehead : *Symbolism : Its Meaning and Effect*, London, 1928.
W-HIL	M. Winternitz : *A History of Indian Literature*, Vol. I, Calcutta University publication, 1927.
WM	Wilfred Meynell in his comment on Francis Thompson's *Sister Song*.

W-PP	George Whalley : *Poetic Process*, Routledge & Kegan Paul, 1953.
Y-R : CY	W. B. Yeats : *Reveries* : Over Childhood and Youth, Macmillan & Co. Ltd., 1917.
Y-NN	Yāska : *The Nighaṇṭu* : *The Nirukta*, ed. by L. Swaroopa, Punjab University Publication, 1927.
	MC=Māṇikyacandra A Commentator on *Sāhityadarpaṇa*.
	KMS=Kāvya Mālā Series.
	OGS=Oriental Gaikwad Series.
	BSS=Bombay Sanskrit Series.
	CSS=Chowkhambā Sanskrit Series.
	KSS=Kāśī Sanskrit Series.
	Illustr. V.=Illustrative Verse.

CHAPTER I

INTRODUCTION

Before giving my readers an idea of the concept of *Citrakāvya* in Sanskrit literature or what I feel about it, I may first define what poetry is and state the place of *Citrakāvya* in *Kāvya* or poetry in general. In fact, in Sanskrit literature, [1]the term *Kāvya* means 'the work or idea of a poet' and denotes prose as well as verse, or even a mixture of both (Campū). Naturally, *Citrakāvya* can find expression both in prose and verse or in the mixed genre. Now, [2]*Kāvya*, or poetry, as it may be broadly called, consists of meaningful words in the first instance. [3]In Sanskrit poetics, all words in relation to the meaning they convey are guided by the three powers of denotation (Abhidhā), indication (Lakṣaṇā) and suggestion (Vyañjanā). They might, we know, convey different meanings in different contexts, or all the three meanings, denotative, indicative and suggestive, simultaneously in the same context. Snatched out of context, they may never mean anything, but may always denote, indicate or suggest in association, implicit or explicit, in a specific syntactical order.

A word, first, gives its conventional sense through the power of denotation embedded in it, according to the *Naiyāyikas*, in consonance with the will of God. It is, actually, quite a different thing that technical words have their meanings ascertained and fixed by the experts. [4]The sense, thus denoted

1. Cf. EV I, p. 17 : Kavayata 'iti kavistasya karma bhāvo vā kāvyam/
2. Cf. BK I, V. 16, p 8. Śabdārthau sahitau kāvyam/
3. Cf. VV, p. 1 : Vṛttayaḥ kāvyasaraṇāvalaṅkāraprabandhṛbhiḥ/
Abhidhā lakṣaṇā vyaktiriti tisro nirūpitāḥ//
4. Cf. RG II, p. 175 : Śaktyākhyorthasya śabdagataḥ śabdasyārthagato vā sambandhaviśeṣobhidhā/

is called the expressed or the direct sense, because it happens to be the original meaning of a word. This power of expression is threefold : customary or conventional (Rūḍhi), etymological acceptation (Yoga), and etymologo-conventional signification (Yogarūḍhi). [1]The first is contained in the word whose meaning has been conventionally accepted, [2]the second is found where the meaning is understood with the help of the etymology, that is, the root part and suffix part of the word and [3]in the third, the power of expression, invested in the various parts of the word, is as much necessary as one compiled the whole. That is, in the last one, the etymological sense goes to strengthen the conventional sense.

But how does a word having multiple meanings give only one meaning in a particular context ? [4]As a matter of fact, there are certain factors like connection disjunction and association etc. which limit its connotation, to one specific meaning, especially in those cases in which the author, or speaker, wants to communicate only one sense. But a poet sometimes uses words with two or more meanings very often deliberately. When this is the case, either both the meanings are of equal importance and relevant to the matter in hand or they are irrelevant to it. The poet uses them as the standard of similitude pertaining to some other object of comparison, or, of the two, one is the thing compared and the other, the standard.

In the first two cases, there is no question of the validity of the operation of the power of denotation which rhetoricians ascribe to the operation of the double entendre. Regarding the third, *Abhinavagupta*, *Mammaṭa* and *Viśvanātha* opine that

1. Cf. VV, p. 1 : Akhaṇḍaśaktimātreṇaikārthapratipādakatvaṁ rūḍhiḥ/
2. Ibid, p. 2 : Avayavaśaktimātrasāpekṣaṁ padasyaikārthapratipādakatvaṁ yogaḥ/
3. Ibid, p. 2 : Avayavasamudāyobhayaśaktisāpekṣamekārthapratipādakatvaṁ yogarūḍhiḥ/
4. Vide VP, quoted KPI II p. 20 :

   Saṁyogo viprayogaśca sāhacaryaṁ virodhitā/
   Arthaḥ prakaraṇaṁ liṅgaṁ śabdasyānyasya sannidhiḥ//
   Sāmarthyamaucitī deśaḥ kālo vyaktiḥ svarādayaḥ/
   Śabdārthasyānavacchede viśeṣasmṛtihetavaḥ//

there, only the meaning relevant to the matter in hand is denotative and the power of denotation cannot operate in the other case. Thus the meaning is suggestive, not denotative. However, a group of rhetoricians, including *Appaya Dīkṣita*, do not subscribe to this view. They hold that under such cases, both the meanings are denotative, and only the figure, establishing between them the relationship of the thing compared and the standard, is suggestive. Normally, *Mammaṭa* and others repudiate the operation of double entendre, and see the possibility of suggestion, based on the signification of a word. However *Dīkṣita* accepts the operation of the figure double entendre. [1]In his view a punning word makes the meaning known, regardless of the subject, through the power of denotation. Further, he suggests that the intention of the old rhetoricians like *Mammaṭa*, is that always in such cases, there is only the suggestion of the figures of sense such as simile, metaphor etc. and they never mean that merely the power of suggestion operates.

With regard to the power of indication, we can say that it is almost an extended form of the power of denotation. [2]It occurs on the denotative sense being impeded. For instance, in the conventional example, 'The hamlet is situated on the Ganges', the denotative sense of the hamlet being situated on the streams of the Ganges, has no explicit meaning. But through the power of indication, the meaning is clarified that 'The hamlet is situated on the bank of the Ganges.' [3]It is first of two types : simple (Śuddhā) and one founded on some resemblance between the primary and secondary sense of a word (Gauṇī). [4]Then again, there are two kinds : one based on the conventional acceptation of meaning (Rūḍhi) and the other which acquires some meaning from outside (Prayojana).

1. Cf. VV, p. 13 : Tadrītyā na kathamcidapi prakaraṇāprakaraṇādiniyamanaṁ śakyaśaṅkaṁ/Tasmāt prastutāprastutobhayapare'pi prastutāprastutobhayavācyārthebhidhaiva vṛttiḥ/
2. Cf. KPI II, V. 9, p. 10 : Mukhyārthabādhe tadyoge rūḍhito'tha prayojanāt/
3. Cf. SD II, V. 14.
4. Ibid, V.9.

Another two : [1]a word used elliptically, besides retaining its own primary sense, conveys another (Upādāna); [2]and a word that sheds its own primary sense, but conveys some other(Lakṣaṇa). [3]Besides, each of these can be divided into one founded on the attribution of the nature or properties (Sāropā), and the other, based on the identification of two things in such a manner that the one is completely absorbed into the other (Sādhyavasānā). The meaning expressed through either of these ways, is called indicative.

But when the powers of denotation and indication fail, the power of suggestion comes into play. As with the power of indication there are again many divisions. [4]The first is when the denotative sense is not intended (Avivakṣitavācya) and this suggestion is founded on indication. The second is when the denotative sense, inherent in suggestion, is intended (Vivakṣitānyaparavācya), and this is based on the power of denotation. [5]The first is of two kinds : one where the denotative sense has continued into some other sense (Arthāntarasaṅkramita) and the other, where it has been completely disregarded (Atyantatiraskṛta). [6]The second also, is of two kinds : one where the process of transfer is not visible (Asaṁlakṣyakrama) and the other, where it is visible (Saṁlakṣyakrama). [7]The poetic emotion or sentiment is expressed within the first. [8]The latter has six divisions : arising of oneself (Svataḥsambhavī) or born of the perfect expression of a poet (Kaviprauḍhoktisiddha) and dependent on the perfect expression of a person speaking on behalf of the poet (Kavinibaddhavaktṛprauḍhoktisiddha). Each of these relates to the suggestion of some fact (Vastu), or some figure of speech (Alaṁkāra). In this limited way, the suggestive meaning, arising from the power of sense (Arthaśakti), multiplies to twelve.

1. Cf. SD II, V.10.
2. Ibid, V.11.
3. Ibid, V.12.
4. Ibid, IV, V.3.
5. Ibid, V.4.
6. Ibid, V.5.
7. Ibid, V.6.
8. Ibid, V.9.

These are the powers which ultimately invest strength in the words which form the poetic organism [1]and which are distinguished from ordinary speech (Vārtā). Among the western critics, [2]some have given precedence to the word or [3]to the sense, but indigenous writers have given equal treatment to both. [4]In fact, there cannot be any polarisation between meaning and word, content and form, because these dualities are apparent only by analytical dissection. In the actual poetic expression they are indissolubly united. Their unity is symbolised by [5]the idea of *Ardhanārīśvara*, or by [6]the 'celebration of the divine nuptials of sound and sense in poetry,' as Wilfred Meynell has called it.

Sanskrit poetics encompass the union of sound and meaning in poetry in terms of the organic, inseparable relation between the two, which implies that the functions of the components are simply complementary. [7]*Kuntaka* propounded that sound and sense should be such that they beautify each other. [8]*Kālidāsa* believed that both should be equally beautiful so that it be impossible to decide which enhances the other. The former expands the concept to cover the continuum represented by an extended poem. Thus, not only should there be

1. Cf. BK II, V.87, p. 63 :

    Gato'stamarko bhātīnduryānti vāsāya pakṣiṇaḥ/
    Ityevamādi kiṁ kāvyaṁ vārtāmenāṁ pracakṣate//

2. Vide H-VM, p. 684 : 'It is not with ideas that one makes sonnets but with words.'
   Cf. C-CO; p. 153 : 'It is not pathetic messages that make us shed our best tears but the miracle of a word in the right place.'
3. Vide F-LLC, p. 187 : 'No ! Form is the flesh itself of the idea, as the idea is the soul of life.'
   Cf. : N-MP, p. 13 : 'The music of poetry is not something which exists apart from its meaning.'
4. Vide B-OC, p. 1087 : 'The idea and form are two realities in one.'
5. Vide RV, I, V.1.
6. Vide WM.
7. Cf. VJI V.17, p. 60 : Sāhityamanayoḥ śobhāśālitāṁ prati kāpyasau/
8. Cf. KS I, V.42 :
   Kaṇṭhasya tasyāḥ stanabandhurasya muktākalāpasya ca nistalasya/
   Anyonyaśobhājananād babhūva sādhāraṇo bhūṣaṇabhūṣyabhāvaḥ//

this functional integration between the sound and meaning, but, in an extended poetic work, such an integration should exist between one word and another, and between one idea and another. When [1]*Abhinavagupta* interpreted poetic utterance as an ideal structure, he believed that the poetic intention could integrate both idea and expression without any compromise in favour of one or the other.

Therefore, poetry consists of tension generated and contained. It is noteworthy that [2]*Kuntaka* once defined literature as consisting of the mutual tension between word and meaning. He termed literature *Sāhitya* and enunciated the concept of the co-existence of sound and sense. This is, in fact, the basic trait of every literary expression. It means that the tension in poetry should be compatible with the basic harmony. That is, in literature one word should vie with the other, and one idea with another. So the poem, or, for that matter, literature generally, is fused out of the said tensions, into an integrated and tranquil whole. Therefore, the form is functional and organic. [3]*Vāmana*, on the other hand, thinks that the insertion and deletion of words occurs only when there is uncertainty of mind. When the poet decides on his choice of vocabulary, the composition is perfected. He goes on to say that the verbalisation is perfected when the words, functionally and poetically, cannot be replaced to advantage by any synonyms. [4]According to *Bhoja*, even the ideas should be irreplaceable, if the poetic sense is not to be destroyed or radically altered.

[5]This brings to mind the concept of *Śayyā* with which the conception of the perfection of both word and meaning, is related in Sanskrit poetics. This, in poetic theory, means the apposite use of words in conjunction. In the final analysis, when the perfection is ideal, the literary value of *Śayyā* is

1. Cf. L-DL, p. 27 : Vakroktiḥ utkṛṣṭā saṁghaṭanā.../
2. Cf. VJI, V-17, p. 60 : Anyūnānatiriktatvamanohāriṇyavasthitiḥ//
3. Cf. KSV, 1.3.15, p. 32.
4. Cf SP, p. 18.
5. Cf. KS, Intro. V.8, p. 4.

realised where meaning is inherent in the words, and where each word, in turn, is integrated into the whole. Thus, without any qualifying clauses, the words and the meanings have appropriate powers of denotation, indication and suggestion at the right places. They are fused into the poetic organism, or the body of the poetry. Thus the words and the sense should have all the qualities enunciated in the works on poetics, in relation to a particular style.

The position regarding the faults, the figures and the evolution of the poetic sentiment is not clear. The rhetoricians generally say that *Citrakāvya* is non-suggestive and from this standpoint, it should have no relation to the above. Therefore, *Viśvanātha* kept this style of poetry apart. To suit our purpose, [1]we shall take up the definition of poetry given by *Mammaṭa*. He has placed *Citra* style of poetry in the last category due to its non-suggestive character. Although he states that the poetic organism should be free of faults, [2]rhetoricians suggest that this complete freedom is but the ideal and is not always possible, although errors should be minimized. So certain faults, such as abstruseness etc., especially in *Śabdacitra*, do not debar *Citrakāvya* from the realm of poetry. So far as *Arthacitra* is concerned in the sense we take it, it should be free from blemishes which may hinder the emotive imagery.

As regards figures of speech, *Rasavādī* rhetoricians like [3]*Viśvanātha* have relegated them to a secondary position and have held that they are not indispensable for the creation of charm in poetry. [4]Therefore *Mammaṭa* pleads that sometimes, poetry should exist even without such figures. This does not give premium to our position. We know that *Citrakāvya* is constituted of figures, *Śabdacitra* of the figures of sound,

1. Cf. KPI I, V.4, p. 3 :
   Tadadoṣau śabdārthau saguṇāvanalaṁkṛtī punaḥ kvāpi/
2. Cf. SD I, p. 10 :
   Kiṁcaivaṁ kāvyaṁ praviralaviṣayaṁ nirviṣayaṁ vā syāt sarvathā nirdoṣasyaikāntamasambhavāt/
3. Ibid X, p. 478 :
   Asthirā iti naiṣāṁ guṇavadāvaśyakī sthitiḥ/
4. Vide Fn. No. I above.

Ubhayacitra of those bordering on sound and sense, and *Artha-citra* of sense only. As a matter of fact, even where there is no figure, there is an image, and in the highest sense if this image is poetic and emotive, as is expounded in detail later. Or, on the other hand, there may be some figure which is not readily perceivable. For instance, in the following verse, there is no apparent figure, but the charm is no less : [1]"As the pleasant breeze slowly stirs you, the cātaka bird, as though in tune with you, sings sweetly to your left. The she-cranes, as if in the sky to renew an aquaintance from the time of their gestation, hover above you, who are so beautiful to their eyes." It does give an image, an emotive image, though not based on similitude. I do not think that even the presence of the poetic naturalism (Svabhāvokti) can be denied here. There is some suggestion of personification in the verse, and the sympathetic induction in the relation of cloud and the she-cranes gives a new contour to the poetic beauty.

The poetic figures cannot be identified with images; they only generate the latter. They are the means to an end, not an end in themselves. Indeed, though these figures are not an integral part of poetry, their importance cannot be gainsaid. [2]Rhetoricians have likened these to such human ornaments as bracelets but they are not always so. The said ornaments can exist away from the body, but there are certain figures of sense which cannot be torn from the poetic context. They are intrinsically related to the poetic organism.

I differ from the generally accepted stand because of the view taken by *Viśvanātha*, a prominent protagonist of the *Rasa* theory. According to this, the figures subserve the poetic

1. Cf. MD I, V.9 :

   Mandaṁ mandaṁ nudati pavanaścānukūlo yathā tvāṁ
   Vāmaśchāyaṁ nadati madhuraṁ cātakaste sagandhaḥ/
   Garbhādhānakṣaṇaparicayānnūnamābaddhamālāḥ
   Seviṣyante nayanasubhagaṁ khe bhavantaṁ balākāḥ//

2. Vide DL II, V.6, p. 204 :

   Aṅgāśritāstvalaṁkārā mantavyāḥ kaṭakādivat/

   Cf. SD X, V.1, p. 477 : Rasādīnupakurvanto'laṁkārāste'ṅgadādivat/

   Cf. CL V, V.1, p. 90 :

   Śabdārthayoḥ prasiddhyā vā kaveḥ prauḍhivaśena vā/
   Hārādivadalaṁkārasaṁniveśo manoharaḥ//

emotion or sentiment. The sentiment exists in the poetic organism, consisting of words and meanings, and the elements instrumental in the evocation of the sentiment are complementary to the beauty of the sound and sense. Thus, while the figures are subservient to the poetic emotion, how can it be said that they are the material and external cause of the poetic beauty ? According to this view, on the one hand, they would feed the poetic beauty, but on the other, merely properties of word and meaning. Where the beauty is engendered in poetry because of the configuration of word and sense, the poetry will lose much of its charm in form and content, if we attempt to do away with the pictorial effects of the figures. [1]*Ānanda*, perhaps, with a view to this, propounds that in the matter of suggestion of the sentiment, the figures of speech will not be considered an extraneous aspect of poetry. Basically, the point is, that when poetic form is dependent upon figures of speech, the evocation of the poetic emotion or sentiment can be achieved in an organic fashion. The relation between the two is not such that they can be picked up separately, or be segregated.

[2]Croce has discussed in a subtle way, both these aspects of a poetic figure. First, he poses a question as to how an ornament, or the figure, can be joined to an expression. If it is joined externally, then, it must remain a separate entity. On the contrary, if it is done internally, then, either it mars the expression, or it does form part of it and becomes a constituent element of the whole. The figures, in whatever form they come, always add intensity to the human emotion, and thus help in evolving the poetic sentiment.

But the figures are related to the denotational power of expression and [3]they constitute a mode of it. They fall within the jurisdiction of the denotative sense and not of the suggestive one, as will be clear later. When the denotative sense surpasses, or is at par with the suggestive, then the latter becomes secondary and the former primary. [4]*Ānanda* states

1. Vide DL II, p. 222 : Na teṣāṁ bahiraṅgatvaṁ rasābhivyaktau/
2. C-A IX, p. 69.
3. Vide DL III, p. 473 :
   Anantā hi vāgvikalpāstatprakārā eva cālaṁkārāḥ/
4. Ibid I, p. 114 :
   Cārutvotkarṣanibandhanā hi vācyavyaṅgyayoḥ prādhānyavivakṣā/

that it should be the poetic beauty which should ultimately determine the greater importance of the denotative or the suggestive sense. He differentiates between the embellisher and the embellished, between the figures and the sentiment, and this is the generally accepted view. But here too I differ. To my mind, the human emotion or sentiment embodied in poetry, is as intangible as the soul itself which, coincidentally, it has been called in relation to the body of poetry. It is as immutable and unaffected as the [1]unconscious which, in modern surrealist terminology, might be said to be [2]the breeding-ground of the best of literary creations, and is treated almost as the western counterpart of the Indian soul-concept.

In other words, figures increase the charm of the poetic organism, but not its actual soul, the poetic emotion or sentiment. However, these figures are an integral part of the denotative meaning and beauty of poetry. Rhetoricians accept the existence of the [3]poetic subversion (Vakrokti) or [4]the hyperbole (Atiśayokti) in almost all the figures and therefore it is not possible to regard an expression as the mere adornment of an idea. It is part of a unified whole. It is also alleged that at certain places in figurative works, everything is emotive and there is no external element, adding to the beauty of the poetry. This is not true. The sentiment of the poetry may, in fact, derive from certain figures of speech. Finally, if the existence of the figures be taken for granted for the generation of beauty in the denotative sense, then, as figures of speech themselves, they would become irrelevant. Thus, such expressions may be suggestive of the essence of poetry, but usually add to the beauty of the essence of denotative contents.

The figures are generally used for enhancing the poetic charm, as we have stated. This charm may relate to the emotions or to the expression. Therefore, the function of the figures is, on the one hand, to dress the thoughts and emotions

1. Vide L-PI, VI, p. 144.
2. Vide H-CEL, p. 30 : "The best specimens of literature only throw out vague suggestion, and their authors are not even aware of the nature of their work—they are hardly conscious artists."
3. Cf. BK I, V-36, p. 19 : Vakrābhidheyaśabdoktiriṣṭā vācāmalaṁkṛtiḥ/
4. Cf. KD II, V. 220, p. 223.

with beauty, and on the other, to render the expression candid and effective. [1]So they should be organised with regard to the relevant sentiment and emotion. Only in this way can they be effective. [2]Poets adept and accomplished in the portrayal of sentiments, are not concerned with figures of speech. Their effectiveness is spontaneous with the real poet. Only those figures which are revealed in a natural way, should be used.

[3]We have hinted that the figures are like the ornaments of thought as well as of language and if they justify this, they are the warp and woof of the work. Only then will they be able to make the language beautiful and thrilling, only then will they be capable of injecting life and power into the emotions. Otherwise, they will be laboured and the poetic composition will suffer. The emotions are more important than the expression and so, if the former be poor, then a beautiful mode of expression will not give validity to the composition. Therefore, the primary need is for a living, poetic organism.

But if the poetic sentiment is not the thing embellished, as we have propounded earlier, why may it not be taken as a figure ? Many rhetoricians of the *Alaṁkāra* School have taken this stand, chief among them being *Bhāmaha*, *Daṇḍin*, *Udbhaṭa* and *Vāgbhaṭa*. In the figures succulent (Rasavat), agreeable (Preyas), mighty (Ūrjasvin) and the composed (Samāhita), different feelings, emotions and sentiments, are made to function as figures. This situation arises when a particular poetic emotion might be subordinated to another. However, to me it appears that the realisation of sentiment is a different dimension of poetry, and the poetic sentiment or emotion has an absolute degree of prominence in relation to the other poetic concepts. In two poetic contexts, two separate sentiments might be inde-

1. Cf. DL II, p. 197 : Rasabhāvāditātparyamāśritya viniveśanaṁ/
   Alaṁkṛtīnāṁ sarvāsāmalaṁkāratvasādhanaṁ//
2. Ibid II, p. 291 : Alaṁkārāntarāṇi hi nirūpyamāṇadurghaṭānyapi rasasamāhitacetasaḥ pratibhānavataḥ Kaverahaṁpūrvikayā parāpatanti/
3. Vide Supra p. 10.

pendently prominent. So far as the aforesaid figures are concerned, they have, from this angle, only an element of sentiment, and they cannot be said to embody the sentiment proper. [1]Quite differently, *Udbhaṭa* thinks that the qualities and the figures both constitute the permanent properties of poetry. He has, in this connection, dubbed the ideas of those who say that qualities are inseparably related to poetry and the figures are incidental, as blind adherence to this point of view. According to him, the figures of sense, such as simile, metaphor etc., are as much inseparable from poetry as the qualities, such as sweetness, perspicuity, etc. Some modern rhetoricians, although they have accepted the difference of embellisher and embellished in the school of suggestion, do not conform to the view that the figures are not indispensable for poetry. [2]*Jaideva* criticizes the assertion of *Mammaṭa* that sometimes, poetry can exist even without figures, and goes on to state further, that the figures as much constitute the essential element of poetry as heat does of fire. From this point of view, the figures might be treated as creative of the poetic charm. [3]*Vāmana* holds a moderate view. To him the figures only enhance the beauty, they are not creative like the qualities inherent in it. The suggestionists, on the contrary, accept only the suggestion or the sentiment as such.

The figures have, moreover, almost an inseparable relation with imagination. In literature the former are complementary to the latter. No unit of thought is independent in itself. The imagination is its carrier. Therefore, the progress of our thoughts depends on that of the imagination. [4]The latter means, in the first instance, the production of vivid images, usually visual images. We sometimes feel the necessity of these images for the expression of our thoughts and emotions.

1. Quot. KPI VIII, p. 181 : Samavāyavṛtyā śauryādayaḥ saṁyogavṛttyā ca hārādayaḥ ityastu guṇālaṁkārāṇāṁ bhedaḥ/ Ojaḥprabhṛtīnāmanuprāsopamādīnāṁ cobhayeṣāmapi samavāyavṛttyā sthitiriti gaḍḍulikāpravāheṇaivaiṣāṁ bhedaḥ/
2. Cf. CL I, V. 8, p. 10. Aṅgīkaroti yaḥ kāvyaṁ śabdārthāvanalaṁkṛtī/
   Asau na manyate kasmādanuṣṇamanalaṁkṛtī//
3. Cf. KSV, 3.1.1—2, p. 69 : Kāvyaśobhāyāḥ kartāro dharmā guṇāh/ Tadatiśayahetavastvalaṁkārāḥ/
4. Vide R-PLC, XXXII, p. 239.

Imagination gives concrete form to the abstract, as the language of inner psychological thoughts. It also makes intelligible the superorganic elements by relating them to the sense-organs. When our thoughts, in moments of stress, flow towards the terra firma of unfamiliar and extraordinary emotions, then they have, of necessity, to be aided by the figures and the imagination.

The imagination, in a way, is the outcome of the emotions and therefore, regardless of logic, makes our expression powerful, profound, colourful and lucid. Consequently, without imagination, emotion cannot be fully verbalised. The mind of a poet is generally very pure and clear like that of the primordial man or of a child, and its thoughts and emotions have an imaginative quality. As we can know the subject-matter of a book by its illustrations and diagrams, so we can know the value of the content, by the imaginative expression. But the function of the imagination is also to arouse in the heart of the readers or auditors, a sense of fascination or repulsion towards the thought of a poet, for the materialisation of sympathetic induction.

[1]The similes and metaphors, among the figures, have separate categories, but an imaginative word-picture may analyse both. [2]The imagery, in fact, is like a small word-picture which the poet uses for the exposition of his thoughts and emotions in order to endow them with clarity and intelligibility. In the absence of such imaginative word-pictures, the emotions become invalid. Thus, we can say that imagination is a virtue which poetry cannot dispense with. Good poetry is often figurative and symbolical, and matter-of-fact expression cannot create good poetry. [3]Even C.D. Lewis, a prominent modern critic, gives great importance to the similes and metaphors used. In his opinion, to invest real beauty in the poetic composition, they must be both original and powerful.

It is these figures which make imaginative word-pictures conform to the actual universe, making them more vital. On the other hand, the imagination, when it seeks to create some

1. Vide M-CM, p. 4.
2. Vide S-SI, p. 9.
3. Vide L-PI, p. 18.

form, or portray some beauty, may utilise certain figures of speech, but only it can create the essence. It also heightens the poetic effect of newly found imageries. The figures and the imagination gain first familiarity in the poets' awakening, with the magic touch of the chords of feelings asleep in the heart. The aesthetics which dissect the formal properties of poetry, of proportion, symmetry, harmony and balance, are influenced, by the forces of imagination which create beauty and generate the readers' sympathy towards its understanding and experience.

The proper commixture of the various physical elements creates the universe, and the productive imagination, with the help of sensual concretisation, creates a novel and beautiful world. But imagination can organise or arrange for new images only where its expression be free from orthodox ideas. The poet must adopt some kind of medium for the successful expression of his experiences and thoughts, his hopes and fears, his pains and pleasures. On the whole, images constitute this medium. This, on the one hand, enlivens the expressions and sentiments, and on the other, limits them within certain boundaries. As a consequence of the inevitability of this medium, imagination takes up various designs and colours, like a rainbow. [1]As opposed to the imagination of a painter, which presents ocular, concretised images, that of a poet creates those both ocular and auricular.

With imagination creating beauty, the improbable, artificial form of a poem changes into a probable, natural one. [2]Much of the charm of imagination is squandered and lost in the use of similes, metaphors etc., effected only for their own sake, for figurative effect. But the same figures, as pointed out elsewhere, can create a greater intensity of effect, endurance and depth, when properly integrated with the imaginative process. The human mind is in the habit of linking the present with the past. Sometimes, it becomes overwhelmed with the recollection of certain past incidents or events. At that

1. Vide KK, p. 17.
2. Ibid, p. 19.

moment, it reaches out to the thoughts and emotions of the past, having completely forsaken the present, and then it experiences an undefinable sense of pleasure. This world of poetic joy is the harnessing ground of poetic sentiment. Psychologically, there is a deep relation between memory and recognition. When one looks to the past, the latter can become realised and can open up a vast vista of imagination.

Ocular and recollected images are generally taken to be the sources of the imaginative images. The latter gather materials for the process of their own creation, from what we have seen or heard in the past, or from the experience of the present. Thus, images endow shape and form to the nature of poetry, and in order to express the poignancy of a thing or idea, present its concrete form before us. Only if this image-creation depends on the allusion of some idea or emotion, and enhances beauty, sweetness, loveliness or brightness etc., will it be of use to poetry. If it relates only to length, breadth, shape or colour etc., then it will be not only futile, but also a positive handicap to the realisation of the poetic sentiment.

Therefore, the imagery of similitude, which awakens the emotions, is alone acceptable in a poem, and not that, which having generated some momentary beauty, becomes ineffective. Thus, being divorced of ocular imagery, the imaginative may create a charm, but it will always be incapable of giving concrete shape to any idea or effect. Poetry does not only give us a meaning, but also portrays the form of the subject-matter. This portrayal always relates to some particular individual or thing, and not anything in general. [1]Imagination is unable to present the concretised idea of any class. Indigenous poets have utilised imaginative image-creation for the sublimation of sentiments, and not for any extraneous effect. In the opinion of F.S. Flint, a lyric is the best medium for the concretisation of ideas or things. In longer poems, the unity, flow, and uniformity of idea and emotion is marred, and so one unitary form cannot arise. This in our own literature is quite commensurate with the stupendous success of *Kālidāsa's Meghadūta* as a small lyrical poem, concretising human emotions.

1. Cf. RM, p. 295.

In poetry, only such standards are taken to be effective and exciting as are in close proximity with our thoughts and emotions, and as have been familiar for some time. They are dependent on the similarity of form, of properties, and of the aggregate poetic effect. In the view of Croce, likeness (Sādṛśya) and the community of properties, (Sādharmya), may not be important from a rhetoric standpoint, but to us they constitute an important concept, because, if we brush them aside, there is nothing left in matter of image-creation. The imagination, to the extent it creates imagery with the help of emotion, is an inexhaustible treasure for poetry. But if it makes an alliance with logic, then it cannot create images and in that event, it will not form the subject of poetry. [1]Even in any of the various relations, the poetic sentiment is satiated with the attribution of the nature or properties of one thing to another, but the logic and thought will remain incomplete.

For resemblance of form in poetry, it is not necessary that there be complete identity in point of appearance or variety, or for likeness in properties of that there be complete similarity of virtues between the standard of comparison and the matter in hand. In poetry, similarity (Sādṛśya) is in the form of '*Bimbapratibimba*'—relation and community of properties (Sādharmya) by way of *Vastuprativastu*—relation which become helpful in the suggestion of sentiments. [2]Therefore, even if the emotions be perfectly sublimated, only at the allusion to this similarity, or the community of properties, will there be no need of their complete attribution.

In the light of the foregoing discussion, we shall look into the main divisions of poetry, and then try to evaluate the place of *Citrakāvya* therein. [3]The power of suggestion is thought to be the very lifeblood of poetry in Sanskrit literature, and so the positive presence or otherwise of it, is the chief determinant, according to Sanskrit rhetoricians, of the said varieties. [4]*Mammaṭa* and many of his ilk, classify poetry into

1. Cf. P-PM. p. 217.
2. Cf. KA, p. 97.
3. Vide Supra, p. 4.
4. Cf. KPI I, p. 4.

three main varieties : suggestive poetry (Dhvanikāvya), the poetry of subordinate suggestion (Guṇībhūtavyaṅgya), non-suggestive poetry (Citra). In the first, there is a predominance of suggestive sense, in the second it is only secondary, and in the third, according to them, there is no suggestive sense whatsoever, and the charm that it has is due to the peculiarity of word or meaning, or of both. This type of poetry, as they feel, is composed to give effect to that very peculiarity. In preferential order traditionally, the first division is the best, the second the second best and the third the worst.

[1]*Viśvanātha* actually accepts only two types, as he excludes the third because it is characterised by the absence of the sense of suggestion, and according to him, suggestion or poetic sentiment is the very soul of poetry. [2]*Jagannātha*, on the contrary, propounds four main types of poetry, to accommodate *Citra* in the poetry of subordinate suggestion (Guṇībhūta-vyaṅgya), and it is he who has salvaged *Citrakāvya* to some extent. His four types are : first, Uttamottama, second, uttama, third, Madhyama, and then Adhama. In the second and third varieties, he treats respectively the two divisions of the poetry of subordinate suggestion, that is, one where the suggestion is explicit (Jāgarūka), and the other where it is implicit (Ajāgarūka). In these two he finds scope for all poetry where the charm is generated chiefly because of the figures of sense. In the last category, he places the verbal peculiarity (Śabda-citra), which gives only intellectual delight and not emotional exhilaration.

When we talk of suggestive poetry, we do not seriously mean that the poetry be all suggestion and no denotation. [3]In this variety, the suggestive element surpasses the denotative one, either in volume or intensity, or in both. To take an example : [4]"The first rain-drops stayed for a moment on *Pārvatī*'s eyebrows, were whipped from her lower lip and

1. Vide SD IV, p. 191.
2. Vide RG, I, p. 11.
3. Cf. CM, p. 23 : Yatra vācyātiśāyi vyaṅgyaṁ sa dhvaniḥ/
4. Cf. KS V, V. 24, p. 79 :

splashed on to her breasts, and then trickled slowly threefold, to her navel."

Here the poet has described the course of the first rain-drops on *Pārvatī's* body. He has suggested its beauty, and has also indicated that she was in a meditative stance.

To be specific, the suggestion is made by the stay of the rain-drops on her eyebrows, of their density; by their stay only for a moment, of their softness; by their having been whipped from her lower lip, of its tenderness; by their splashing on to her breasts, of the latter's firmness; and through their termination in her navel, of its depth and capacity. In the phrase 'first rain-drops' the word 'first' suggests that the drops were few, but the plurality of the word 'rain-drops' denotes their capacity. Also, the delineation of the first rain-drops on *Pārvatī*'s body is suggestive of her erect position, and through it in turn, is made the suggestion of her meditative posture being unimpeded even with the falling of the first cool rain-drops giving relief from the prolonged and scorching summer.

Thus *Pārvatī*'s perfect meditative posture is suggested in the verse. The stay of the rain-drops on her brows, suggests that she was looking, with her eyes half-closed, towards the tip of her nose. Had her eyes been completely open or closed, then the tips of the brows would have been either upturned or downturned, and it would not have been possible for the water-drops to stay on her brows. It is also suggested that she had her mouth closed, for otherwise, as the drops fell from the eye-brows, they would have entered the mouth and would not have fallen downwards. Had she not been firmly erect in her meditative posture, the rain-drops would not have splashed directly from her lower-lip on to her breasts. Also, they would not have then trickled into her navel. Moreover, had the navel been fleshy, the rain-drops would not have terminated there. As the drops fell from brows to lower lip, and from the latter to the breasts, and from them to the navel, it sug-

Sthitāḥ kṣaṇaṁ pakṣmasu tāḍitādharāḥ
Payodharotsedhanipātacūrṇitāḥ/
Valīṣu tasyāḥ skhalitāḥ prapedire
Cireṇa nābhim prathamodabindavaḥ//

gests that she was motionless, or else the water-drops would not have fallen in that manner. Here it is clear that the suggestive sense excels the ordinary or the denotative sense.

With this background, let us take an example of the poetry of subordinate suggestion. [1]"'O beloved one, will you return at the end of a watch (i.e. a period roughly of three hours), or at midday, or in the afternoon, or in the evening ?' With streaming tears, the girl implores her lover not to journey to a place which takes hundred days to cover." It is suggested that the girl would be unable to endure a separation of more than a day. It is clear in the verse that if the lover goes, it will take him hundred days to reach the destination, but the deadline that the beloved sets, is the eventide. Without expressing her disapproval directly, she is suggesting it very clearly, whether innocently or intentionally. It is said that at the time of a person's departure, one should not call that person back. The suggestion here might be taken to be in conformity with this convention. The beloved's tears add to the first suggestion that she cannot bear to be parted for more than a day. This is also in consonance with the idea generally given vent to by poets, that it is in the atmosphere of the night that lovers feel most deeply their separation, as they might pass the day in varied preoccupations. The way the beloved gradually, though with growing disapproval, extends the deadline, shows her heart-breaking effort and courage. It also suggests that as time passes from a watch to midday, from midday to afternoon, and from afternoon to dusk, she would be experiencing an increasing degree and intensity of unhappiness.

The first deadline is the watch and it shows that she could easily pass the first three hours of separation. After that, she would lose patience with the passage of time, till evening, when even the patient has no patience, and she would die. The direct or the expressed sense, is the beloved's dissuasion

1. Cf. Praharaviratam madhye vāhnastato'pi pare'thavā
Kimuta sakale yāte vāhni priya tvamihaiṣyasi/
Iti dinaśataprāpyaṁ deśam priyasya yiyāsato
Harati gamanam bālā-lāpaiḥ savāṣpagalajjalaiḥ//

of the lover from going, and according to *Dīkṣita*, the suggestions strengthen that denotative sense. To *Paṇḍitarāja*, this is an instance of suggestive poetry, embodying the sentiment in separation, and surpasses the expressed sense. The latter might have criticised the former quite justly elsewhere, but here I think, in pursuance of the traditional exposition of the poetry of subordinate suggestion, *Dīkṣita* is right in calling it the same. To my mind, the chief difference between suggestive poetry and the poetry of subordinate suggestion, should be of volume or intensity or both. That is, if the volume or intensity or both of suggestion, is more than that of the direct expression, then it will be suggestive poetry. If the volume or intensity or both of denotation is more than that of suggestion, then the poetry will be one of subordinate suggestion.

There is no question of suggestion being subservient to the sense of denotation, because wherever there is suggestion, it will more often than not, under very exceptional cases like the one above quoted, subserve the denotative sense, as the former may or may not be present in a particular verse, but the latter should always be. Both are separate entities and should be treated, as such, on individual merit. Moreover, if suggestion is the better and more desired thing, which certainly it is, how can it assist the denotation? Even popularly speaking, the master is always the master and the servant the servant. The difficulty is all the more great if the figures are used alongside the suggestion, or still greater when the figures used are themselves suggestive.

In the latter eventuality, it is difficult to keep suggestion from the figures, or for that matter, from the direct sense, and the total effect should be suggestive. As I have stressed that there are some figures of sense which are very directly related to the sense of suggestion, or even to the poetic sentiment or emotion in the ultimate analysis, and as the figures are traditionally taken to be the decoration of the denotative power of expression, one would like to strip them of the suggestive garb and proclaim them subservient to the direct sense. As a result, the accruing poetry is one of subordinate suggestion. There is nothing wrong with figurative expression in poetry; it may heighten the general poetic tone and effect if it is accompanied with the suggestive emotion, giving a unitary impression to the reader. The emotion is the most important thing in poetry, and if it is present then the other factors will help it, and if it is not, then the so-called figurative expression will not be emotive.

The instance of suggestive poetry we have quoted above, pregnant with so many suggestions in an apparently bizarre-looking verse, is rare, and I doubt whether all the suggestions that the rhetoricians have pointed out can be revealed as existing in the poet's mind. The figurative expression, in its own right, cannot be decried. Although there can be verses with many and beautiful figures as suggestions, we quote only an exquisitely simple, though beautiful verse which, according to the traditional standard, should have a predominant denotative sense, or at best, it would be an instance of the poetry of subordinate suggestion owing to the most enchanting simile used, coupled with emotive and organic suggestions. The poetry here, in the final analysis, should be called suggestive. [1]"About to choose her husband, she passed along the row, giving a radiance to the kings, like the flame of a lamp in the night on the deserted mansions of the highway."

The occasion is the husband-choosing ceremony of *Indumatī*. The kings have come in their best and are sitting in a line. Each of them thinks that he deserves the garland of *Indumatī* and will get it. The princess would go through the row with a garland in her hand, which she would fling round the neck of the one she would choose as her husband. She arrives and commences. She stops before one king while the latter is being described. The particular king is aglow with the prospect of being chosen, but she does not like him and moves ahead. His face hopefully lit, is now dark with despondency. This happens with the other kings whom she visits. The poet here has likened the beautiful princess to the flame of a

1. Cf. RV. VI, V. 67 :
Sañcāriṇī dīpaśikheva rātrau yaṁ yaṁ vyatīyāya patiṁvarā sā/
Narendramārgāṭṭa iva prapede vivarṇabhāvaṁ sa sa bhūmipālaḥ//

lamp and the dressed-up kings, seated in the row, to the majestic edifices on the public highway. It is said that beauty has a light about it. The princess is fair-complexioned and the suggestion is that she radiates the white gleam of her face. This is the physical aspect of the simile, commensurate with the physical focusing of light on the mansion at which, at a particular moment of time, somebody with a lighted lamp in his hand, happens to pass. More than this is the spiritual aspect, where the beauty of *Indumatī* as an aesthetic ideal, or the hope of gaining her, kindles the hearts of the kings. The face is the index of the mind, or, the other way round, what happiness or sorrow, hope and despondency, there is in the mind, is visible upon the face. *Indumatī*, therefore, as a glowing light enlightens the faces as well as the hearts of the suitor-kings.

It is also significant that the lamp is almost suggested to move itself. It has its own beauty. It is said to move in the night and justifies its utility and beauty, as well as the appropriateness of the simile. It is noteworthy that the poet chooses a simile which agrees with the matter in hand even in respect of gender and number. This adds to the compactness and beauty in the simile that has made the poet immortal. To my mind, the use of the word *Bhāva* in *Vivarṇabhāvaṁ* is quite important. The poet might have used *Rūpa* instead, but that would not highlight the metamorphosis of feeling that was going on in the inner recesses of the minds and hearts of the kings. The word *Vivarṇa* in the compound, is no less remarkable because it suggests that the kings who were rejected, were so saddened that they lost the usual colour of their faces. Thus the simple, though powerful words used, plus the lucidity and forcefulness of style, compactness, suggestiveness and appropriateness of the figure, together with the use of telling adjectives and the vivacity and emotional potency of the suggestions and the images they evolve, make the verse better than one where there is only multiplicity of pure suggestions. In all, this may be called an instance of suggestive poetry.

Thus, what is called Citrakāvya, especially the one endowed with *Arthacitra*, can be poetry of a very high order, provided there be concord between them and the images evolved, and the consistency of impression. The figures, of which this division of poetry is constituted, are not irrelevant and contribute in evoking a fine poetic sense, or an equally superb poetic image. All this is related to the creative imagination of a poet. The secret of originality in the evocation of a good visual image is first, the perceptive eye, and then the interpretive imagination. With these is created a poetry which both inspires and impresses.

CHAPTER II

DEVELOPMENT OF CONCEPTS

Citrakāvya consists in the peculiarity attendant on word (Śabdacitra), on the meaning (Arthacitra), and of word and the meaning (Ubhayacitra). The effect must in all the three cases, be qua poetic figure. The three varieties are generally characterised by the absence of the power of suggestion (Vyañjanā). Embellishment is taken to be the secondary sine qua non of poetry, and *Citrakāvya* is that which embellishes word (Śabda), meaning (Artha) or both (Ubhaya). This sort of poetry falls within the third division, as determined earlier.

[1]Among many dictionary meanings of the word *Citra*, two are prominent : 'peculiar' (as adjective), and 'image' (or 'picture', as noun). In *Citrakāvya*, [2]a sense of wonder is generated owing to the peculiar handling of certain metres etc; or due to the use of poetic designs (Bandhas) representing pictures of certain specific types in verses, depending on the skill of the poet in the arrangement of letters. Secondly, it may be interpreted to mean something an image or picture in poetry may denote, which the various poetic designs or the poetic or emotive images, might reflect. In the coming chapters, it will be evident that both these interpretations have to be taken in order, to cover the whole field of the traditionally accepted sub-varieties of the three said divisions of *Citrakāvya*. Thirdly, as a corollary to the second interpretation [3]we might say that *Citrakāvya* is only the image of true poetry (Kāvya), not the poetry itself. In this case, it merely imitates poetry

1. Vide SKD Vol. II, p. 448.
   Cf. VP Vol. IV, p. 2942.
   Cf. MW SED, p. 396.
2. Cf. EV VII, p. 190 : Aho yena krameṇa gatā varṇapaṁktistenaiva krameṇa pratyāgatetyāścaryakāritvād vā citram/
3. Cf. DL III, p. 495 : Na tanmukhyaṁ kāvyaṁ/Kāvyānukāro hyasau/

without ever becoming so, and is therefore, an exercise for a novice talent.

[1]Following *Mammaṭa*, we find that the expression 'Citra' denotes figures of speech and literary excellence. Consequently, the belles lettres endowed with the figures of sound, or sense, or both, and the requisite literary excellence, are styled *Citrakāvya*. I think this is the most comprehensive view as it subsumes within it all the possible ramifications of the foregoing interpretations.

The first interpretation is, undoubtedly, based on the concept of *Citra* as a figure of speech (Citrālaṁkāra). Even among the rhetoricians, this idea seems to have gained currency, and *citrakāvya* might owe its origin to this. [2]*Ruyyaka*, [3]*Jayadeva*, [4]*Viśvanātha*, and others like *Bhānudatta* and *Keśava miśra*, mention *citra* only as a figure and have enumerated it among the figures of sound. It is noteworthy that none of the most celebrated rhetoricians has defined and dealt with *citra* as a figure in the sense the above have, with the sole exception of *Viśvanātha*. The modern, and most prevalent, concept of *Citrakāvya*, is an extended version of the current meaning of *Citrālaṁkāra*, and in the implications of the latter we find the seed of the former. But to differentiate, *Citrālaṁkāra* deals with *citra*, as we have just averred, as a figure of sound, whereas *Citrakāvya* treats it as a figure pertaining to sound or sense or both. The former stands for a particular variety of the figure of sound, consisting mostly of the poetic designs (Bandhas), while the latter includes within its jurisdiction all the figurative peculiarities of word or meaning or both.

With [5]*Mammaṭa*, only the later rhetoricians [6]*Vidyādhara* and [7]*Vidyānātha*, speak of *citra* both as a division of

1. Cf. KPl I, p. 5: Citramiti guṇālaṁkārayuktam,.... /
2. Vide AS, p. 30.
3. Cf. CL V, p. 100.
4. Vide SD X, p. 514.
5. Cf. KPl I, p. 5; IX, p. 214: Yadyapi śabdātmakānāṁ varṇānāṁ khaḍgādyākārahetutā nāsti, tathāpi tadvyañjakānāṁ lipyātmakavarṇānāṁ tathātvena tathātvamupacaryate/
6. Cf. EV VII, p. 189.
7. Vide PY, p. 71 and pp. 345-349.

poetry, and as a figure of speech. [1]*Ānanda* and [2]*Dīkṣita* refer to it only as a variety of poetry because the former has to deal with poetry alone, on the basis of the presence or otherwise, of suggestion, and for the latter it would have been beyond his scope to treat any other matter. It is surprising that *Bhāmaha*, *Daṇḍin* and *Udbhaṭa*, though dealing with the figures of sound, the latter even elaborately, do not name *citra* as a figure. [3]*Rudraṭa* does not name it as figure, but [4]*Namisādhu*, in his comments, does so clearly. *Kuntaka* treats every poetic concept in the light of the evasive speech qua poetic figure (Vakrokti) and hence, though knowing, might not have found scope for its clear mention. [5]*Bhoja*, on the contrary, while making an elaborate treatment of the six varieties of *citra*, takes it as an axiom and feels that he is dealing with *citra* as a figure. The position with [6]*Hemacandra* is stranger. In connection with his treatment of the varieties of poetry, he dubs the non-suggestive type as the worst, but does not mention that it is called *citra*. He mentions it while dealing with the figures of sound.

The third interpretation is not very reasonable, and having basis in *Mammaṭa*, we shall here try to make an exposition and application of the second, especially in relation to the poetic image (Arthacitra), [7]which is near the Western concept of 'image poetry'. With respect to *Śabdacitra*, as we shall elaborate later, it is best to interpret 'citra' as a certain uniqueness or peculiarity wrought in poetry. The idea of image-making in poetry might originally have been borrowed from the field of painting. The principles underlying them were

1. Cf. DL III, p. 494 : Pradhānaguṇabhāvābhyāṁ vyaṅgyasyaivaṁ vyavasthite/Kāvye ubhe tato'nyadyat taccitramabhidhīyate//
2. Cf CM, p. 11.
3. Cf. RK V, V. 1, p. 119.
4. Ibid : Yatra kāvye vastūnāṁ cakrādīnāṁ rūpāṇi saṁsthānāni racyante nibadhyante taccitraśādṛśyādāścaryād vā citraṁ nāmālaṁkāraḥ/
5. Cf SKB II, p. 265.
6. Vide H-KN II.58, p. 157 : Avyaṅgyamavaram/
7. Vide Appendix No. I.

called Citrasūtras. [1]*Viṣṇudharmottara* unhesitatingly states that the art of image-making cannot be understood except by one who has studied *Citrasūtras* which, in turn, cannot be known without mastering the art of dancing. Further, dancing (Nṛtta) does not exist without the accompaniment of musical instruments and proficiency in the latter is unattainable without the study of singing as an art.

In [2]*Kuṭṭanīmata*, we find the *citrasūtras* mentioned as one of the subjects to be studied by the accomplished courtesans, along with *Bharata*, *Viśākhila* and *Dantila*. [3]In *Viṣṇudharmottara* a fine image is described which a poet may try to imbibe and emulate in the poetry of *Arthacitra* : "The surface glistens, and appears to come to meet the spectator (or reader as we may add in case of such poetic image) : the sweetness seems as if smiling, and appears as if endowed with life." *Citra* is described as one where the representation is like an image. [4]It is surprising to find here that even the concept of sentiment (Rasa) has been extended to all the arts except that of architecture. In literature (Kāvya) it is *Kāvyarasa*, in painting (Citra) it is *Citrarasa*, and so on. Moreover, we find such ideas as *Rasacitra*, *Bhāvacitra* and even, *Dhūlicitra* prevalent quite long ago. In the context of imagery in poetry, the word *Ālekhyaprakhya* was, perhaps, current. *Ānanda* uses it in the *Vṛtti* and it is amazing that [5]*Rājaśekhara* borrows it in a different context.

Among the peculiarities pertaining to sound (Śabdacitra), alliteration (Anuprāsa) is mentioned by almost all the rhetoricians except *Ānandavardhana* and *Dīkṣita* for the reasons mentioned. Among its varieties, most of the rhetoricians give *Chekānuprāsa* and *Vṛttyanuprāsa*. [6]*Ruyyaka*, [7]*Jayadeva*,

1. Cf. VD Vol. II, III.II, p. 4.
2. Cf. D-KM, V. 123, p. 30 :
   Bharataviśākhiladantilavṛkṣāyurvedacitrasūtreṣu/
   Patracchedavidhāne bhramakarmaṇi pustasūdaśāstreṣu//
3. Cf. VD Vol. I, III, Chap. 43, V. 21, p. 155.
4. Ibid : Vol. II, III, Sec. XII, p. 217.
5. Cf KM XIII, p. 211.
6. Cf. AS, p. 28.
7. Cf, CL V, p. 95.

[1]*Mammaṭa*, [2]*Viśvanātha*, [3]*Vidyādhara* and [4]*Vidyānātha* also add *Lāṭānuprāsa*. [5]*Viśvanātha*, with [6]*Daṇḍin* and some others, enumerates *Śrutyanuprāsa* in the list. It is peculiar that [7]*Jayadeva* names *Sphuṭānuprāsa*, and [8]*Bhāmaha* together with [9]*Udbhaṭa*, mentions *Grāmyānuprāsa*, which the former annotates as *Komalānuprāsa*. Besides, [10]*Udbhaṭa*, [11]*Jayadeva* and [12]*Viśvanātha* each respectively adds *Paruṣānuprāsa*, *Arthānuprāsa* and *Antyānuprāsa*. [13]*Hemacandra* mentions by name only *Lāṭa*. As for the repetition of both letters or words, he gives two varieties each : One where the repetition is only once (Sakṛdāvṛtti), and the other where it is many times (Asakṛdāvṛtti). [14]*Rudraṭa* bases his division of alliteration on his concept of *Vṛttis* as does *Bhoja* also.

[15]The latter makes almost a complete departure from the traditional treatment of alliteration and enumerates a vast variety. First, he gives three broad varieties based on the repetition of sounds (Śrutyanuprāsa), of letters (Varṇānuprāsa) and of words (Padānuprāsa). Then he classifies the first into three : *Grāmya*, *Nāgara* and *Upanāgara*; dividing the first into three again—constituting the repetition of soft letters, of hard letters and of medium letters; the second into two—constituting the repetition of letters having either the same place or organ of utterance, or a different one; and the third into four—making up the repetition of ḍa, la, or ra, la, or na,

1. Cf. KPl IX, p. 195.
2. Cf SD X, p. 486.
3. Cf. EV VII, p. 192.
4. Vide PY, p. 341.
5. Cf. SD X, p. 484.
6. Vide KD III, 55-60, pp. 54-59.
7. Vide CL V, p. 96.
8. Cf. BK II, V. 6, p. 31.
9. Cf. KSS, p. 5.
10. Ibid, p. 4.
11. Cf. CL V, p. 97.
12. Cf. SD X, p. 485.
13. Cf. H-KN II, p. 295.
14. Cf. RK, V. 19, p. 41.
15. Vide SKB II, pp. 228-265.

ṇa or dental and palatal sounds; thus making in all, nine sub-varieties. Of the second, the rhetorician gives twelve divisions i.e. the repetition of letters constituting bunches, occurring at particular spots, having some other letter or letters in the middle, lengthening and shortening at places, continuing and discontinuing, consisting of the growing number of letters in an order, consisting of repetitive letters in a reversed order, a group with the occurrence at the beginning and end of each foot, occurring only in the middle of each foot joining the parts, occurring at very close intervals till the end of sentence or the verse, quite different from the above, and interspersed with stressed letters. Of the third, the extra divisions are: words consisting of disjunct syllables, of conjunct letters, constituting smooth repetition with soft syllables made up of the various modes of repetitive words and somewhat tautologous. This as well as those resembling the first, second, fifth, eighth and ninth varieties of the second type of alliteration, together with a series of repetitions, form the abovesaid eighth and ninth varieties.

Bhoja has given much importance to alliteration and has derived and classified the *Vṛttis*, or the particular styles of composition, on its basis. For example, *Kārṇāṭī* (i.e. the style of composition connected with the Karṇāṭa country) consists of guttural alliterations, *Kauntalī* (i.e. connected with the Kuntala country) of palatal, *Kauṅkī* (i.e. related to the Koṅka country) of cerebral, *Auṇḍrī* (i.e. related to Oṇḍra) of conjuncts having the same place or organ of utterance, *Pauṇḍrī* (i.e. of the Puṇḍra country) of dissimilar conjuncts, *Kauṅkaṇī* (i.e. of Koṅkaṇa) of dental letters, *Vānavāsikā* (i.e. of Vanavāsa) of labials, *Tāmraliptikā* (i.e. one relating to the Tāmralipti country) of conjuncts formed with the last letters of each class, *Māthurī* (i.e. one of Mathurā) of the sibilants, *Drāviḍī* (i.e. of Draviḍa country) of the semi-vowels, *Mātsyā* (i.e. connected with Matsya country) of the repetition of letters taken from two or three such classes, and *Māgadhī* (i.e. relating to Magadha) of letters of one class made to look like *Vaidarbhī* (i.e. of Vidarbha country) by certain interceptions. The alliteration of words bordering on chimes, might form different subdivisions due to the intermingling of the compounded and the uncompounded words, and of those intercepted and unintercepted. [1]Striking at the root of the alliterations evolved, *Bhoja* has shown that they are possible owing to many human feelings, such as ecstasy, wonder, excitement or flurry, or any two or three of these.

[2]It is peculiar to realise that what *Kuntaka* meant by the circumlocution or undulation of speech belonging to the arrangement of letters, is this very alliteration. Here it has been split into three varieties according to whether there is repetition of one, two, or more letters. In another way also, the writer classifies it threefold : firstly, where the repetition is of letters, guttural, palatal, cerebral, dental and labial, mixed with their final nasals; secondly, where ta, la and na sounds are repeated mostly in twos; and thirdly, where there is repetition of the rest consonantal sounds in conjunct form. This treatment, it goes without saying, resembles that of *Bhoja*. Also there is some similarity in that *Kuntaka* includes in this class the styles of composition like *Upanāgarikā* etc., and also the chimes or the verbal juggleries similar to these.

Of chimes mention is made by almost all rhetoricians except *Udbhaṭa*, *Ānanda* and *Dīkṣita*. The first and the last were dealing with a different type but *Ānanda* should have treated it. Among older rhetoricians, [3]*Bhāmaha* names only five broad types, including the complicated *Saṁdaṣṭaka* and *Samudgaka*. As a refreshing contrast, [4]*Daṇḍin* gives forty-three varieties of ordinary chimes, over and above thirteen types of *Samudgaka*,—and the *Saṁdaṣṭa* and *Mahāyamaka* of which he offers only one illustration, but [5]*Premacandra*, in his commentary, says that a large number of varieties of it could be possible. In elaboration, only [6]*Bhoja* has been able to match, and even

1. Vide SKB II, pp. 256-257.
2. Cf. VJ I, p. 66 : Etadeva varṇavinyāsavakratvaṁ cirantaneṣvanuprāsa iti prasiddham/
3. Vide BK II, V. 10, p. 33.
4. Vide KD III, pp. 334-388.
5. Ibid, p. 384 : Atyantabahavasteṣām bhedāḥ sambhedayonayaḥ/
6. Cf. SKB II, pp. 198-221.

surpass *Daṇḍin*. He goes more subtly into the divisions and discovers that among chimes occurring at different places of the feet i.e. at the beginning, middle and end, all combinations are not possible, as illustrations are not available in all cases. Among such varieties are the unseparated one (Avyapeta), occurring at the beginning or end of only one foot of a verse and the separated one (Vyapeta), occurring at the middle of only two feet. With regard to the unseparated one occurring at the middle, he says that it can be possible only with respect to its occurrence in the fourth foot. Moreover, he treats almost a new style of chimes, where the position rules are not obeyed (Asthānayamaka). In one foot itself, two or more sets of words are repeated, in separated or unseparated way. This can happen with regard to other feet as well. Also, the repetition can be very minute to the extent of the reverberance of letters in a long series, continuing up to even more than one foot. This, in this position, or when extended, forms *Varṇacitra* of the rhetoricians.

In a novel way, [1]*Bhoja* invents a new name, the girdle-chime (Kāñcīyamaka), for one of the complicated varieties. [2]But the importance of *Rudraṭa* in this connection cannot be gainsaid. He devotes a full chapter to the discussion of chimes, and he is more concerned with their classification. He has given some new names under this head like *Garbha*, *Puccha*, *Paṁkti*, *Vaktra*, *Śikhā*, *Mālā* etc. but, in fact, this is not a new idea. Thus, superficially only, he gives new orientation to the discussion of chimes. [3]To the *Rasavādī* rhetoricians like *Mammaṭa* and *Viśvanātha*, complicated chimes and bandhas were a positive evil and so they made only passing reference to the possible varieties, and have not treated them in detail. [4]*Vidyādhara* has shown a little more academic interest in the chimes, and has dealt with the desirability or otherwise, of their use in literature. It is peculiar that he

1. Cf SKB II, p. 216.
2. Cf. RK. III, pp. 49-83.
3. Cf. KPI IX, p. 199 : Tadetat kāvyāntargaḍubhūtaṁ....../
   Cf. SD X, p. 516 : Kavyāntargaḍubhūtatayā tu neha prapañcyate.
4. Vide EV VII, p. 189 : Prāyaśo yamake citre rasapuṣṭirna dṛśyate/

prohibits chimes occurring in only three feet of a verse. He is also against their general use in poetry, because they might prove detrimental to the realisation of a particular sentiment.

Of the reversed designs (Vilomacitras), few among the rhetoricians have made any mention, and very few have treated them. When extended in certain order, they are called all-moving (Sarvatobhadra) or, the half-moving (Ardhabhrama). Most are dealt with, among the old rhetoricians by [1]*Daṇḍin*, and among the new by [2]*Vidyādhara* and [3]*Kavikarṇapūra*. But of the poetic designs, mention is made by [4]*Hemacandra* of only the sword and the drum, and [5]*Mammaṭa* adds the lotus to it. With *Bhāmaha*, *Daṇḍin* keeps complete silence, but [6]the latter mentions the conventional *Gomūtrikā*. [7]*Rudraṭa*, again, comes to the fore. He treats all the designs mentioned, and innovates new ones like the bow, the arrow, the lance (Śakti), the plough, the horse-step, the elephant-step, the pestle and trident. In recent times, [8]*Vidyādhara* is elaborate in dealing with most of these, adding the mountain-design, while [9]*Vidyānātha* mentions the wheel-design with the eight-petalled lotus, and adds the serpent-design. To these, as extra designs, [10]*Kavikarṇapūra* adds the umbrella, the banner and the club. It is surprising that *Viśvanātha* does not name any. Perhaps he felt that they detracted from the realisation of the poetic sentiment.

[11]In this context, the novelty of *Bhoja* lies in the elaboration of the manifold sub-varieties of the lotus-design, the wheel-design and the *Gomūtrikā*. As for the lotus-design itself, he treats the four-petalled, the eight-petalled, the sixteen-petalled, and the special eight-petalled one bearing the name of the poet. Of the wheel also, he gives a few different designs

1. Cf. KD III, pp. 386-394.
2. Cf. EV VII, p. 191.
3. Cf. K-AK II, 7.
4. Vide H-KN, p. 314.
5. Vide KPl, p. 217.
6. Cf. KD III, p. 390.
7. Cf. RK V, pp. 121-142.
8. Cf. EV VII, p. 190.
9. Vide PY, pp. 346-349.
10. Vide K-AK II. 7.
11. Vide SKB II, pp. 272-276 & 280, 284-293.

like the *Dviśṛṅgāṭaka*, the *Viviḍita* etc. Of the conventional *Gomūtrikā*, he treats over twelve varieties consisting in one foot, two feet, hemistich, one full verse, of reversed order, of varied metres, and of more than one language. Sometimes one verse can form many and varied types of it. He also gives the sky-design and the *Śarayantrabandha*, and cites verses which can give a hundred, a thousand, ten thousand, a lakh, a crore, or even countless verses at will. In [1]*Viloma-citra*, he introduces verses where the reversed form is made up of, and written in a different language. In [2]*Varṇa-citra*, he gives yet a more elaborate treatment of verses consisting of only one consonant, or two, or three etc, havving no dental or labial or cerebral or palatal letters or any two or three of these or having only short or long vowels or in a different way qualitatively short or long or both in a certain pattern.

With regard to the figures of both sound and sense (Ubhayālaṁkāras), falling under the peculiarities pertaining to both (Ubhayacitra), [3]*Vidyānātha* is, perhaps, the first to make clear mention. [4]Among these, the subversive speech qua poetic figure is several times mentioned by *Bhāmaha*, but perhaps he took it in a general sense. It is queer that *Daṇḍin*, *Udbhaṭa* and *Jayadeva*, do not enumerate it. Following [5]*Mammaṭa* and [6]*Viśvanātha*, [7]*Vidyādhara* and [8]*Vidyānātha* also give its two types, but [9]*Bhoja* and [10]*Hemacandra* do so in a different way. [11]*Mammaṭa* and [12]*Viśvanātha* place

1. Vide SKB II, pp. 277, 278.
2. Ibid, pp. 265-272.
3. Cf. PY, p. 337.
4. Cf. BK I, Vs. 34,36; II-Vs. 85 86; VI-V. 66.
5. Vide KPI IX, p. 192.
6. Vide SD X, p. 490.
7. Cf. EV VII, p. 326.
8. Cf. PY, p. 411.
9. Cf SKB II, p. 296.
10. Vide H-KN II, p. 332.
11. See Fn. No. 5 above.
12. See Fn. No. 6 above.

it as a figure of sound, while [1]*Ruyyaka*, [2]*Vidyādhara*, [3]*Vidyānātha* and *Dīkṣita*, think it is a figure of sense. As for paranomasia, [4]*Bhāmaha* and [5]*Daṇḍin* both mention it, but do not split it into two as the unbroken (Abhaṅga) and the broken (Sabhaṅga), as the later writers have done. Only [6]*Bhoja* treats its six varieties, and [7]*Viśvanātha* eight. [8]*Rudraṭa* treats it as a figure belonging both to sound and sense, and deals with it in two separate chapters. He gives many new varieties of both. It is peculiar that *Vidyādhara* and *Vidyānātha* do not name it at all. Jayadeva, on the other hand, classifies it differently. As for its historicity, it is an old figure, but about its nature rhetoricians hold varied views. Some take it as a figure of sound, some of sense, and some both. Actually, it all depends on the particular verse being capable of alteration in words without any change in the meaning. If there is such capacity, the figure will be treated as that of sense, otherwise, paranomasia is a figure of sound. The maxim holds good with all the figures having dual nature. The same figure can be both of sound and sense when a particular arrangement of words can, or cannot, be altered without affecting the meaning. Incapability of being altered (Parivṛttyasahiṣṇuttva), is the sine qua non of the figures of sound, and so they excite appreciation only when set in a particular fashion. Thus alliterations and chimes are possible only when there is repetition of particular letters, or groups of letters, at certain regular and close intervals. Of the poetic designs (Bandhas on the other hand, there must be, like the Euclid, certain suppositions regarding certain letters at particular points.

According to [9]*Ruyyaka*, the seeming tautology (Punaruktavadābhāsa) is a figure of sense, but to [10]*Mammaṭa* and

1. Cf. AS, p. 219.
2. Vide Supra p. 33, Fn. No. 7.
3. Vide Supra p. 33, Fn. No. 8.
4. Cf. BK. III, p. 73.
5. Cf. KD II, p. 290.
6. Cf. SKB II, p. 221.
7. Cf. SD X, p. 492.
8. Vide RK IV & X.
9. Cf. AS, p. 20.
10. Cf. KPl IX, p. 219.

[1]*Śobhākara*, it is that of sound only. It must be mentioned here that [2]*Mammaṭa* takes one of its varieties as representing both the figures, and in that sense, it is an *Ubhayālaṁkāra* forming basis of the *Ubhayacitra*. Among other rhetoricians [3]*Udbhaṭa*, [4]*Hemacandra*, [5]*Vidyādhara* and [6]*Vidyānātha*, treat it. [7]*Jayadeva* mentions it as *Punaruktapratīkāśa*. Among older ones, *Bhāmaha* and *Daṇḍin*, and later even the omnivorous *Bhoja*, do not mention it. As for the insinuatory speech (Chekokti), it is also a new figure but [8]based on the *Chekokticcāyā* of *Bhoja*. Among other dual figures accepted here for discussion, the concealing speech (Gūḍhokti), and the contriving speech (Yukti), have been treated by both *Dīkṣita* and [9]*Bhoja*. *Dīkṣita* has innovated a new figure in the revealing speech (Vivṛtokti).

[10]As for the contriving speech (Yukti), it, though a new figure, is actually an offshoot of the conventional covert allusion (Vyājokti). In it there is the concealment of what is not formal, but in the latter, there is the concealment of form itself. According to another view, in the former there is concealment by verbs of some secret, but in the latter, it is through the statement of some fact only. It is worthy of mention here that [11]*Bhoja* has taken it as a figure of sound and has dealt at length with its six varieties. [12]Sometimes a

1. Cf. Vide AR, p. 1.
2. Cf. KPl IX, V. 9, p. 220.
3. Cf. KSS, p. 3.
4. Cf. H-KN II. p. 338.
5. Cf. EV VII, p. 184.
6. Vide PY, p. 343.
7. Vide CL V, p. 98.
8. Vide SKB II, p. 165.
9. Cf. SKB II, p. 298.
   Cf. Ibid, p. 172.
10. Ibid, p. 257.
11. Vide Supra Fn. No. 11, p. 35.
12. Vide KN, p. 151 : Tvatkhaḍgakhaṇḍitasapatnavilāsinīnāṁ
    Bhūṣā bhavantyabhinavā bhuvanaikavīra/
    Netreṣu kaṅkaṇamathoruṣu patravallī
    Colendrasiṁha ! tilakaṁ karapallaveṣu//

different figure, such as incongruity (Asaṅgati), can display a striking meaning with verbal manipulations.

Among these, the subversive speech (Vakrokti) deserves special treatment, as quite a new school of thought in poetics was woven round this concept. *Kuntaka*, in his chef d'oeuvre (Vakroktijīvita), invested the concept with a new life and represented the deviant expression as the very life-force of poetry. Although this gave importance to figurative speech at the cost of the suggestive speech, this movement initially gathered much momentum and attracted serious attention.

About figures of sense, I have nothing to say here, except that in order to create the peculiarities with regard to meaning or the poetic image (Arthacitra), there must be, as discussed later in detail, the reflection of the object compared in that to be compared (Bimbānubimbabhāva), to show the essential qualities of both. Other figures of sense come under the second order, of those capable of exciting an appreciative audience with regard to the sense. But the poetic figurations (Vicchittis), with respect to surpassing the standard of comparison by the object (Vyatirekavicchitti), and that regarding concealment of the real and the display of something else as real, would stand on the borderland of *Ubhayacitras*.

[1]But it is still more surprising to find that besides paranomasia (Śleṣa), and the subversive speech qua poetic figure (Vakrokti), some scholars have treated apparent incongruity (Virodha), model metaphor (Samāsokti), circumlocutory speech (Paryāyokta), figurative reference (Anyokti), concealment (Apahnuti), illusion (Bhrāntimān), metaphorical hyperbole (Rūpakātiśayokti) and subtle reference (Sūkṣma), under the head of poetic tricks (Kūṭas). These poetic tricks can safely be placed under the peculiarities pertaining both to sound and sense (Ubhayacitras), because some of these poetic tricks are founded on puns (Śleṣa), and some owe their origin to the poetic subversion of speech (Vakrokti), and the two have characteristic features of both the figures of sound and sense.

1. Vide KKA, p. 47.

Unintelligibility or abstruseness is the basis of *Kūṭa*. Poetic tricks (Kūṭas) gave rise to riddles or the conundrums, under the criteria of *Ubhayacitras*. Alliteration and chimes or some striking image or meaning, should not be enough to entitle any piece of poetry to selection as *Ubhayacitra*, as has generally been done by the rhetoricians. This would at best produce collocation (Saṁsṛṣṭi), or commixture (Saṁkara), of figures of sense, or of sound, or both. To make up this variety of *Citrakāvya*, there should be some sort of verbal jugglery, together with some fine imagery, or at the least, there should be some exciting or striking meaning mingled together. These elements with the suggested sense without prominence, would not debar any piece of poetry from *Citra* variety.

As a matter of fact, poetry which is understood without reference to the sense and context of the words used, is *Kūṭa*. Here, something is said for effecting poetic charm in concealing the sense in a parade of pedantries From the point of view of content, the concealment of meanings and the clever use of words, are two conditions mecessary for *Kūṭa* poetry. In understanding the meaning, one has to ransack one's brain and imagination, but once discovered, the meaning gives a high degree of delight.

There is some difficulty in grasping the meaning in suggestive poetry after the abandonment of the directly conveyed sense, but that does not give *Kūṭa* poetry the status and importance of the suggestive class. In fact, a poet need not make skilful use of words or of other means, such as the creation of figures, in the composition of *Kūṭa* poetry, in giving vent to suggestive poetry. Besides, the mysterious sense of the former cannot be equated with the suggested sense (Dhvanyartha). It is the expressed sense (Vācyārtha), derived through the contextual interchange of words. Thus, difficult words and figures are used in almost all varieties of *Citrakāvya*, but they are not all *Kūṭas* because the meaning is not always inscrutable or ambiguous.

Kūṭa has been very popular with scholars of discrimination, to the extent that in modern times we are accustomed to the word *Kūṭakāvya* on the analogy of *Citrakāvya*.

Indeed, [1]*Kūṭa* is a specific form of poetry-writing representing the oblique style of expression where the desired sense is concealed and couched in occult words. But, broadly speaking, it might be called a distinct branch of poetry. [2]Poetry is the art of the embellishment of thoughts, and the expression of emotions and sentiments. A poet's expressions become ecstatic, and his words create pleasure. When the style becomes musical, the verbalisation of thought is sublimated by the imagination. Simplicity is the ornament of the descriptive style, and strangeness that of reflective writing.

Perhaps *Kūṭa* is of recent origin, but [3]*Prahelikā* is an old word found in *Amarakoṣa*, together with *Pravahlikā*, and dealt at length in [4]*Viṣṇudharmottarapurāṇa*. It seems to be a literary diversion from very ancient times. In the Vedic age, mention is made of the latter in the *Brāhmaṇas* of the *Ṛgveda*, such as [5]*Aitareya*. The reference is about certain laconic verses of the [6]*Atharvaveda*. A different type of riddle namely theological, is also referred to in the *Brāhmaṇas*, under the name of [7]*Brahmodya*. The attraction of this kind of literary activity seems to have been considerable, and it is mentioned as one of sixty-four arts in the [8]*Kāmasūtras* of *Vātsyāyana*, and is referred to by [9]*Yaśodhara* in his comments on it, as one well-known (Lokapratīta) in society. He gives two varieties of it, viz., one for diversion (Krīḍārtha), and the other for discussion (Vādārtha). [10]*Viṣṇudharmottara* gives twenty-four varieties based on *Daṇḍin's* sixteen divisions, of which[11] the latter has dubbed fourteen as riddles based on the faults of poetry (Duṣṭaprahelikās).[12] *Bhāmaha* describes it as one employ-

1. KKA, p. 1.
2. Ibid.
3. Cf. AK I-IV, p. 58.
4. Cf. VD III, Vol I, p. 35.
5. Vide AB XXX VII, p. 788.
6. VINS Vol. II, p. 40.
7. Ibid, p. 80.
8. Cf. VKS I-III-16, p. 29.
9. Cf. VKS I-III-16, p. 32.
10. Cf. VD III. II, Vol. II, p. 22.
11. Cf. KD III, V. 106, p. 410.
12. Vide BK II, Vs. 9-10, p. 10.

ing chimes (Yamaka) and having recondite meanings through the variety of root-meanings. He further adds that such a literary form could be understood, like the *Śāstras*, only with the help of commentaries, and it is a source of pleasure to the sharp-witted, but humiliation for the lesser so. Among later writers, to mention only a few, *Mammaṭa* dees not even mention it, and[1] *Viśvanātha* states emphatically that it is unfavourable to sentiment (Rasa). It is of interest to note here, that [2]the *Preraṇa*-variety of *Geyaprekṣakāvya*, full of humour, and replete with erotic suggestions, consists of such riddles.

In [3]*Viṣṇudharmottara*, there is a general instruction that a riddle should be expressed only through one or two verses. This explains why *Ubhayacitra* is difficult to compose, for there it is necessary to maintain poetic interest in a number of verses. According to [4]Winternitz, the riddle queries and riddle gambols were originally the recreation of the vedic age, and sometimes formed part of the sacrificial rituals. Besides, in those ancient days, such poetry was to endow the elements of nature with anthropomorphic forms, to strike wonder and curiosity in the breasts of human beings, and to give brevity of expression in meaning, as well as to keep the secrets of mysticism concealed. It was possible because of the high development of the sensibilities and sentiments expressed. With respect to such poetry, mostly in *Kūṭa*, the language used is generally symbolical or mystical, the symbols often taken from the universe of nature. [5]Sometimes, the experience of the mystical and metaphysical, being itself inexpressible, makes one take recourse to such symbols and metaphors. Like a dumb person, the mystical seer could experience only within himself, and could express this to others only with the help of symbols and gestures.

From the works of Sanskrit poets, like [6]*Bāṇa*, it is

1. Vide SD X, V. 13.
2. Cf. H-KN VIII, p. 446.
3. Cf. VD III, II, Vol. II, p. 19.
4. Vide W-HIL Vol. I, p. 184.
5. Vide KKA, p. 50.
6. Vide KB, p. 15: Kadācidālekhyavinodena...kadācidakṣaracyutakabindumatīgūḍhacaturthapādaprahelikāpradānādibhirvanitāsaṁbhogaparāṅmukhaḥ....

evident that people in general used to take an interest in this sort of poetic recreation. As a result of this high sensibility for poetry and art, and owing to the social conditions prevailing in the middle age of Sanskrit literature, a vast literature of the ilk of *Kūṭas*, *Citras* and *Prahelikās* was produced. [1]The propensity of the poets towards this kind of literature was also because of their liking for copious use of figures, both of sound and sense, bordering on the *Kūṭas*. Among these figures, with respect to *Kūṭa* poetry, the figures of sound are styled *Śabdālaṁkārakūṭa*, and those of sense, *Arthālaṁkārakūṭa*. Thus, the figures have special importance in *Kūṭa* composition, but they are only the properties making poetry more beautiful. They conceal the real beauty which, when unravelled, gives unique delight to the reader.

Here we may point out that [2]*Keśavamiśra* classifies the figure concealed (Gūḍha), and the poetic interrogations, (Praśnas), under the figures of sound.[3] With him, [4]*Bhoja* puts riddles (Prahelikās) under the same head, and adds *Jāti*, *Rīti*, *Vṛtti*, *Chāyā*, *Śayyā*, *Mudrā*, *Gumphanā*, *Paṭhiti* and *Bhaṇiti*, which are exposed to the charge of over-extension. Among these, we have seen how [5]*Śayyā* is, essentially, a part of the concept of style (Rīti), and [6]how *Vṛtti*, though helpful in the determination of a particular style, is conducive to the creation of certain figures like alliteration and chimes. *Chāyā* is not of much importance. Of *Mudrā*, *Gumphanā*, *Paṭhiti* and *Bhaṇiti*, I think that the first three could be placed under the categories pertaining to both word and sense (Ubhayacitra).

Bhoja classifies all of these into six varieties, with perhaps, the intention of maintaining uniformity. [7]Among the varieties of the first, relating to the word, sentence, case, number and the juxtaposition (Samuccaya), the one per-

1. Vide Supra, p. 36.
2. Cf. Aś X, pp. 30-31.
3. Ibid.
4. Vide SKB II, p. 141.
5. Vide Supra p. 6.
6. Cf. Supra p. 30.
7. Cf. SKB II, p. 166.

taining to word is important as there is some concealed purpose to be expressed through the power of indication (Lakṣaṇā). [1]*Gumphanā* is the appropriate arrangement of word and meaning, and hence, might be conducive to any of the divisions of *Citrakāvya*. Besides those varieties relating to the word, meaning and sentence, it is also one connected with the use of synonyms, and the conventionally accepted successive order of words in a sentence. [2]As for *Paṭhiti*, it might promote *Ubhayacitra* by giving some particular sense in a verse through reading it with a change of voice (Kāku), accentuation, splitting of words and sentences, gesticulation and chiming. [3]*Bhaṇiti*, on the contrary, is an expression endowed with periphrasis (Bhaṅgin) or beauty (Vicchitti). It thus lies on the borderland of deviant expression (Vakrokti) when subversion or evasion of speech is meant, of conception qua poetic figure (Utprekṣā) where thc poetic beauty is generated because of the probability of the similitude offered, and of exaggeration (Atiśayokti) where the similarity drawn is improbable in the material world. According to *Bhoja*, it is also where something more is suggested in the particular verse than what is stated, when one part of the statement is covered by another part in the style of self-comparison (Ananvaya), and when something more is to be imagined in the verse from outside in order that full sense be carried through.

Coming to the three varieties of *Citrakāvya* themselves, it is the most commonplace view that of the three, the verbal peculiarity (Śabdacitra), mainly based on the figures of sound, is the least important. The reason for this is that it is generally regarded as an impediment to the maturing of a particular sentiment desired by a poet. [4]Of the particular figures of sound constituting it, especially the highly spun chimes, some rhetoricians are very critical. The criticism is justified, and these figures are good only insofar as they

1. Cf. SKB. II, p. 180.
2. Ibid, p 191.
3. Ibid, p. 177.
4. Vide Supra p. 31. Fn No. 3.

are in proportion and aid the particular prevailing sentiment, without divesting from it.

[1]*Bhoja* has named these figures as *Citra*, forming the kernel of *Citrālaṁkāra*, and classified it into six varieties. The first and second varieties, *Svaracitra* and *Vyañjanacitra*, constitute *Varṇacitra*. The third is *Sthānacitra*, dependent upon the use of letters in poetry and produced vocally from one, two, or more places of pronunciation in the mouth. The fourth and fifth, *Ākāracitra* and *Bandhacitra*, resemble each other and have very slight difference. The sixth is *Gaticitra*, embodying the *Vilomacitras*, the *Ardhabhrama*, *Sarvatobhadra* etc. figures, where a striking verbal effect is created through the movement of certain letters or groups of letters in a particular order.[2] It may be mentioned that *Hemacandra* has also given attention to these *citras*.

Lastly, we must treat some concepts enunciated by *Kuntaka*, which, though not directly related to *Citra*, are vital to the discussion. [3]Besides the periphrasis belonging to the arrangement of letters dealt with elsewhere, [4]that relating to the first part or the root part of a word, is most vital and is of eight kinds : the one dependent on the peculiarity of convention (Rūḍhivaicitryavakratā), that depending on the use of synonyms (Paryāyavakratā), that pertaining to attribution (Upacāravakratā), the one belonging to the use of adjectives (Viśeṣaṇavakratā), one based on concealment (Saṁvṛtivakratā), that attached to the grammatical use of Vṛttis (Vṛttivakratā), one relating to the peculiarity in the use of gender (Liṅgavaicitryavakratā), and the one related to the peculiarity of the verbal form (Kriyāvaicitryavakratā).

[5]Among these, the first one, in point of poetic beauty, is dependent on the power of indication, and *Ānanda* has dealt with it in connection with suggestion having a transfer of sense (Arthāntarasaṅkramitavācyadhvani). [6]*Kuntaka* has

1. Cf. SKB II, p. 265.
2. Vide H-KN V, p. 307.
3. Vide Supra p. 30.
4. Cf. VJ, I, pp. 66-81.
5. Cf, VJ, II, p. 192.
6. Cf. DL II, p. 167 & p. 170.

taken examples from *Dhvanyāloka* itself. As for the second, the [1]suggestionists have included it under *Paryāyadhvani* and the [2]*Alaṁkāravādins* under the figure *Parikara*. These two might come under the aegis of *Arthacitra*. With regard to the production of image,[3] we are more concerned with the third. Here, even with scanty relation, the properties of the standard of similitude are attributed to the matter in hand in such a way, that the difference between the two is eliminated, which gives rise to an identity, although the fundamental nature of the two differs in that one is abstract and animate, while the other is concrete and inanimate. Among these, where the attribution is of concrete on the abstract, we might get a true image, but where it is of the animate on the inanimate, it is so to a lesser extent. On the contrary, where the attribution is of the abstract on the concrete, we have very touching poetic beauty and sometimes imagery. [4]According to *Kuntaka*, this forms the foundation of beauty, born of the indicative sense, especially *Gauṇī*, and of the figures of sense like mataphor etc.

The fourth is also important. [5]In another context we have dealt with the power of appropriate adjectives related either to the cases or to the verbal forms. The nouns are endowed with beauty, which the particular adjective reveals. When it creates additional beauty, it might do so by giving rise to some figures of sense. [6]*Kuntaka*, very scientifically, stresses here the appropriateness of adjectives to the matter, sentiment, or the figures etc. Among these, those of imagist character are helpful in portraying the picture of the thing described, those which are sensuous awaken the sensibilities, and those intellectual provoke thought. Sometimes they also have the quality of expressing some idea succinctly.

1. Cf. SD X, p. 670.
2. Cf. CL V, p. 125.
3. Vide VJ II, p. 223.
4. Ibid, II, V. 14 : Yanmūlā sarasollekhā rūpakādiralaṁkṛtiḥ/
5. Vide Supra p. 22.
6. Cf. VJ II. 15, p. 236 :
   Svamahimnā vidhīyante yena lokottaraśriyaḥ/
   Rasasvabhāvālaṁkārāstad vidheyaṁ viśeṣaṇam//

What a sentence may not be able to express, an adjective may do. With the contact of the periphrasis dependent on attribution, the importance of the use of adjectives increases.

Among the later varieties, only the fifth and the eighth, especially the latter, bordering on poetic tricks (Kūṭas), concern us, and are relevant to the discussion in that they bring concealment and augment poetic beauty. Of the periphrasis pertaining to the latter part or the suffix part of a word, there is no importance in this context except [1]in the case of a particular variety of it, where the cases in a particular sentence are reversed, and some sort of *Kūṭa* is perceptible.

1. Ibid, illustr. V. 97, p. 275 :
Yācñāṁ dainyaparigrahapraṇayinīṁ nekṣvākavaḥ śikṣitāḥ
Sevāsaṁvalitaḥ kadā raghukule maulau nibaddho 'ñjaliḥ/
Sarvaṁ tadvihitaṁ tathāpyudadhinā naivāparodhaḥ kṛtaḥ
Pāṇiḥ samprati te haṭhāt kimaparaṁ spraṣṭuṁ dhanurdhāvati//

CHAPTER III

ŚABDA CITRA

In the peculiarities pertaining to word (Śabdacitra), ingenuity is displayed in the arrangement of letters, or in the combination of letters making different words or senses. The verbal figures of speech on which this depends, or from which the charm of *Śabdacitra* originates, are, broadly speaking, alliteration (Anuprāsa) and chime (Yamaka). The former is of two kinds : the alliteration of letters (Varṇānuprāsa), and the alliteration of words (Padānuprāsa). The former itself is of two classes : dexterous alliteration (Chekānuprāsa) consisting of repetitions of one or more consonants, and repetitive alliteration (Vṛttyanuprāsa) comprising of the repetition of a single consonant. Besides these, [1]as we have just seen, alliteration may be of many types, determined by different points of view, of which most come within the said categories. Of these, only *Lāṭānuprāsa* needs special mention. Here the letters and the sense are the same, but there is difference in the syntactical relation (Anvaya).

It may be pointed out that rhetoricians have generally accepted only two categories of alliteration, the repetitive and the dexterous one, and what in the more descriptive manner above is called the alliteration of words, is something very close to chime. To me this appears to be the more scientific view of the two and I deal with only those two categories which can be illustrated within the space of single verse : "[2]The female bees, making much noise, were excited by the

1. Vide Supra pp. 27-30.
2. Cf. SV. VI, V. 20 :

Madhurayā madhubodhitamādhavīmadhusamṛddhasamedhitamedhayā/
Madhukarāṅganayā muhurunmadadhvanibhṛtā nibhṛtākṣaramujjage//

pollen of the *Mādhavī* creeper, which was rich due to the advent of spring, and sang in steady, but sweet tones." There is a recurrence of *m*, *dh* letters on the one hand, and even of a group of these letters, construed as *mādhavī* on the other, intensifying the striking verbal expression produced by the repetition of a regular group of sounds, *nibhṛtā*.

Chime is a permutation or reverberation of words. It occurs when the same letter is repeated, or when the same word is repeated with different meanings, with regularity at the beginning, middle or end of a foot, or a whole foot in alternative feet by alterations of caesura. The latter is of three kinds : that occurring on the transference of it by the separation of an entire letter (Śṛṅkhalā), one on the resumption by a letter of its own form on the cessation of its conjunction with another letter (Parivartaka), and that on the disappearance of a word on the disruption of conjunct letters (Cūrṇaka). This classification of chime on the basis of caesura is only artificial, and here we shall avoid *Rudraṭa* and *Bhoja*, and follow *Daṇḍin*, and take it up in the various permutations and combinations of the differing varieties.

To take first the chime of the unseparated (Avyapeta) variety occurring in the beginning of a foot : "[1]Oh friend, do not show this jealous anger to your beloved; being broken-hearted, you should make him feel ashamed by clinging to his neck." Here, the chime is in the beginning of the first foot of the verse, in *mānena-mānena* (mā+anena). It may occur in the beginning of the second or third or fourth foot.

Again, there can be chiming in the beginning of the first and second feet. [2]"O one with lotus-like face, please tell (me) whether the vernal season is making your eyes have sweet

1. Vide KD III, V. 4, p. 337 :

   Mānena mānena sakhi praṇayo 'bhūt priye jane/
   Khaṇḍitā kaṇṭhamāśliṣya tameva kuru satrapam//

2. Ibid . V. 8, p. 339 :

   Madhuraṁ madhuraṁbhojavadane vada netrayoḥ/
   Vibhramaṁ bhramarabhrāntyā viḍambayati kiṁ nu te//

dalliance, mistaking it to be the black-bee !" Here, we find chime in the beginning of the first foot, *madhuraṁ-madhuraṁ* (+bhoja), and in the beginning of the second foot, *vadane-vada ne* (+trayoḥ). There can also be chime in the beginning of first and third feet, first and fourth feet, second and third feet, second and fourth feet, and third and fourth feet.

We shall now come to a verse having three chimes in the beginning of the feet. [1]"Frantic cranes were plunging into the water of the pond and the white swan, with its reviling cries, was about to kill me". Here the chime occurs at the beginning of the first, second and third feet in *viśadā-viśad* (+āmatta), *sārase-sārase*, and *kurute-kurute* (neyaṁ), respectively. In this way, this may occur in the beginning of the first, second and fourth feet, first, third and fourth feet, and second, third and fourth feet.

There could be chimes in all the four feet and everywhere in the beginning : [2]"May my charming beloved, with pale-red silken garments of *Pāṭala* colour, be like the pink rays of the sun, or like the wine-coloured western horizon (at the sunset time) !" Here chime is seen in *ramaṇī-ramaṇī* (+*yā*), *Pāṭalā-pāṭalā* (+ṁśukā), *vāruṇī-vāruṇī* (+bhūta), and *saura-bhā-saurabhā* (+spadam), respectively in the beginning of the first, second, third and fourth feet. Also, there can be many subdivisions of *yamaka*, found in the middle or end of the first, second, third, fourth feet or any of two, three, or all the four feet of the verse.

Coming to the separated (vyapeta) variety, we find that whereas chimes were always in pairs without any words intervening between them in the above instances, here there may be a word or words coming between a set, or sets of pairs. First, to take the first and second feet making up this pair : [3]"(The spring season) makes the pride (or jealous anger) of

1. Cf. Ibid : V. 14, p. 342 : Viśadā viśadāmattasārase sārase jale/
Kurute kuruteneyaṁ haṁsī māmantakāmiṣam//
2. Ibid : V. 18 p. 345 : Ramaṇī ramaṇīyā me pāṭalāpāṭalāṁśukā/
Vāruṇīvāruṇībhūtasaurabhā saurabhāspadam//
3. Ibid : V. 20 : Madhureṇadṛśām mānam madhureṇa sugandhinā/
Sahakārodgamenaiva śābdaśeṣaṁ kariṣyati//

those (women) with eyes, charming like those of the female gezelle, remain in word (or name) only, as if, with sprouting of the new bunches of blossoms of *sahakāra*, sweet and fragrant !" Here the chime occurs in *madhureṇa—madhureṇa* pair, the first one in the beginning of the first foot as part of the word *madhureṇadṛśāṁ*, and the second in the beginning of the second foot as an independent word.

Such chimes can take place between first and third feet, first and fourth feet, second and third feet, second and fourth feet, and third and fourth feet, always in the beginning. This can also occur with three groups of sounds, words, or parts of words, in the beginning of any of the three feet, finally culminating in the beginnings of all thc four feet : [1]"In the battles, the elephants, trickling with blood, having been killed with your hands, putting an end to the enemies, looked beautiful like the evening clouds !" Here, the chime is consummated in *kareṇa-kareṇa-kareṇa* in the beginning of the first, second and third feet. It is to be pointed out that *Kareṇa* is a part of the word *antakareṇa* in the second foot, and of *Kareṇavaḥ* in the third foot. It needs no mention that in the instance above, other words intervene between *kareṇa* occurring in the different feet.

There can be two sets of equal groups of sounds in different combinations, i.e. one set occurring in the first and second feet, and the second in the third and fourth, one set in the first and third feet, and the other in the second and fourth, and first as well as fourth feet constituting the first set, and the remaining second and third making up the other set. Let us take the first variety :[2] "The damsels, ornamented with jewelery, danced, with their beautiful and intoxicating eyes and lips capable of creating pleasure, and making their lovers wait upon them." Here, the first set of words occurring in the first and second feet is *mudārama*, where in the first foot, *mudā* is a separate word and *rama* is part of the word *ramaṇam*, and in the second foot, it is made out of the word

1. Ibid: V. 26, p. 348 : Kareṇa te raṇeṣvantakareṇa dviṣatāṁ hatāḥ/
Kareṇavaḥ kṣaradraktā bhānti saṁdhyāghanā iva//
2. Ibid : V. 30, p. 349 : Mudā ramaṇamanvītamudāramaṇibhūṣaṇāḥ/
Madabhramaddṛśaḥ kartumadabhrajaghanāḥ kṣamāḥ//

udāramaṇi with prior euphonic combination with *m* sound of the word *anvītam*. The word in the second set is *madabhra*, part of *madabhramaddṛśaḥ* in the third foot, and of *adabhraja-ghanāḥ* with euphonic combination with *m* sound of the word *Kartuṁ* in the fourth foot.

We should remember here that in the previous variety, where pair chimes take effect, all the sub-varieties could be possible if the chimes occur in the middle or end of the foot in combinations of first and second, first and third, first and fourth, second and fourth, and third and fourth feet. This could happen in all the four feet as well. Where there are three equal chiming groups of sounds, the combinations in the middle or end of any three feet out of the four, can be among first, second, third feet, first, third, fourth feet, and second, third and fourth feet.

Going back, in the unseparated (Avyapeta) variety, the chimes arising in the beginning of one foot and in the middle or end of another, or in the middle of one foot and end of another i.e. in the beginning of the first foot and middle or end of the second, in the beginning of the first and middle or end of the third foot, and in the beginning of the first and middle or end of the fourth foot, would make some more divisions, viz., in the middle of the first foot and beginning or middle or end of the second, in the middle of the first and beginning or middle or end of the third, and middle of the first as well as the beginning or middle or end of the fourth foot. From the point of view of the chime in the end of the first foot, the following combinations would turn out : end of the first and beginning or middle or end of the second, end of the first and beginning or middle or end of the third, and end of the first and beginning or middle or end of the fourth foot.

Naturally, in most of the above cases, when more than one set of 'pair-chimes' are met with, both unseparated and separated varieties of chimes occur. In the following, one set of identical pair chimes occurs in the beginnings of the first and second feet, and the other set in the beginnings of the third and fourth feet : [1]'She is unable to look to that *Sāla* tree whose blossoms hang down, as also she is incapable of bearing the sight of the black-bees nestling on the *Vakula* trees, and of her female friends lying to her !' Here, the chime in the first half is in *Sālaṁ-Sālam.* The first pair in the beginning of the first foot consists of *Sālaṁ*, and the identical part of the word *Sālambakalikā.* In the second pair, both the words are independent. Thus, in the second half, the beginning of the third foot consists of *Nālī-nālī* of which both constitute parts of separate words. The second pair, commencing with the fourth foot, comprises of *Nālī* existing in the compounded word, and the identical word as part of *nālīkinīrapi* where *na* and *alīkinīrapi* are euphonically combined.

Among this mixed variety, more combinations are possible as one set of pair-chimes can occur in the beginning of first and fourth or first and third, and the other pair in the beginning of second and third or third and fourth feet. Combinations could be had from the occurrence of the first set in the beginning or middle or end of first foot, and the middle or end of the second, as well as of the second set in the beginning or middle or end of third, and middle or end of the fourth feet. The occurrence of the first set can be in the beginning or middle or end of the first, and middle or end of the third feet, as well as of the second set in the beginning or middle or end of the second, and middle or end of the fourth feet; as also the occurrence of the first set in the beginning or middle or end of the first foot, and middle or end of the fourth, as well as of the second set in the beginning or middle or end of the second foot, and middle or end of the third foot.

Likewise, a single set of pair-chimes might occur in the beginning, middle or end of all the feet : [2]'In the long night of three watches, may I get at death, because she is, as if, fading

1. Ibid : V. 34, p. 351 :
   Sālaṁ sālambakalikāsālaṁ sālaṁ na vīkṣituṁ/
   Nālīnālīnavakulānālī nālīkinīrapi//
2. Ibid : V. 36, p. 353 :
   Yāma yāmatrayādhīnāyāmayā maraṇaṁ niśā/
   Yāmayāma dhiyā'svarttyāyā māyā mathitaiva sā//

away with inner pangs on account of the length of night whose vicinity I reached mentally !' Here, the pair-chime *yāma-yāma* occurs independently, or as part of other word or words euphonically combined in all the four feet in the beginning. In this way, this single-set of four-pair chimes can be found in the beginning of one, or more than one, but less than four feet, and the middle or end of the remaining feet. Going back to the separated variety, the chimes may eventuate in the beginning of the first foot and middle or end of the second, third, or fourth feet, in the middle of the first foot and beginning or middle or end of the second, or third, or fourth feet, and in the end of the first as well as the beginning or middle or end of the second, third, or fourth feet. Retracing our steps, we find only one pair-chime twice in all the four feet; one in the beginning and the other in the end, or one or more but less than four in the beginning, and remaining in the middle or just before the end, or one or more but less than four in the end and the remaining in the middle or just after the beginning, or one pair in all the four feet, or one in the middle and in the end in all the feet uniformly.

Take for example, the first sub-variety among the above-mentioned[1] : "O guileless and pitiful friend, please make my union with her possible, who is afflicted like the moon, troubled with the increase and decrease of his digits and because in the night whose watch-period does not end and who is (hence) lustreless, (and) from whom I have myself got this love-languor." Here, the chime-pair *mayā-mayā* of the unseparated variety, made up of independent or euphonically combined sounds, occurs in the beginning and end of all the feet, making also the separated variety of chime because of the intervening words between the two sets of identical pair-sounds, in each of the feet.

1. Ibid : V. 48, p. 363 :

Mayāmayālambyakalāmayāmayā
Mayāmayātavyavirāmayāmayā/
Mayāmayārtiṁ niśayāmayāmayā-
Mayāmayāmūṁ karuṇāmayāmayā//

Like the above there can also be only one pair-chime occurring thrice, or even more times, depending on the length of the foot in a particular metre accommodating the pairs, as well as the intervening words, and this can happen in all the four feet, or in other possible combinations discussed above. Here we shall take the case of three pair-chimes in each of the four feet—in the beginning, in the middle and in the end: [1]"O one with dark complexion like that of the black throat of *Śiva*, or of *Yama*, or of the laboun, O conversationalist like those cooing at the time (i.e. rainy season) of the moist, dark clouds (that is, peacocks), O *Kriṣṇa*, the destroyer of the Supreme Destroyer, the Death to the *Kali* (or sinful) Era, may the soft-speaking damsels with dark locks of hair looking beautiful on their heads, be attracted (towards you)!" The chime-pair occurring throughout at the said places is *Kāla-Kāla*. Also, there is a high order of alliteration on account of the commixture of some similar sounds in the gaps. One thing may be said here, that with the increase of pairs in a foot, the possibility of combinations increases, but the other way round, with the lessening of gaps between the pairs, this possibility might decrease.

Now we propose to deal with more complex forms of alliteration, of chime as well as the pictorial poetic compositions (Citrabandhas) etc. When a poet chooses to compose a verse with the fewest of letters, the alliterative effect is heightened. First, to take a verse made up of only two letters running throughout in any combination: [2]"He, with adroit spies, making vacuum of the enemies, looking beautiful with the waving clothes, refulgent and adept in the warfare, moved with peculiar steppings." There are only two letters *ca* and

1. Ibid : V. 50, p. 365:
   Kālakālagalakālakālamukhakālakāla
   Kālakālaghanakālakālapanakāla kāla/
   Kālakālasitakālakā lalanikālakāla
   Kālakālagatu kālakāla kalikālakāla//
2. Vide KJ, XV, V. 38 :
   Cāracañcuś cirārecī cañcaccīrarucā rucaḥ/
   Cacāra ruciraś cāru cārairācāracañcuraḥ//

ra occurring throughout this verse. This can also happen with each of the four feet having repetitions of one or two letters of different sound-groups, even in various combinations. For example, we may take each foot out of four with a different letter : [1]"With sword, with arrows and the bow, proceeding having acquired gold and elephants etc., and, thus, fortune favouring and of resplendent demeanour, though grave, and with the ability of killing even the son of *Śiva* (i.e. Skanda), *Arjuna*, jumping (as if with verve and jubilance), suddenly looked beautiful !" The first foot here is made up of *sa*, the second of *ya*, the third of *la* and the fourth again, of *śa* letters. This can eventuate in only one or two or three feet.

Now to take an example of a verse consisting of only one letter in all the four feet : [2]"O multifaced one, he is not a man to be hurt by any ordinary person, and the person who hurts an inferior one, is not really a man (i.e. he lacks manhood); and he cannot be one hurting his master, and one hurting such, who, very much already hurt, is not free of fault (i.e. it is a blemish in just warfare)." Here *na* letter runs throughout. Other letters in the constituent words are, inevitably, vowels combining euphonically with the recurrent *na* sound. These constitute the *Vyañjanacitra* of *Bhoja*, leading to the striking effect created out of the repetition of a certain number of consonants. As for the *Svaracitra*, we take here only one example, with all the letters having 'ai' vowel : [3]"May I be prosperous with (attainment of) the gods like

1. Ibid, V. 5 :
   Sa sāsiḥ sāsusūḥ sāsoyeyāyeyāyayāyayaḥ/
   Lalau līḷāṁ lalo'lolaḥ śāśīśāśiśuśīḥ śaśau//

2. Ibid, V. 14 :
   Na nonanunnonunnono nānā nānānanānanu/
   Nunno'nunnonanunnenonānenānunnanunnanuṭ//

3. Vide SKB II illustr. 277, p. 271 :
   Vaidhairainairaiśairaindra iraijairailairjainaiḥ saiddhaih/
   Maitrairnaikairdhairyairvaira irdaiḥ svaiḥ svairairdaivaistaistaiḥ//

Brahmā, *Viṣṇu*, *Śiva*, *Indra*, *Kāma* (i.e. Cupid), *Ilā* (i.e. Earth), *Buddha*, the *Siddhas*, *Mitra*, *Kubera* and those over and above these, and with the patience and opulence of sundry kinds, all well-known !" Of the *Sthānacitra*, it is not proposed to give here any illustration, as unless limited to the use of only one or two letters, having identical pronunciation where it would be a de facto case of *Varṇacitra*—it does not generally evoke wonder at first sight.

Coming to the more complex varieties of chime, to take first what is called 'Chaining chimes' (Śṛṅkhalāyamaka), so named as one word of the chime-pair comes in the end of a foot and in the beginning of the consecutive foot, thus connecting the two : [1]"*Śiva*, with mercy, not that did not speed the arrows, dreadful, with their heads spilling away the fears and capped with the feathers of peacocks." The first pair in the first two feet is *Bhīmā-bhīmā* and the second in the third and fourth feet is *Śikhā-śikhā*. Besides the above, there could also be one connecting chime-pair between the end of the second and the beginning of the third foot. In all, there being three chime-pairs, this variety is named *Sandaṣṭa* : [2]"That woman (lit. the weak one) whose love is brimming due to enebriety (or intoxication) and who has pangs of cupid within, did not prove to be so much heat-giving (or afflicting) to me, having been accompanied by me, in spite of being enraged on account of my offences." The pair connecting the first and second feet is *madena sā-madenasā*, while the second pair connecting the second and third feet is—*na yojitā*—*na yojitā-* and the third one connecting the third and fourth feet is *gatāpitā-gatāpi tā-*.

Among the most complex, there could be the repetition of a foot in different combinations i.e. in first and second, in

1. Ibid, V. 42 :

   Tena vyātenire bhīmā bhīmārjunaphalānanāḥ/
   Na nānukampya viśikhāḥ śikhādharajavāsasaḥ//

2. Vide KD III, V. 52, p. 368 :

   Upoḍharāgāpyabalā madena sā madenasā manyurasena yojitā/
   Na yojitātmānamanaṅgatāpitāṅgatāpi tāpāya mamāsa neyate//

first and third, in first and fourth, in second and third, in second and fourth, or the first three feet can be the same, or the first two and fourth, or the last three. For instance : [1]"I, the stupid one who did not shun the jealous wrath tenaciously, and whose heart and soul both are pitiless, did not embrace my lover, fallen on my feet, in a way so that I could have pressed my two breasts against his bosom !" The first foot *Namandayāvarjitamānasātmayā* is repeated in the second. All these are called foot-chimes (Padābhyāsayamaka), but when all four feet are the same, it is the chime superior (Mahāyamaka) : [2]"The arrows of *Arjuna* (lit. the overlord of the world) disseminated (in different directions). In the world the arrows of *Śiva* were made to go the adverse way; the *Gaṇas* of *Śiva*, capable of killing the demons, felt jubilant and those looking for *Śiva* (i.e. gods and the sages) took to heaven (lit. the moving place of the birds) !" Here, *Vikāśamīyurjagatīśa-mārgaṇā* is repeated in the four feet.

There is, also, a variety called *Samudgaka* where half the verse, consisting of two feet, is identical : [3]"We have swiftly moving chariots, we have dexterously trotting horses, we have divine elephants sounding sweetly and we have a distinguished infantry capable of getting over all odds." The first root is identical with the third and the second with the fourth. So the hemistich comprising of the first two feet *Syandamāno chaturagāḥ surebhāvāvipattayaḥ* is repeated in identical manner. Two more combinations can be possible here,

1. Vide Ibid III, V. 57, p. 372 :

    Na mandayāvarjitamānasātmayā namandayāvarjitamāna-sātmayā/
    Urasyupāstīrṇapayodharadvayaṁ mayā samāliṅgyata jīviteś-varaḥ//

2. Cf KJ. XV, V. 52 :

    Vikāśamīyurjagatīśamārgaṇā vikāśamīyurjagatīśa mārgaṇāḥ/
    Vikāśamīyurjagatīśamārgaṇā vikāśamīyurjagatīśamārgaṇāḥ//

3. Ibid XV, V. 16 :

    Syandanā no chaturagāḥ surebhāvāvipattayaḥ/
    Syandanā no cha turagāḥ surebhāvā vipattayaḥ//

first where the first foot is repeated in the second and the third in the fourth, and second, where the first foot is identical with the fourth and the second with the third. To crown all, even one separate verse could be repeated verbally in another verse, both having different meanings : [1](i) "O king, on account of your muscular and stout arms, unequalled in destroying the strong foes, this earth has become dreadless". (ii) "Your enemies who are leaderless, whose weapons are placed on the funeral pyre, whom affluence (or sovereignty) and friends have bereaved, and who are afraid, have climbed the scale of *Yama* (i.e. have died)." One verse having the identical groups of sounds repeated in the other is *Vināyakena bhavatā vṛttopacitabāhunā/ Svamitroddhāriṇābhītā pṛthvī yamatulāśritā//* This is called verse chime (Ślokābhyāsayamaka).

It is a difficult art in which a poet reverses a particular verse in another verse : [2](i) "O immortals, our adversaries, endowed with sharp swords, fearless, resplendent, (and) beautiful, and capable of putting up with the strains of battles, do not in the matter of strength feel shaky." (ii) "Shining with armour, gleaming with the fire of energy and with glowing high breasts, who, fearless, relishes the battle-field, devouring (people) with (roaring) sounds." The first verse is *Niśitāsirato 'bhīkonyejate 'maraṇārucā/ Sārato na virodhī na svābhāsobharavānuta //*', repeated in reverse order in the second verse, beginning from the end of this verse and ending with the beginning. In the like manner, when half the verse is repeated in reverse order, we can have the reversed

1. Vide KD, Vs. 68-69, p. 382 :

   Vināyakena bhavatā vṛttopacitabāhunā/
   Svamitroddhāriṇā'bhītā pṛthvī yamatulāśritā//
   Vināyakena bhavatā vṛttopacitabāhunā/
   Svamitroddhāriṇā'bhītā pṛthvī yamatulāśritā//

2. Cf. KD XV, Vs, 22-23 :

   Niśitāsirato'bhī konyejate'maraṇārucā/
   Sārato na virodhī naḥ svābhāsobharavānuta//
   Tanuvārabhasobhāsvānadhīrovinatorasā/
   Cāruṇā ramate janye ko'bhītārasitāśini//

half verse chime (Pratilomaślokārdhayamaka) : [1]"I, who am plunged in meditation of *Brahman*, have no love for worldly pleasures, or the pangs of Cupid, or any sad thought wearing the bliss which overcomes even time." The first two feet repeated in reverse order consist of *Nādinomadenā dhīḥ svā na me kācana kāmitā/*. Likewise, there can be the reversed verse-foot chime (Pratilomapādayamaka) where at the end of a foot, the consecutive foot begins with the ending letters of the former and goes on to end in the reverse way : [2]"O one lording over the demons even in the Heaven, will you be able to go to conquer the different directions (i.e. regions situated in different quarters), being endowed with indifferent notions, in the mountains difficult of access (by enemies) on account of dense forest trees, quite unshakable and where foes cannot get hold of you ?" Here, *Vetraśākakujeśaile* of the first foot is repeated in the second in reverse order, and *yāta kiṁ vidiśo jetuṁ* of the third foot, is reversed in the fourth.

In what is called the half-moving (Ardhabhrama), the letters in all the feet are so arranged that the first, second, third and fourth letters, in descending order, as well as in ascending order the last the penultimate letters, the third from last and the fourth from last, when read together would give the first, second, third and the last foot of the verse. The most noteworthy thing here is that each foot would have only eight letters, otherwise the letters of one side would not correspond to the letters of the other side, and all the letters would not make the whole verse exactly. It is obvious that the letters making the last foot stand close to each other in all the feet. [3]From the figure it is clear that there are

1. Cf. KD III, V. 75, p. 387 :

   Nādino madanādhī svā na me kācana kāmitā/
   Tārnikā na ca kāmena svādhīnādamanodinā//

2. Vide KJ, XV, V. 18 :

   Vetraśākakuje śaile' leśaije'kukaśātrave/
   Yāta kiṁ vidiśo jetuṁ tujeśodivi kiṁ tayā//

3. Vide Appendix No. II, Figure No. 1.

four linings of arrows, first coming down and then moving up in a half-moon, forming the four feet of the verse. Had the said linings made a circle or moved all round, it would have been all-moving (Sarvatobhadra), but as they move in a half circle, it is called half-moving.

[1]With the aforesaid all-round moving, the arrangement of letters is such that besides the respective co-ordination of first letters to the last, of the second to the penultimate ones, of the third to the third from last, and of the fourth to the fourth from last letters to make up the four feet, respectively in descending and ascending order, the resultant foot would prove itself even though read either way. So, in the *Ardhabhrama* variety, for example, the first letters of all the four feet in descending order, would make the first foot, read or written from the righthand side, only when taken together with the last letters of the four feet in ascending order. But in this variety, the first letters and the last in descending and ascending order respectively, would make the first foot of the verse, read or written even from the lefthand side. Therefore, with a view to the formation of a particular foot, let us first come down and then, moving horizontally, go up in respect of the reading of a particular set of letters, and then move to the right and get the first foot in the same order as one would get in reading the same to the left from the same point from where one started reading the first letters of all the feet. The most remarkable feature here is that out of the eight letters of which each foot of this variety consists, four from the beginning are the same as the next four in reversed order, and so, the last letter of the first group is the same as the first of the other group, the penultimate letter of the first is identical with the second letter of the second group, and so on. One thing more. The first letters and the last, in the said order, form the big circle or half-circle, the next correlating letters the smaller, the next yet smaller, and the next the smallest. Among the four feet in criss-cross fashion, there are,

1. Vide Appendix No. II, Figure No. 2.

in all, twenty-one squares. As the two four-letter-groups in each foot are reversible to each other, each letter in each foot comes twice in identical manner. It is noteworthy that the above few, according to *Bhoja*, constitute the *Gaticitra*. The above figures may be called subtler varieties of chime (yamaka), requiring more poetic skill.

Of *Gomūtrikā*, though *Bhoja* treats it among the *bandhacitras*, [1]he says that it depends on the peculiarity of movement (Gativaicitrya) and hence, we classify it under *Gaticitras*. [2]It has several varieties : that constituting two or more feet of the verse called *Pādagomūtrikā*, one constituting it in a verse and then giving rise to another verse called *Ardhagomūtrikā*, one constituting of two verses which is called *Ślokagomūtrikā* etc. Moreover, sometimes we have the last-mentioned variety where the two verses are composed in two different languages, or even in two separate metres, and then there is *Gomūtrikādhenu* and its sub-varieties, which give rise to a hundred, a thousand, or any number of *gomūtrikā* verses. This is really a marvellous feat of which Sanskrit poetry might be proud. [3]It may be pointed out here that this variety of *Citrabandha* is called *Gomūtrikā* because the system of reading out the verse it follows, is in a cut-cross fashion like that of the sprinkling urine of a moving cow.

Avoiding detail, we treat here only [4]*Pādagomūtrikā* as a representative variety. We first make an elongated rectangle and bisect it lengthwise. Then, starting from the lefthand side corner below, we draw eight parallel lines upward meeting

1. Vide SKB II, p. 284 : Udāharaṇamātraṁ caitat, tena gativicitrādigomūtrikādayo 'nye'pi citraprakārā bhavanti.
2. Vide Ibid : pp. 284-293.
3. Ibid : V. 115, p. 284 :

   Gatiruccāvacā yatra mārge mūtrasya goriva/
   Gomūtriketi tatprāhurduṣkaraṁ citravedinaḥ//
4. The illustr. V. :

   Kāṁkṣan pulomatanayāstanapīḍitāni
   Vakṣaḥsthalotthitarayanchanapiditani/
   Pāyādapāyabhayato namucipraharī
   Māyāmapāsya bhavato'mbumucāṁ prasārī//

on the upper line of the rectangle, so that the eighth line meets half-way on the righthand side vertical line. Then, starting from the lefthand side corner above, we draw parallel lines so that these lines meet the previously drawn lines on points where they touch the upper or the lower horizontal lines of the rectangle. Now the first two pattern-gaps, one just above the other, on both left and right sides, are to be left out, and starting from the lefthand side, in the next pattern-gap every letter is to be placed on the bisecting line, and in the previous adjacent ones, the letters are to be kept in the middle. It is peculiar that every following letter, even in the second foot, is identical with that in the first, and so, after filling the upper half of the rectangle, when we fill the lower half, every successive letter of the foot coincides on the bisecting line and only the previous ones have to be filled up in the aforesaid manner. Likewise, the next two feet of the verse have also to be filled up in a separate figure.

Unlike *Gomūtrikā*, [1]*Turaṅgapadabandha* comes within *Gaticitras*, in its own right. [2]Here, when all the four feet of the verse are written out in four lines in a systematic way, each letter within a separate pattern, quite a different verse arises when letters are sorted out from the patterns to be covered, as through the movement of a horse in chess i.e. with the movement of two-and-a-half patterns away. To come to the other verse, we move from the first pattern in the first line to the third in the second, then to the fifth in the first, the seventh in the second, the eighth in the fourth, the sixth in the third, the fourth in the fourth, the second in the third, the third in the first, the fifth in the second, the seventh in the first, the eighth in the third, the sixth in the fourth, the fourth in the third, the second in the fourth, the first in the second, the third in the third, the first in the fourth, the second in the second, the fourth in the first, the fifth in the third, the

1. Ibid : p. 279.
2. The illustr V.:

Bālā sukālabālā kā kāntilālakalālitā/
Sasvā sutavatī sārā darpikā vratagardhita//

seventh in the fourth, the eighth in the second, the sixth in the first, the seventh in the third, the eighth in the first, the sixth in the second, the fifth in the fourth, the fourth in the second, the second in the first, the first in the third, and then to the third in the fourth and the last line. For a simple understanding of this movement, we have, in due order, to put numbers in different patterns in the figure given.

Quite similar to this is [1]*Śarayantrabandha*, as here also we move with chess-steps, but in a different way. [2]The four feet of the verse are written out in four lines but as we move with chess-steps to the last among the four feet, we gradually get all these four feet again and not a different verse altogether, as in the previous figure. For the first two feet, this movement will be downwards and for the last two upwards. For every successive letter in all the feet, we have to move out into the other feet, otherwise, for every alternate letter, we have to come to the particular foot undertaken. So in the figure cited, to make up the first foot, one moves for the second, fourth, sixth and eighth letters of the first foot to the identical letters in the third foot, and for giving rise to a similar second foot for the letters in the identical positions already mentioned, we move to identical positions in the fourth foot. Likewise, for the third and fourth feet respectively, we have to move up for the letters in the identical positions to the first and the second feet.

Now to deal with the poetic designs (bandhas). Among them, we have seen that [3]*Rudraṭa* has illustrated some new varieties. In fact, this literature has been growing even in modern times and newer types are still being evolved. Roughly, *bandhas* come up to more than a hundred and fifty in number and some of them bifurcate into many divisions. As the aim is only to introduce the reader to the subject and not

1. Ibid, p. 282.
2. The illustr. V. :

Namaste jagatāṁ gātra sadānavakulakṣaya/
Samaste'ja satāṁ nātra mudāmavana lakṣaya//

3. Vide Supra Chap. II.

to make an elaborate treatment of it, we shall treat only a few important and much-known *bandhas*. [1]It may be pointed out that *Bhoja* has divided them into two varieties : *Ākāracitras* and *Bandhacitras*, and accordingly, though the division is quite artificial, we follow it for convenience. [2]It is peculiar that among the former, only several varieties of *Padmabandha* (lotus-design) and *Cakrabandha* (wheel-design) are taken, and in the latter all the rest are included.

Among the *Ākāracitras*, to first take the lotus-design. This could be of many kinds, such as the four-petalled ones, the eight-petalled ones, the sixteen-petalled ones etc. and, those with the names of the poets related to them. The latter could be possible in all the varieties. Among these, [3]we illustrate for convenience, only the eight-petalled one. In this, there are eight petals, with eight petal-shaped patterns, and there is also one middle filament-portion displaying one round pattern. All the 'yā' letters in the verse in point, are represented by a single such letter placed in the middle pattern. In this case, on two petals there is only one letter each, as against two on every other petal. Otherwise, to make two on all uniformly, of the sixth, eighth and ninth 'yā' letters of the second hemistich, the first two have to be written on separate petals, with the closest associative or concomitant letters, i.e. with 'dhi' and 'mā' letters respectively. Now, beginning with the initial letters of the verse, let us start from the central 'yā' letter, and in the vertical petal above, let first *śri*, and then above it 'tā' letters, be placed in order to make *yāśritā*. Then, place in the petal left to it 'pā' first, and then 'va' above it, then, from the position in the petal still left to it, place 'na', and 'ta' below it, going back to the central 'yā' making up *Pāvanatayā* with these two petals combined, as against the former which alone made up the previously combined whole *yāśritā*.

1. Ibid, p. 265.
2. Ibid, pp. 272-276.
3. The illustr. V. :

Yāśritā pāvanatayā yātanacchadanīcayā/
Yācanīyā dhiyā māyā yāmāyāsaṁstutāśriyā//

Starting from the same central place and coming back in a centrifugal manner to the same petal, viz., first to 'ta' and then to 'na' and then to the petal left to it, first place *ccha* and then 'da' above it, and going above to the petal still left to it, placing first 'nī' and then 'ca' below it, and going back to the central 'yā', makes *yātanacchadanīcayā*, thus ending the first hemistich of the verse. Now, coming up from the central 'yā' to the same petal in order, first to 'ca' and then to 'nī', and then going back to the same 'yā', constitutes *yācanīyā*. Likewise, starting fresh from the top of the petal left to it, viz, from 'dhi' and then to 'yā' below it, shapes *dhiyā*, and then to the petal still left to it, going bottom to bottom, we get 'mā', and then 'yā' just above it, making *māyā*, and then retracing from above to below and going to the central 'yā', forms *yāmāyā*. Ultimately, moving from the central 'yā' to 'saṁ' below 'stu' on the petal left to it, and then to the latter and then again going to the petal still left to it, top to top, to 'tā' from 'stu' and latterly to *śri* below it and to the central 'yā', makes up *Saṁstutāśriyā*, thus, ending the second half of the couplet. One important fact is that in the sixth and seventh petals, 'yā' letters might be disposed of, giving these two petals only one letter each, as against two on every other petal. In that case, the letters on the said petals, whenever required, would be construed with the central 'yā'. This is partly shown in the miniature figure where 'yā' letters have been retained in the petals. In the other figure, all possible relations have been shown with the central 'yā', or with 'yā' in the petals, whichever is more expedient. The relation of the letters on the petals with that in the centre is either centripetal i.e. when it comes from the petal to the centre, or, centrifugal i.e. when it emanates from the centre towards any of the petals.

Next the [1]wheel-design. Here also, many varieties might be possible, dependent on the number of spikes in a particular

1. The illustr. V. :

Śuddhaṁ baddhasurāsthisāraviṣama tvaṁ rugjayātisthira
Bhraṣṭoddharmarajaḥpadaṅgavi gavākṣīṇena cañcadbhruvā/

wheel, such as the six-spiked one, the eight-spiked one etc. To avoid detail, we illustrate only the six-spiked one. Here, every foot of the verse begins and ends on a separate spike, where, except the first and last letters which are on the circumference of the wheel, the middle letter is always in the midpoint and which, in the first three feet, invariably is so. Thus, the central letter is construed with all the three feet except the last one, which forms the circumference with spacing of the gaps. These two letters have no relation with those on the spikes or with that in the centre, there being two letters in each gap. The letters on the circumference coincide with every fourth letter of the fourth and the last foot, and do not have to be rearranged. As against the lotus-design illustrated, the letters, except those on the circumference or in the centre, forming the spikes, are running as naturally as in a verse and are not all related to each other in the same way as in the former figure, where the cross-relations among each and every letter are shown through the arrow-marks.

To deal with the poetic designs (bandhas), we take up a few representative ones among the many. First, the [1]umbrella design (Chatrabandha). Here, characteristically, we would have the first foot of the verse reversed in the last foot so that both, being one, would form the handle of the umbrella, and the second and the third feet in continuous order, would together fill up the seven gaps in between the eight stretching bars. Starting from the righthand side, the first three gaps would have in natural order, firstly, three letters, and then two each, and then from the fourth gap onwards the rest of the letters would place themselves in reverse order i.e. the letter coming first would be placed upward and the one coming next beneath that letter. In this way the fourth, fifth, and sixth gaps, would have two letters each, and the seventh would get a

Tathyaṁ cintitaguptirastavidhidigbhedannacakraṁ śucā
Cāro 'prāṁśuradabhramugratanu me ramyo bhavānīrucā//

1. The illustr. V. :
Tanutāṁ tanutāṁ rādhākriṣṇayoścaritaśrutiḥ/
Hṛttāpānāṁ sudhāsindhudhārā tāṁ nu tatāṁ nuta//

quota of three letters. As will be clear from the figure given, starting from the lower part of the handle upwards, and then at the end diverting to the right and starting from the first gap to the last, in the order required as mentioned, and then starting from the uppermost part of the stick downwards, we have an umbrella in verse-form.

Like the above, in what is called the [1]banner-design (Patākābandha) there are only eight letters in each foot but the difference is that in the stick part of the banner we will not give a whole foot, the first foot, nor only the first foot is the same as reversed form of the last or fourth foot, rather, the whole first two feet are identical with the next two feet when reversed. So in the stick portion, only the first six letters of the first foot would be placed, one below the other, in vertical form, and out of the remaining letters of the first and second feet combined, the first and the uppermost linear gap has four letters and the next two below this have three each, all horizontally written in the natural order. It will be obvious that beginning with the letters of the banner-pole in ascending order, and at the end moving on to the first linear pattern, and then the second and the third horizontally, we have the first two feet or the hemistich. After that, reading back from the end of the third linear pattern, then the second, then the first, from left to right, and coming to the pole, reading back in descending order would give the other hemistich or the last two feet. This poetic structure is nothing more than the reversed half-verse chime (Pratilomaślokārdhayamaka) with the difference that whereas in the former each foot should consist of only eight letters, there can be no such restriction in regard to the latter.

The same verse can be cast in the club figure (Gadābandha) order when, beginning upside down in the handle of the club, having only one letter in the first and uppermost pattern followed by two such patterns with three letters each in descending vertical order, and then among three such patterns on the club itself, giving each one three letters in hori-

1. The illustr. V.: Rāsataṁsarasārambhe rādhā sā'raramādhavaṁ/
Bandhamārarasādhārābhe'raṁ sārasataṁsarā//

zontal natural order, we get the hemistich. Going up, reading the same letters in the opposite way, we come to the other half of the verse and the whole verse is complete. The first thing to be noted is that the total number of letters in the handle part is seven, while in the previous structure it was only six. But with this divergence, we have in all the patterns, three letters consistently, except the one remnant letter which is kept separately in the uppermost stripe. In the previous pattern we begin in the ascending order, in this design we start in descending order of the polar part of the club as is evidenced from the figure. From the point of view of symmetry and consistency, one more element is noticeable, that in the second and third pattern-shreds of the handle respectively, we find 'ta' letter flanked by 'sa' letter, and 'sā' letter flanked by 'ra' letter.

Finally, [1]the drum-design (Murajabandha). Here we have first two strings tightened on the opposite sides. The first one is bound up to the lefthand side corner above, and touching the middle of the lower portion meets the righthand side corner above, and the second one, on the opposite side, bound up to the lefthand side corner below and bisecting the upper portion, comes down to the righthand side corner beneath. The first forms the first foot of the verse and in the second are placed the letters constituting the fourth foot. These two make a rectangle in the middle having the common letters *Nā-ga-ma-nā* in the same order as read from the half above and half below. There are two rectangles from both sides, having almost the same area, meeting in an artistic way in the middle of the previously mentioned rectangle. Among these two rectangles, that at the lefthand side makes up the second foot, where the letters are placed in an order starting from the left corner and coming, upside down, near the same position, and one at the righthand side consisting of the third foot where the letters are read from the right corner, upside down, close to the same point.

With the intersection of these three rectangles, ten

1. The illustr. V. : Sā senā gamanārambhe rasenāsīdanāratā/
Tāranādajanā mattadhīranāgamanāmayā//

small rectangles are formed consisting of four letters in a systematic way which produce no meaning. In consonance with a regular system, the letters are always placed after the intersection. If the corner has no such intersection, then on two flanks of the corner, two letters are placed. What is noteworthy is the production of twelve triangles on the four sides of the drum-figure and surprisingly, if the placing of letters be accurate, methodical and artistic, all the four feet of the verse would be read out, one after another, in four lines, as if in a natural way.

In the above *Citrabandhas*, whether *Gaticitras*, *Ākāra-citras* or the *Bandhacitras*, the most common thing is the repetition of certain letters in certain positions, which enhances the sense of wonder produced in a particular variety. Thus, alliteration and chimes might be said to be at the root of these poetic designs. [1]The particular verses quoted as illustrations corroborate this idea. In *Gomūtrikā*, the word *Pīḍitāni* occurs at the end of the first two feet and in the beginning and end of the last two feet respectively, occur the alliterative words *Pāyādapāya* and *Māyāmapāsya*, *Prahārī* and *Prasārī*. In *Turaṅgapada*, the first two feet have several alliterations, and in the beginning of the third it is found in *Sa sva su*, and likewise the words *Darpikā* and *Gardhita* occurring respectively in the beginning and end of the fourth foot. In *Śarayantra*, the first and third feet are similar in sound and so are the second and the fourth. In *Padmabandha* there is a recurrence of similar sounds in *Pāvanatayā*, *Nīcayā* and *Yācanīyā dhiyā māyā yāmāyā* etc. and so in the *Cakrabandha* in *Śuddhaṁ baddha*, *Gavigavā*, *Guptirasta* and *Radabhramugra* etc. Likewise, there are alliterations and chimes in *Tanutāṁ tanutāṁ*, *Sudhāsindhu-dhārā* and *Tāṁ nutatāṁ nuta* in *Chatrabandha*, in *Rāsataṁ sara-sārambhe*, *Rādhāsāra* etc. in *Patākābandha* and in *Murajabandha* in *Sā senā* and *Rasenā*, and in *Tāranā* and *Dhīranā*, respectively in the beginning of the first and second, third and fourth feet. In the last-mentioned variety, in the middle of the first and fourth feet, the word *Gamanā* recurs, adding to the total effect.

1. Vide Supra, pp. 59-66.

CHAPTER IV

UBHAYACITRA

In this chapter we propose to deal with the second division of the third variety of poetry, namely, the peculiarity pertaining to both word and meaning (Ubhayacitra). Both word and the meaning together should give charm to a particular verse. Here, we should be clear that the striking effect pertaining to the word (Śabdacitra), or that pertaining to the meaning (Arthacitra), can be found singly in a set of verses constituting a separate body of poetry. But this second division can be found only in a few individual and scattered verses. I do not mean to say that the striking qualities pertaining to both word and meaning (Ubhayacitra), running continuously and consistently throughout a number of verses, is an impossibility. This is generally not possible insofar as this variety of *Citrakāvya* embodies within itself a commixture both of the figures of sound and of sense. We try to establish in further chapters that the riddles (Prahelikās), or the poetic tricks (Kūṭas) etc., also constitute this variety of poetry and we might get them running throughout a number of verses.

Here, we may give passing reference to the fact that [1]this division has not been accepted by all the rhetoricians and is missed by even the magnum opus, *Dhvanyāloka*. But this might have been done mainly through omission or commission. Those rhetoricians who relied, for this classification, on the concept of the figures of speech, of both sound and sense, have not generally felt the necessity of recognising this division. According to them, only two could be possible

1. Cf. DL III, pp. 494-495.

concomitant with the two types of figures of speech. In fact, this division consists in the sum-total of striking effects generated by both the figures of speech, and in this case is homogeneous, incapable of being separated or demarcated as that of word or of sense. Here I differ from the view of *Dīkṣita* and others, that a verse containing both the figures of sound and sense might be taken as an instance of *Ubhaya-citra.*

In this division may be included the particular figures utilising the striking qualities of the two kinds of figures of speech (Ubhayālaṁkāras) standing on their borderland, chiefly the poetic tricks (Kūṭas), in which might come different varieties of riddles, controverted points (Praśnas), and other verbal tricks effective through concealment, placement, and dropping of letter etc. Here we may note that sometimes *Kūṭas* themselves take help of, or are born out of, some particular figure of sound (Śabdālaṁkāra) or of sound and sense (Ubhayālaṁkāra). It is seldom the case that a particular verse, forming *Kūṭa*, arises on some figure of sense (Arthālaṁkāra).

Firstly let us examine the dual nature of the aforesaid figures. Among these, the [1]concealing speech is that which is not addressed to the person for whom it is intended : "O bullock, be off another's field; the guardian of the field is coming." Here the speaker exhorts somebody, engaged in amorous antics with the wife of another, and tells him of the danger of staying. On the contrary, only the first part of the illustration covers the [2]revealing speech qua poetic figure. In both places there is use of some word or words having more than one meaning. In the above example, such a word is *Kṣetra* meaning both 'field' and 'wife'. The real purport of the speech is not intended for a neutral audience, and the second sense is always a suggestive one. The dual character of these two figures is due to the double entendre present. In

1. Cf. KN, V. 154, p. 252 :
   Gūḍhoktiranyoddeśyaṁ ced yadanyaṁ prati kathyate/
   Vṛṣāpehi parakṣetrādāyāti kṣetrarakṣakaḥ//
2. Ibid., V. 155, p. 253 : Vivṛtoktiḥ śliṣṭaguptaṁ kavināviṣkṛtaṁ yadi/
   Vṛṣāpehi parakṣetrāditi vakti sasūcanam//

[1]contriving speech there is also concealment, but of one's own motive and actions, as a result of which, not only the motive is concealed, but the person to whom it remains undisclosed is duped: 'She was drawing your picture but seeing somebody coming, gave it in hand the bow of flowers'. [2]This is similar to the use of certain words with particular motive in *Kūṭa* poetry. The [3]*Sūkṣma* figure is likewise similar.

[4]In insinuatory speech, a skilled speaker, having used a proverb, wants to suggest a concealed sense : "O friend, only a serpent knows the steps of a serpent." Here the conduct of a bad man is made known from that of another such person, perhaps on the basis of the pun on the word *Bhujaṅga*, meaning both 'serpent' and a 'bad character.' [5]Even in subversive speech, there is pun, and through it some other meaning is suggested : "O beloved, shun your jealous anger; the day has come. *Nandī* is not here; he is near *Śiva*." The second part of the speech is a clever subversion of the first, which, in that sense is construed differently, meaning, 'Don't leave *Nandī* who is come.' As for the seeming tautology, it consists in the use of different words which appear to give one meaning but have many.

Among *Kūṭas*, we illustrate first one based on chimes : [6]"O *Jānakī*, *Rāma* has sent you this ring of brilliant colour, of gold, pure, and with the letters of his name inscribed." Here, the word *Suvarṇa*, in genitive, has been repeated four

1. Cf. KN, V. 156, p. 256 :
   Yuktiḥ parātisandhānaṁ kriyayā marmaguptaye/
   Tvāmālikhantī dṛṣṭvā'nyaṁ dhanuḥpauṣpaṁ kare 'likhat//
2. Cf. SRB 198-67, p. 540.
3. Cf. KN V 151, p. 248.
4. Cf. Ibid. V. 158, p. 257 :
   Chekoktiryatra lokokteḥ syādarthāntaragarbhitā/
   Bhujaṅga eva jānīte bhujaṅgacaraṇaṁ sakhe//
5. Ibid V. 159, p. 259 :
   Vakroktiḥ śleṣakākubhyāmaparārthaprakalpanam/
   Muñca mānaṁ dinaṁ prāptaṁ neha nandī harāntike//
6. Cf. SRB 194-8, p. 532 :
   Suvarṇasya suvarṇasya suvarṇasya ca Jānaki/
   Preṣitā tava Rāmeṇa suvarṇasya ca mudrikā//

times. The meanings in respective order are : of brilliant colour, pure, with letters (inscribed), and golden. Sometimes, this striking sense is generated through the use of symbols and metaphors, generally taken from the phenomena of nature. Often a letter or even a number is sufficient to convey the idea[1] : "The eagle (Garuḍa), swan and bullock (in reverse order), are carriers who have in their hands trident, conch-shell and disc (respectively). Such gods (namely *Śiva*, *Brahmā* and *Viṣṇu*) may stay in your house with *Pārvatī*, *Sāvitrī* and *Lakṣmī* (respectively as spouses)." Here, the first letters of the words stand for the whole and are compounded in normal order. These words are : *Vihaṅgaḥ* standing for *Garuḍa*, the king of birds, from *viḥ* meaning 'bird', for *Haṁsa* from *Haṁ*, and for *Vṛṣabha* from '*Ga*' signifying '*Go*' meaning 'bullock', *Tricakaṁdharapāṇayaḥ* where *Tri* stands for *Triśūla*, *Ca* for *Cakra* and *Kaṁ* for *Kambu*; and *Pāsālasahitāḥ* where *Pā* is for *Pārvatī*, *Sā* for *Sāvitrī* and *La* for *Lakṣmī*. Again, there might be use in a specialised sense, of words with manifold meanings: [2]"Having seen a corpse fallen in the waters, the black crow became happy; all the jackals are weeping: O god, why did he go (out of hand) !" The words *Keśava*, *Droṇa* and *Kaurava*, are not used in the conventional sense of *Kriṣṇa*, *Droṇācārya* and the *Kauravas*. In respective order, they mean 'the corpse in water,' 'the black crow' and 'the jackals'. The apparent contradiction in actions in respect of the conventional meanings of the words used, engenders the striking effects.

Sometimes a long series of compounded words stand for and mean one object : [3]'May *Kṛṣṇa*, having eyes like lotuses, the ally of *Arjuna*; the husband of *Draupadī* : the sister of

1. Cf. SRB 195-28, p. 532 :
   Vihaṅgā vāhanaṁ yeṣāṁ tricakandharapāṇayaḥ/
   Pāsālasahitā devāḥ sadā tiṣṭhantu te gṛhe//
2. Ibid. 194-1, p. 532 :
   Keśavaṁ patitaṁ dṛṣṭvā droṇo harṣamupāgataḥ/
   Rudanti kauravāḥ sarve hā keśava kathaṁ gataḥ//
3. Ibid, 197-9, p. 539 :
   Vāyumitrasutabandhuvāhanārātibhūṣaṇaśirovalambinī/
   Tajjavairibhaginīpateḥ sakhā pātu māṁ kamalalocano hariḥ//

Śikhaṇḍī : the foe of *Bhīṣma*, begotten of the *Gaṅgā* whom *Śiva* carried on his head, who himself makes ornaments of the serpents; the enemy of rats; the carrier of *Gaṇeśa* : the brother of *Kārttikeya*; the son of *Agni* : the friend of *Vāyu*, protect me !" Almost the whole of the first three feet of the verse mean *Arjuna*. This is possible because of the far-fetched application of the power of indication which is, actually, a [1]blemish in poetic constructions but is sublimated in *Kūṭa* because of the sense of wonder it creates. The whole compound may be resolved thus : The companion of *Vāyu*=*Agni*; his son=*Kārttikeya*; his brother=*Gaṇeśa*; his carrier=rat; its enemy=serpent; one making it a decoration=*Śiva*; one having been kept on his head=*Gaṅgā*; one born of her=*Bhīṣma*; his foe=*Sikhaṇḍī*; his sister=*Draupadī*; her husband =*Arjuna*. This can happen in a series of words even without a compound : [2]"May *Viṣṇu*, the lord of *Lakṣmī*, the progeny of waters : the enemy of fire, the offspring of the inner part of (the trunk of) the fig-tree, be pleased with me !" Here the difference lies in the use of the word *Garbha* in more than one shades of meaning. First and foremost, this is used in the sense of 'inner part' and then it means 'progeny.' The exposition is : the inner part of the fig tree; its progeny=*Agni*; its enemy=water; its progeny=*Lakṣmī*; her lord=*Viṣṇu*. Thus the use of words in meanings not in vogue brings forth *Kūṭa* : [3]"In *Kali* age the countryside would commerce in foodgrains, the brāhmins in the Vedas and women in their secret parts." Here also the poetic charm, however artificial, emerges out of a blemish. The exposition of the illustration lies in the knowledge of the meanings of the [4]words *Aṭṭa*, *Śūla*, *Śiva*,

1. Vide Kumārila :
   Nirūḍhā lakṣaṇāḥ kāścit sāmarthyādabhidhānavat/
   Kriyante sāmprataṁ kāścit kāścinnaiva tvaśaktitaḥ//
2. Cf. SRB 195-26, p. 534 :
   Śamīgarbhasya yo garbhastasya garbhasya yo ripuḥ/
   Ripugarbhasya yo bhartā sa me viṣṇuḥ prasīdatu//
3. Ibid. 194-15, p. 533 :
   Aṭṭaśūlā janapadāḥ śivaśūlāścatuṣpathāḥ/
   Pramadā keśaśūlinyo bhaviṣyanti kalau yuge//
4. Ibid. notes :

Catuṣpatha and *Keśa*, which here mean respectively, 'food-grains', 'selling', *Vedas*, *Brāhmaṇa* and 'the secret part of woman.'

Sometimes, there is mystery in meaning due to difficulty in construing the words properly, which, in turn, leads to *Kūṭa* : [1]"Having seen the birth of a child to the demons, *Rāma* having eyes like lotuses, chief (or famous) in the lineage of *Raghu*, gave thought (to their destruction)." There is contradiction, more apparent than actual, in the prose order which, when kept properly, gives the right meaning. Here, the words after the first one in the second hemistich, would be construed with *Raghuvaṁśe* and the first with the rest. Besides, in the strangeness due to compounds (Samāsakūṭa), one word is to be construed differently because of different compounds applicable to it : [2]"O king, myself as well as yourself, both are *Lokanātha*. (The difference is :) I am *Bahuvrīhi* compound i.e. one whose master is the world, and you are genitive *tatpuruṣa* i.e. master of the world." By way of a panegyric, a bard says to a king that they both are *Lokanātha*; the only difference is that he is *Bahuvrīhi* (i.e. *Lokaḥ nāthaḥ yasya* viz.; a suppliant) while the king is genitive *Tatpuruṣa* (i.e. *Lokasya nāthaḥ*, viz., lord of the world). Similarly, in the mystery due to the use of the nominal root (Nāmadhātukūṭa), the striking effect is generated because of the use of such verb or verbs : [3]"O beloved, how your burden (or braid) of hair can be capable of being served by the ageless ones (that is, gods), as

Aṭṭamannaṁ śivo vedo brāhmaṇaśca catuṣpathaḥ/
Keśo bhaga iti proktaḥ śūlo vikraya ucyate//

1. Cf. SRB 195-32, p. 535 :
Kumārasaṁbhavaṁ dṛṣṭvā Raghuvaṁśe mano'dadhat/
Rākṣasānāṁ kulaśreṣṭho Rāmo rājīvalocanaḥ//

2. Ibid, 195-22.
N.B. :—Here we may point out that grammatical symbols have been used to enhance the beauty of the paradox :
Ahaṁ ca tvaṁ ca Rājendra lokanāthāvubhāvapi/
Bahuvrīhirahaṁ rājan ṣaṣṭhītatpuruṣo bhavān//

3. Ibid, 195-22, p. 537 :
Kati te kabarībhārāḥ sumanaḥsaṅgāt priye'tinīlatvāt/
Bhavati ca kalāpavattvānnirjarasevyaḥ kathaṁ vā syāt//

it acts like *Brahmā* on account of its attachment to flowers (or, gods, in case of Brahmā), like *Viṣṇu* owing to its being blue (or, black) and is like *Siva* because of carrying ornaments (in the case of Śiva : in the shape of serpents)." Here also, the peculiarity lies in the two meanings displayed by the three verbs, *Kati*, *Ati* and *Bhavati*, that are used. The first two are indeclinables, ordinarily while the third remains a verb. These nominal verbs are derived respectively, from *Ka*=creator, *A* =*Viṣṇu* and *Bhava*=Śiva.

We have seen above that double entendre plays an important role in the formation of the poetic charm, pertaining to both word and sense. Now, we see that the indicative signification of word (Lakṣaṇā) is very helpful in the composition of *Kūṭa* poetry, belonging to this second division of *Citrakāvya*. We have already seen a very occult instance of it, in the illustration of *Kūṭa* arising out of a compounded series of words (Samastaśabdamālākūṭa). In the verse below, we find a beautiful example—where, for the blooming of the lotuses, the poet resorts to the power of indication : "[1]This sun (lit. one having odd number of horses) shining (even) in the cloudy sky and having attained the lustre of *Viṣṇu*, makes the slumber of the lotuses go." The *Kūṭa*, again, is accentuated by the use of words, not in vogue in the sense they are used i.e. *Vārivāraṇamastaka* for culvert, *viṣa* for water and *Kṣaya* for dwelling place : [2]"O Devara (that is, husband's brother), I have seen a goat on the culvert (lit. on the head of that, obstructing waters) that went to its place, having consumed the leaves of the sun-plant and having taken water." The latter can also be said to be an illustration of *Kūṭa* arising out of certain euphonic combinations (Sandhikūṭa), as here two quite separate words, when euphonically coalesced, give a different word, altogether changing the tenor of the whole verse. For

1. Cf. SRB 196-43, p. 537 :
   Prābhrabhrāḍ viṣṇudhāmāpyaviṣamāśvaḥ karotyayam/
   Nidrāṁ sahasraparṇānāṁ palāyanaparāyaṇām//
2. Ibid, 195-31, p. 535 :
   Devarājo mayā dṛṣṭo vārivāraṇamastake/
   Bhakṣayitvārkaparṇāni viṣam pītvā kṣayaṁ gataḥ//

instance, the word thus formed here is *Devarājaḥ* (Devara+Ajaḥ), giving the surface meaning *Indra*, and the latter is said to have been seen on the culvert and having consumed the leaves of the sun-plant and swallowed them, is stated to have met with destruction.

Among *Prahelikās*, there are certain ones which are *Kūṭa* poetry as well : [1]"O one with lotus-like eyes, I want to drink water from you. But if you are a female servant (: sense taken of a *Śūdrā* woman), I won't; if you are not, certainly I will." It is a *Sandhikūṭa*, as also a *Prahelikā* based on pun: the former because the effect is heightened because of the euphonic combination in the word *Dāsyasi* occurring twice, and the latter on the score of apparent-looking verbal form, *Dāsyasi* being repeated in a contradictory manner. Very often a certain object is described in such manner in a conventional paradox, and after reading the verse, the object described is found :"[2](That is) legless but goes afar, having letters but is not a paṇḍita (i.e. scholar), though mouthless, speaks clear; one who understands, is a paṇḍita." Here, the object described is a 'written letter.' In an extended form, this is found in interrogative verses where generally, the answer or clue is supplied in the last foot. This interrogative riddle (Praśna) as it is called, is broadly of two kinds : reply to the queries asked by only one person (Ekapṛṣṭapraśnottara), and reply to the queries asked, generally between two persons mutually questioning and answering (Dvipṛṣṭapraśnottara). The second one is also called simultaneous question-answer (Yugapatpraśnottara), as replies are being given and questions asked simultaneously. This is also said to be mutual speech and counter-speech (Uktipratyukti) for the same reason.

Of the two, the former is of six sub-divisions : reply consisting within the verse itself (Antarālāpa); reply to be made outside the verse (Bahirālāpa); replies where words from

1. Cf. SRB & SM, p. 351 :

   Pānīyaṁ pātumicchāmi tvattaḥ kamalalocane/
   Yadi dāsyasi necchāmi no dāsyasi pibāmyaham//

2. Cf. SRB No. 1, p. 528 :

   Apādo dūragāmī ca sākṣaro na tu paṇḍitaḥ/
   Amukhaḥ sphuṭavaktā ca yo jānāti sa paṇḍitaḥ//

outside have to be construed, perhaps on the basis of those existing within the verse (Bahirantarālāpa); *Jātipraśna* where the questionnaire, consisting of both question and answer (Praśnottarajāti), is supplied by the two answers of two different questions, of which the second answer is the reverse, in the order of letters, of the first reply; *Pṛṣṭapraśna* where the questions themselves provide answers when words are construed differently; and *Uttarapraśna* where replies to the queries in first three feet of the verse are generally supplied in the last foot, as also the overall answer of the whole query in the verse given in the last foot, is, the other way round, characterised by certain adjectives in that very last foot. As for the latter kind, there cannot be any distinct types, but is of various shades.

To take first one. First of all, it is of two types, one where answers of the queries of the first three feet of the verse consist in the last foot, and the other where generally, queries are put not in all the feet, but whatever the query, the answer lies in construing the letters of one word : [1]"From whom is the musk produced ? Who kills the herd of elephants ? What should a coward do in battle ? From deer, the lion, retreat." Here, uncompounded three words of the fourth foot, respectively give answer to the queries put in the first three feet. [2]"Who moves in the sky ? Who is charming ? What is to be uttered in prayer ? What is the decoration ? Who is to be respected ? *How (was) Laṅkā* ? The bird, the Lakṣmī, the Ṛk (Veda), the bracelet, the father (Shaken by the brave monkeys !) !" On the other hand, this highlights a different shade where in first three feet, two questions are asked. In all, six queries are asked and replies to all these queries, except the last one, are supplied in the fourth foot in a compounded,

1. Cf. SRB No. 1. p. 550 :

    Kastūrī jāyate kasmāt ko hanti kariṇāṁ kulam/
    Kiṁ kuryāt kātaro yuddhe mṛgāt siṁhaḥ palāyanam//

2. Ibid, No. 2, p. 550 :

    Kaḥ khe carati kā ramyā kā japyā kiṁ vibhūṣaṇam/
    Ko vandyaḥ kīdṛśī laṁkā vīramarkaṭakampitā//

compact fashion, which itself is a cogent answer to the last query. For the first five queries the answers, respectively, in the last foot are, *viḥ* (i.e. bird)+*Ramā* (i.e. Lakṣmī)+Ṛk (i.e. Vedic stanza)+*Kaṭakaṁ* (i.e. bracelet)+Pitā (i.e. father), euphonically combined. From the first verse, it differs in that there, the fourth foot, though on the surface having some meaning, is at best contradictory and not cogent grammatically, whereas it is so in the second illustration : [1]"What is ornament for the breasts ? How is *Umā* ? From where is the light of the moon ? *How does Sītā weep, having been carried away by Rāvaṇa* ? The pearl-necklace, devoted to *Śiva*, from night [*O Rāma, O Devara (i.e. Lakṣmaṇa), O father, O mother* !]." Here also in the first three feet there are many questions asked though not as many as in the previous one, and the fourth foot answers the last query. But in respect of answering the previous queries, the fourth foot should be resolved letter by letter in as many parts as are the queries. The following is the most sophisticated : [2]"Who is the beloved of *Śiva* ? What is as beautiful as the moon ? What does the serpent do to the face of its counterpart ? Who is the husband of *Lakṣmī* ? *What is odd among the even* (i.e. exciting thing) ? *Gaurī*, face, kisses,—*Vāsudeva*. (Also, *Vāsudeva* kisses *Gaurī's* face !)." This illustrates a type having many queries in the first three feet whose answers, except the last one's, are pointed out in respective order in the words constituting the last foot, which is itself a cogent clause and an answer to the last query. One more thing to be noted here is the apparent contradiction found in the last foot.

1. Cf. SRB No. 19, p. 551 :

   Vibhūṣaṇaṁ kiṁ kucamaṇḍalānāṁ
   kīdṛśyumā candramasaḥ kuto bhāḥ/
   Sītā kathaṁ rauti daśāsyanītā
   hā Rāma hā devara tāta mātaḥ//

2. Ibid, No. 16, p. 551 & SP No. 3 (p. 88), SM No. 27, p. 352 :

   Kā śambhukāntā kimu candrakāntaṁ kāntāmukhaṁ kiṁ kurute bhujaṅgaḥ/
   Kaḥ śrīpatiḥ kā viṣamā samasya gaurīmukhaṁ cumbati vāsudevaḥ//

Coming to the other type, we get only two shades generally, one where the whole word answers the question and the other, where requisite letters construed out of a single word provide clue to the answer : [1]"Only highly intelligent people know from where the three worlds are (generated), and on being born they (i.e. the three worlds) are full of love, (the answers being) placed in this verse in the beginning." Here, the word *Ādau* in the beginning portion of the verse where the clue is said to exist, when resolved as *Āt+Au* provides, in respective order, two answers to the two queries found in the last two feet of the verse. The first question is : *Kutaḥ bhuvanatrayam* ? (whence the three worlds), and the answer is : *Āt* (from *Viṣṇu*). The second question is : *Kasmin samutpanne sarāgam bhuvanatrayam* ? (On whom being born, the three worlds become full of love-sentiment ?)—and the answer is : *Au* (On cupid being born). Here the word *Bhuvanatrayam* is to be construed with both the interrogative clauses. As against it is the following verse : [2]"The cave says : Who am I ? What is the answer (embedded) in this query ? Why, even told, you do not understand, O friend, that you are slighting!" The answer from the verbal form *Kadarthayasi* (i.e. why despise ?) from which we fetch out, according to our convenience, the letters *dar+ya+si*, which when euphonically coalesced, form the word *Daryasi* (i.e. you are a cavern), providing the answer.

In *Bahirālāpa* we get such shade : [3]"Tell me, O good boy, how is your father (to you), and how is the ocean with waves swayed by the wind ?" Here we have two queries in

1. Cf. SRB No. 24, p. 351 :

 Śloke'trādau vinirdiṣṭaṁ vijānanti mahādhiyaḥ/
 Kutaḥ kasmin samutpanne sarāgam bhuvanatrayam//

2. Ibid, No. 23, p. 351 :

 Kā 'hamasmi guhā vakti praśne'muṣmin kimuttaram/
 Kathamuktaṁ na jānāsi kadarthayasi yat sakhe//

3. Ibid, No. 25, p. 352 :

 Bhadra māṇavakākhyāhi kīdṛśaḥ khalu te pitā/
 Vātāndolitakallolaḥ kīdṛśaśca mahodadhiḥ//

answer to which a word is adeptly evolved. When dissolved in two different ways it gives answers to the queries The said word is evolved from outside the verse of which there is no clue whatsoever. This word is *Majjanmakaraḥ*, which, when disjoined like '*Mat+janmakaraḥ*', provides answer to the first question. When it is euphonically disjoined like *Majjat+Makaraḥ*, it answers the second query. At both places, the word respectively means 'giver of my birth' and 'the place where alligators emerge and submerge.' On the contrary, in verse that follows, there is some difference : [1]"Which upheld *Viṣṇu* bearing the appearance of a pig ? Which the king wants foeless ? By whom is cupid produced ? Through which is adorned the face of the damsel ?" The difference is that there is some clue for making out the word which provides answers to all queries, and this clue lies in the answer of the fourth foot of which only parts are answers to the three preceding queries, consisting in three previous feet of the verse. This also makes some difference in the nature of this interrogative paradox, as contrary to this, in the previous verse, the whole word provided reply to both the questions. Here, the answers of the first three feet are, respectively, *Kuṁ* (i.e. the earth)+*Kuṁ* (i.e. the earth)+*Ena* (i.e. through Viṣṇu), together making the reply to the fourth foot in *Kuṁkumena.*

Sometimes the answers to be made out for the separate queries, as well as the aggregate answer, are all grammatical, or might be technical terms : [2]"Whom the wicked does not like (or praise) ? What is *Suptiṅanta* ? Please tell the appellation of the nine *lādeśa tiṅ* (or, the verbal tense roots)." The answer of the first query is *Parasmai* (i.e. for other), and of the second *Padam* (i.e. the word), and of the third constituting the third and fourth feet, amounting to *Parasmaipadam* (i.e. a voice for another). Thus, we might have a *kūṭa* like this :

1. Cf. SRB No. 24, p. 352 :
   Kāṁ harirabharat śūkararūpaḥ kāmarirahitāmicchati bhūpaḥ/
   Kenākāri ca manmathajananaṁ kena virājati taruṇīvadanam//
2. Ibid No. 19, p. 555 :
   Na ślāghate khalaḥ kasmai suptiṅantaṁ kimucyate/
   Lādeśānāṁ navānāṁ ca tiṅāṁ kiṁ nāma kathyatām//

[1]"Who keeps closely embraced on the chest of *Viṣṇu* ? Who, in the *Nandana* forest, is happy on account of the pollens of lotuses ? What is the metre of verse, having short and long letters ?" 'Here, of the last query constituting the last two feet, the answer is the name of a metre, made up of the answers of the first two feet of the verse. So, in order of the three queries, the answers are : *Mā* (i.e. Lakṣmī)+*Alinī* (i.e. black-bee)=*Mālinī* (metre). Again, we find an increase in the complexities in composition : [2]"Who moves in the sky ? By whom was killed the lord of the demons (viz. Rāvaṇa) ? Who sinks in the sea ? How is the sportive gait of a young woman ? Who is beloved of the king ? What is the carriage of the monarch ? What is charming in the waters ? Who was abductor of *Rāma's* wife ? What constitutes the middle letters of my replies to the questions, constitutes benediction to you." There are eight queries, the answers of which, respectively, are : *Graheśaḥ* (i.e. the lord of constellations), *Rāmeṇa* (i.e. By *Rāma*), *Mainākaḥ* (i.e. the mountain of the same name), *Mantharam* (i.e. slow), *Sacivaḥ* (i.e. the minister), *Turaṅgaḥ* (i.e. the horse), *Rājīvam* (i.e. the lotus) and *Rāvaṇaḥ* (i.e. the demon of the same name) of which the middle letters, as per instructions in the last foot, form the benedictory message viz., *He me nātha ciraṁjīva* (i.e. O my lord, may you live long !). Still further, let us see the complexity : [3]"Which does the

1. Cf. SRB No. 97, p. 561 :

    Urasi murabhidaḥ kā gāḍhamāliṅgitāste
    Sarasijamakarandāmoditā nandane kā/
    Girisamalaghuvarṇairarṇavākhyātisaṁkhyai-
    Rgurubhirapi kṛtā kā chandasāṁ vṛttirasti//

2. Ibid, No. 116, p. 563 :

    Kaḥ khe yāti hato niśācarapatiḥ kenāmbudhau majjati
    Kaḥ kīdṛk taruṇīvilāsagamanaṁ ko nāma rājñāṁ priyaḥ/
    Patraṁ kiṁ nṛpateḥ kimapsu lalitaṁ ko Rāmarāmāharo
    Matpraśnottaramadhyamākṣarapadaṁ yat tat tavāśīrvacaḥ//

3. Ibid, No. 121, p. 563 :

    Kṣoṇī kaṁ sahate karoti divi kā nṛtyaṁ śivāyāḥ pati-
    Rbhūtānāṁ kamayuṅkta jīvaharaṇe kā Rāmaśatroḥ purī/
    Kaṁ rakṣanti ca sādhavaḥ paśupateḥ kiṁ vāhanaṁ procyatām
    Ālomapratilomaśāstracaturairekaṁ dvayoruttaram//

earth bear ? Who does dancing in the heaven ? Whom did the lord of *Pārvatī* (i.e. Śiva) deploy from amongst the imps for extricating life ? Which is the city of the enemy of *Rāma* (i.e. Rāvaṇa) ? Whom do the good people protect ? Tell which is the carriage of *Śiva* ? One each, in normal as well as in reversed order, is the answer for two consecutive queries." The peculiarity here lies in the fact that the answer of one query is always found reversed in the adjacent one. For instance, the answers of the first two queries are *Bhāraṁ* (i.e. the burden) and *Raṁbhā* (i.e., the celestial nymph of the same name), of the next two *Kālaṁ* (i.e., the particular Bhūta) and *Laṅkā* (i.e. the city of the same name), and still of the next two *Dīnaṁ* (i.e. the poor) and *Nandī* (i.e. the bull of the same name). These queries constitute the first three feet, and the last foot only renders help in finding out the answers. The answers of each pair of queries are the same but in reversed order.

In the SKB of *Bhoja* under the head *Ekapṛṣṭapraśnottara*, there are four more varieties. In *Bahirantarālāpa*, let us take just one example:[1] "Who married *Subhadrā* ? What reply is here in this query, that stands for what (synonym of) monkey ? Whence is the complete sustenance (possible) in heaven (or sky) ?" There are three questions. The answer of first one is somehow supplied by the second in the shape of some synonym of *Kapi* (i.e. the monkey), and from amongst many such synonyms the answer is specified by the third, viz, *Vāyutaḥ* (i.e. through air), which is itself the answer of the third query. With regard to the synonyms of the word *Kapi* which should be *Vāyukta* (i.e. endowed with the particle Vā), the word is specifically ascertained as *Vānaraḥ*, which in turn is the answer of the preceding three queries. Really, *Vāyutaḥ* is the direct answer to the third query, and with respect to the first one, it is something outside, but when out of it comes the word *Vānaraḥ*, it becomes directly related to the first question. In a way, the second and third questions only provide clues to the answer of the first question. Therefore, from this point of view, there is answer within answer, and so

1. Cf. SKB II v. 374, p. 303 :

Subhadrāṁ ka upāyaṁsta praśne 'muṣmin ya uttaraḥ/
Sa kīdṛk kapimācaṣṭe vyomni pūrṇasthitiḥ kutaḥ//

there is something like *Antarantarālāpa* instead of *Bahirantarālāpa*.

Now *Jātipraśna* : [1]"From what nature of landscape the king is conjectured as having bathed ? When asked to dress up the courtyard, what did the reluctant ones tell ?" The first half of the verse and the second half form two queries, and of the first the answer is *Haimavārakarañjinā*, and of the second, *Nājiraṁkaravāmahai*, which is just the reversed form of the first. Likewise, to illustrate *Pṛṣṭapraśna* : [2]"What is it that is one-fourth of *Yojana* ? What is equal to two thousand of *Daṇḍas* (equivalent to four Hastas in measure) ? What is black ? What is sweet ? What is (comfortable) for parrots, the vast shady grove ?" Here all the five queries occur having within them the answers. For instance, *Ko so joaṇavāo* as a query, is rendered in Sanskrit *Kaḥ sa yojanapādaḥ* (i.e. what is it that is one-fourth of a Yojana ?), and in the form of answer is rendered as *Krośo yojanapādaḥ* (i.e. Krośa is that which is one-fourth of a Yojana). In the same way, for *Ko daṇḍāṇaṁ dve sahassāīṁ*, the question is : *Ko daṇḍānāṁ dve sahasre* (i.e. what is equal to two thousand of Daṇḍas ?) and the answer is : *Kodaṇḍānām* (i.e. it is two thousand of Kodaṇḍas). In the second half of the verse there are three queries : *Kā kālī* (i.e. what is black ?), *Kā madhurā* (i.e. what is sweet ?) and *Kiṁ śukapṛthukānanacchāyaṁ* (i.e. what is the shady grove for the parrots ?). The answers are : *Kākālī* (i.e. the row of crows), *Kāmadhurā* (i.e. the highest place of cupid), and *Kiṁśukapṛthukānanacchāyaṁ* (i.e. the shady grove of Palāśa trees). Then *Uttarapraśna*: [3]"What is food for the trees in spring time, asked the fisherman (lit. the tapper of the fish etc.). What reply these two (i.e. first two feet of the verse) got ? The rows of cuckoos, darker than the darkness, devouring the forest region." The words, wanted

1. SKB. II illust. 375;
   Kīdṛśā bhūmibhāgena rājā snāto 'numīyate/
   Prāṅgaṇaṁ kurutetyuktāḥ kimāhustadanicchavaḥ//
2. Ibid, II illust. 376 :
   Ko so joaṇavāo ko daṇḍāṇaṁ dve sahassāīṁ/
   Kā kālī kā madhurā kiṁ śukapṛthukānanacchāyaṁ//
3. Ibid, II, illust. 377, p. 304 :
   Kiṁ vasantasamaye vanabhakṣaḥ pṛṣṭavān sa pṛthulomavilekhaḥ/
   Uttaraṁ ca kimavāpaturetat kānanādatimirādapikālī//

as answers for the first three feet, have been placed in the fourth foot in such an order, that taken as one whole they form the answer directly to the third foot as well. The peculiarity lies in the derivative word *Pikālī* (i.e. row of cuckoos) being qualified by adjectives making the whole of the fourth foot viz. *Kānanādatimirāt api kālī*, and this ultimately is answer to the chief query found in first foot of the verse.

As for queries asked and answers supplied mutually (Dvipṛṣṭapraśnottara) between two persons, there is not much to say. We shall see a few shades that would suffice from the point of view of x-raying its nature. First, there is a simple type in reversing the speech, almost like a logical rebuttal : [1]"Meaningless became the birth of the lotus-plant that did never see the disc of the moon. Also quite futile was the origin of the moon who did not behold the blossoming lotus-plant." By way of *Anyokti*, the lover poet means to say that the birth of the beloved princess is fruitless as she has not seen (yet) the beautiful face of the former. In another half of the verse, the beloved retorts that futile too is his origin, who has not beheld her blossoming countenance. But a definite poetic charm is created out of the subversion of speech (Vakrokti) in retort in the following verse : [2]"Oh ! by whom has the ruthless intellect of yours been devised ? The intellect is heard to consist of the three properties (viz. Sattva, Rajas and Tamas), but never made of wood !" The poetic subversion is based on a pun in the word *Dāruṇā*, used here in fem.nom.sing. of *Dāruṇa* (i.e. rough or ruthless), but is subverted to be understood in instr. sing. of the word *Dāru* (i.e. wood), as is clear from the biting and satirical second half of the verse. To take one more example, to get a different shade though based on pun as before : [3]"Please describe the *Mahābhārata*, the sugarcane-

1. SP No. 17 : Nirarthakaṁ janma gataṁ nalinyāḥ yayā na dṛṣṭaṁ tuhināṁśubimbaṁ/
   Utpattirindorapi niṣphalaiva dṛṣṭā vinidrā nalinī na yena//
2. Ibid & No. 11 (p. 89), SRB No. 3 (p. 564) :
   Aho kenedṛśī buddhirdāruṇā tava nirmitā/
   Triguṇā śrūyate buddhirna tu dārumayī kvacit//
3. Ibid, No.1, p. 64 :
   Bhārataṁ cekṣudaṇḍaṁ ca sindhuminduṁ ca varṇaya/
   Padamekaṁ pradāsyāmi pratiparvarasodayaḥ//

stick, the ocean and the moon. I will give only one foot (of the verse) : *there is rise of Rasa in every Parvan.*" Here the whole tenor of the verse is changed because of the double entendre in the word *Pratiparvarasodayaḥ*, which in respect of the great epic, means 'the evolution of sentiments in every chapter named *Parvan*', with regard to stick of the sugarcane, 'the existence of juice at every knot', with respect to ocean, 'the rise of tide (whether nip or ebb) at every knot (or joint) of the month i.e. on full-moon day or new-moon day', and in relation to the moon, 'the waxing of the digit on every full-moon or new-moon day.' The first half of the verse is traditionally said to be the speech of *Bhoja*, and the second half that of *Kālidāsa.*

We have seen above that concealment brings purpose to *Kūṭas* or the riddles. This concealment can be of the finite verb, of any of the various cases, of compound, of gender, of the case-ending, or of the verbal ending (i.e. Tiṅ) in many ways. For example, in the following verse the finite verb is *Aduḥ*, of which the initial letter is concealed, being euphonically combined with the word *Sarve* before *Duryodhanasamīhayā*, of which again, the initial letter is actually the final one of the aforementioned finite verb : [1]"All the *Pāṇḍavas* who had come gave a cow, gold and varied jewels to him who was in search of riches." So even the word *Duryodhanasamīhayā* can be broken like this : *(A)duḥ+yaḥ+dhanasamīhayā*, giving the proper meaning, otherwise there is apparent contradiction in the verse. Sometimes this concealment is effected through a euphonic combination in a straight style throwing challenge : [2]"O king, the bird wandered in the township from one bamboo tree to another. Here, the verb is concealed. He who knows, is a pundit." The verb *Āṭa* (i.e. past perfect third pers. sing. of √Aṭ) is concealed, being euphonically combined with *Viḥ* (i.e. bird) making a normal word *Virāṭa*, which followed by the word *Nagare*, appears to give a cogent sense and hence eludes the reader.

1. SRB. No. 1 (p. 545), SP No. 1 (p. 82) :
   Āgatāḥ pāṇḍavāḥ sarve'duryodhanasamīhayā/
   Tasmai gāṁ ca suvarṇaṁ ca ratnāni vividhāni ca//

2. Cf. SRB No. 9, p.546 :
   Virāṭanagare rājan kīcakādupakīcakaṁ/
   Atra kriyāpadaṁ guptaṁ yo jānāti sa paṇḍitaḥ//

With regard to the concealment of cases, let us first examine how the nominative case is concealed and the poetic curiosity generated : [1]"O *Brāhmin*, the prosperous one gives on the river-bank, food, raiment, gold and various jewels. Go at once." We find in this instance that the nominative is *Ibhyaḥ* (i.e. prosperous) euphonically combined with the vocative *Brāhmaṇa* in such a way, that the whole word gives the semblance of a dative case, amply justified by the use of the finite verb *Dadāti*, making the confusion more. In the following verse we find the accusative case in *Saraḥ* (i.e. the pond) concealed, having euphonically coalesced with *Javanamārutaḥ* (i.e. the speedy breeze), making the whole word look cogently different in *Sarojavanamārutaḥ* (i.e. the breeze of the cluster of lotus-plants) : [2]"The robust, speedy wind, carrying the moisture-particles, agitates the pond, as if with exhalations of the wives of the passers-by !" Below, the instrumental case is in the word *Mahānasā* (i.e. through a big cart), which when combined euphonically with *Āyātaḥ* (i.e. came) makes a different sense altogether : [3]"This (person) who has come by a big cart, is like a netherworld to you. I have consumed the meat etc., O *Baka*, know me *Bhīma* !" It must be noted that *Mahānasa* (when the final vowel is not elided), means 'cooking place (or kitchen)'. Then, to take illustration of the concealment of the dative : [4]"The damsel, replete with devotion, having bathed in the waters of the small pond, offers to cupid the lotus-flower, meant to augment good fortune." Here the dative case is in *Aye* (from the word Iḥ=cupid) which is so adeptly coalesced with the preceding *Ambhoruhaṁ* (i.e. the lotus) that it goes to make a new and cogent word, qualifying *Vāpī-*

1. SRB No.2 (p. 546), SP No. 3 (p.83) :
   Annavastrasuvarṇāni ratnāni vividhāni ca/
   Brāhmaṇebhyo nadītīre dadāti vraja satvaraṁ//
2. Cf. Ibid. No. 1, p.547, SM No. 8. p. 349 :
   Śīkarāsārasaṁvāhī sarojavanamārutaḥ/
   Prakṣobhayati Pānthastrīniḥśvāsairiva māṁsalaḥ//
3. Cf. Ibid. No. 2, p. 547 :
   Ahaṁ mahānasāyātaḥ kalpito narakastava/
   Mayā māṁsādikaṁ bhuktam bhīmaṁ jānīhi māṁ baka//
4. Ibid. No. 1, p. 547, SM No. 10, p. 349 :
   Aṁbhoruhamaye snātvā vāpīpayasi kāminī/
   Dadāti bhaktisaṁpannā puṣpaṁ saubhāgyavardhanaṁ//

payasi, (i.e. in the waters of the small pond). When *Aye* is separated, and rightly so, with the use of *Dā* root, the word *Ambhoruhaṁ* qualifies *puṣpaṁ* (i.e. flower).

Likewise in the instance below, we get the ablative character of the word *Alinaḥ* (from Alin i.e. the black bee) concealed because of its euphonic combination with *Atyantaṁ* (i.e. very much), giving rise to a new, cogent word, *Atyantamalinaḥ* (very much dark or pallid), qualifying *Ripuḥ* (i.e. enemy): [1]"O brave one, the enemy has been vanquished by you with irresistible arrows, like one overcome by the black bees anxious for flowers in the forest, who get very much frightened of them." As for concealment of the genitive case, we may illustrate thus : [2]"The splendour of a man is generated owing to *Lakṣmī* or *Sarasvatī*. Here the genitive case is concealed. The time-limit (for finding it out) is ten years." In *Bhānuḥ* (i.e. sun) the word *Nuḥ* (from Nṛ i.e. man) is the genitive, which being placed with the word *Bhāḥ* (i.e. lustre) and euphonically coalesced, makes the aforesaid new word give sense. Again, the locative case in the word *E* (from A Viṣṇu or Kṛṣṇa) is concealed below with the word *Kānte* following, forming a word itself : [3]"She (Lakṣmī), having abode among the lotuses, who has made love in secret with *Viṣṇu*, purifies men with her glances." There is a beautiful instance of the vocative of word *Vaṭo* (from Vaṭu=a boy), having been concealed because of its being coalesced with the following word *Ṛkṣaḥ* (i.e. bear), giving rise to a new word *Vaṭavṛkṣaḥ* (i.e. the fig-tree) : [4]"O boy, this big bear is there, obstructing the road. You should not go until and unless it goes elsewhere."

1. Cf. SRB No. 1, p. 547, SM No. 11, p. 349 :
   Śilīmukhaistvayā vīra durvārairnirjito ripuḥ/
   Bibhetyatyantamalino vane'pi kusumākulaiḥ//
2. Cf. Ibid. No. 2. p. 547 :
   Bhānurvai jāyate lakṣmyā sarasvatyā'thavā matā/
   Atra ṣaṣṭhīpadaṁ guptaṁ maryādā daśavārṣikī//
3. Ibid., No. 1, p. 547 :
   Yā kaṭākṣacchaṭāpātaiḥ pavitrayati mānavaṁ/
   Ekānte ropitaprītirasti sā kamalālayā//
4. Ibid, No. 4, p. 548, SP No. 6, p. 84 :
   Vaṭavṛkṣo mahāneṣa mārgamāvṛtya tiṣṭhati/
   Tāvat tvayā na gantavyaṁ yāvannānyatra gacchati//

On the surface, this verse also shows apparent contradiction in meaning.

Before ending this part of the discussion, we must say that the concealment of more than one case is possible : [1]"Be, O hand, always worshipful towards *Śiva*. He, who understands (here) the nominative, the accusative, and the verb concealed, is a pundit." The finite verb, together with the nominative and accusative cases, is concealed. As we see from the dissolution of the word *Bhavāniśa karomeśaṁ* into *Bhava* (i.e. Be)+*Aniśam* (always)+*Kara*, (O hand !)+*Umeśaṁ*, the word *Bhava* is the finite verb, *Umeśaṁ* the accusative case, and *Kara*, though standing for the nominative, is actually the vocative case. In almost all the instances above, the euphonic combination is the cause of concealment. In most of the places after this euphonic coalescence, the words are formed in such a way that the coalescence itself is not easily marked out. This is called *Saṁhitāgupta* (or, Sandhigupta). Wherever with the emergence of new words a sort of apparent contradiction is generated in the verse, the paradoxical or enigmatic effect is all the more heightened. We get such a thing in the last verse as well, where in the new word *Bhavānīśaṅkaromeśaṁ*, there is a separate indication of *Bhavānī*, *Śaṅkara* and *Umeśa*.

The concealment of a compound generally occurs in a word which otherwise is formed in the shape of a derivative etc. So, in compound and in derivative the same word may give different meanings, and hence, this type of concealment might be based on pun : [2]"One in the habit of eating poison, consumes the alms, (and) accompanied by his wife, never leaves the mountain. O brave one, even though enraged you treat your enemy like *Śiva*." The word *Viṣādī*, when expounded, will give the meaning 'one who takes poison', otherwise, it means 'afflicted.' Again, *Sadārogaṁ na muñcati* means (without compound) : 'Always suffers from some malady', but

1. Cf. SRB No. 1, p. 548 :
   Bhavāniśaṅkaromeśaṁ prati pūjāparāyaṇaḥ/
   Kartṛkarmakriyāguptaṁ yo jānāti sa paṇḍitaḥ//
2. Ibid : Viṣādī bhaikṣyamaśnāti sadārogaṁ na muñcati/
   Ruṣṭenāpi tvayā vīra śaṁbhunāririva kṛtaḥ//

when taken in compound it means : *Sadāraḥ* (i.e. accompanied by wife) *agaṁ* (i.e. the mountain) *na muñcati* (i.e. does not leave). In respect of the concealment of gender, we cite the following : [1]"O friend, this lover, having a truly clear heart, has come. Because of his intense love, seeing you after a long time, he will, having embraced, enjoy you." On the surface, masculine nominative *Preyān* (i.e. lover or, the lovely one), coordinate with the neuter *Nitāntasvacchahṛdayaṁ* (i.e. having highly clear heart), looks incongruous, and when we probe deep, we find that there are really two words in the latter, *Nitāntasvacchahṛt* (i.e. having highly clear heart), and *Ayaṁ*, euphonically combined. Both these being masculine are commensurate with the masculine *Preyān*. Here, the concealment is of the masculine gender in *Ayaṁ*, euphonically merged in the neuter *Hṛdayaṁ*. Even in the following, where a case-ending is concealed, that case-ending being nominative singular in the word *Rāḥ* (i.e. wealth), there is an apparent incongruity of use of the singular finite verb *Janayati* (i.e. produces), with the plural-looking *Sadārāḥ* (i.e. those having wives) qualifying *Gṛhamedhinaḥ* (i.e. the householders) : [2]"The opulence always engenders happiness among householders (as opposed to the ascetics), if righteousness and worldly pleasure both be accomplished together." In the same way, in the next instance, plurality of the verb is concealed in singular-looking *Paripṛcchati* (formed with Yaṅ-luk suffix meaning *Atiśayena pṛcchanti* (i.e. ask too much) used with the nominative plural *Sakhyaḥ* (i.e. the friends) : [3]"On yourself being present, female friends ask her oftentimes : 'Why are you emaciated ?' Please say, whether she can make reply to them !"

Finally, we add concealment of a foot, of some intention (of the speaker), or of a fact according to *Bhoja*, over and above those already noted. Let us take the first one : [4]"The row

1. SRB : Nitāntasvacchahṛdayaṁ sakhi preyān samāgataḥ/
Tvāṁ cirāddarśanaprītyā yaḥ samāliṅgya raṁsyate//
2. Ibid : Pramodaṁ janayatyeva sadārā gṛhamedhinaḥ/
Yadi dharmaśca kāmaśca bhavetāṁ saṅgatāvimau//
3. Ibid : Kasmāt tvaṁ durbalāsīti sakhyastāṁ paripṛcchati/
Tvayi saṁnihite tāsu dadyāt kathaya sottaraṁ//
4. Vide SKB II, p. 302, illustr. No. 369 :
Dyuviyadgāminī tārasaṁrāvavihataśrutiḥ/
Haimīṣumālā śuśubhe (vidyutāmiva saṁhatiḥ) //

of arrows reaching up to the heaven and the sky, (and) obstructing the sense of hearing with high-pitched sounds, looked beautiful (like the linings of lightnings) !" The second, first, seventh, fifth, eleventh, ninth, thirteenth and sixteenth letters of the first half of the verse, constitute the fourth foot, shown in brackets, when taken together in the order indicated. So finally we find one whole foot concealed in the verse. Then the second : [1]"If the wife of the servant is asked by her husband's brother to go to the king's place with sword in her hand, then why did she look to the bed smilingly ?" Here, the man having seen red dye etc. on the feet of woman, thinks that she wants to gain upper hand in the course of sexual action, and the woman smilingly looks towards the bed with the intention that the former does not employ her in the action. This very intention is concealed in the verse and has to be construed to bring forth the full meaning. As for the third, the foregoing illustration Pānīyaṁ pātumicchāmi works here. There in the apparent verbal form *Dāsyasi*, the fact of being a *Dāsī* i.e. maid-servant, is concealed.

With the dropping of half a syllable, one full syllable, *Bindu*, *Visarga* or a letter, it is necessary that we should arrange the words in such manner that even after such dropping, the metre of the verse is not affected. In such a case, sometimes the stress of the dropping syllable or letter etc. is shifted to the adjacent, preceding, or following syllable, or the stress is merely loosened. Likewise, with the placing of a half syllable or full syllable, *Bindu* or *Visarga* or a letter, poetic curiosity can be aroused in a particular verse with a vast difference in the meaning with a slight change. Both these droppings and placings are only two facets of one thing. In relation to the change in meaning wrought by the dropping of a syllable etc., the previous meaning of the particular verse can be said to be brought out in a condition when the same syllable etc. is placed after it was dropped out.

1. SKB. illustr. No. 370 :

   Pr—Jai deareṇa bhaṇiā khaggaṁ ghethuṇa raulaṁ vaccā/
   Tā kiṁ sevauṇavahue hasiuṇa valoiaṁ saaṇaṁ//
   Skt.—yadi devareṇa bhaṇitā khadgaṁ gṛhītvā rājakulaṁ vraja/
   Tatkiṁ sevakavadhvā hasitvā'valokitaṁ śayanaṁ//

In the aforementioned order, we are first going to deal with the dropping or placing of half a syllable : [1]"In the sky overcast with clouds and marked with the streaks of lightning, is the newly risen moon, beautiful, and the darling of all, not attainable." The other meaning : "In the sky overcast and streaked with lightning, Oh girl, a lover whom all will like, is very difficult to get !" Here in *Bālenduḥ khe na labhyate* (i.e. the newly risen moon is not available in the sky), if we drop the nasal letter, conjunct with the glide *Duḥ* in *Bālenduḥ*, quite a different meaning is produced in *Bāle duḥkhena labhyate* (i.e. O girl, the Kānta or lover is to be attained with difficulty). With the loss of the nasal here, half a syllable is lost, but, generally speaking, it can be said to be a case of the dropping of a *Bindu* or a consonant also. As against it, in the following, the dropping of a full syllable constituting *ī* in the word *Nīraṁ* (i.e. water), leaves out the word as *Naraṁ* (i.e. man) and consequently gives a new twist in the meaning of the verse : [2]"O people, fatigued on account of lying on the earth (in summer season), take to water, good and clear, for allaying your heat." Other meaning : "O people, vexed of living with the wicked take recourse to a man, noble and clean, for the alleviation of your agonies." Here as in the previous verse, as also in the cases following, it is to be noted that other words in the particular verses are so used as to give double meaning in the case of the dropping of a syllable etc., and here the pun comes into play.

Now to take an example of the dropping of a *Bindu* : [3]"As this *Vakula* tree of mine is of good breed, shady, and situated on a good roadway, so it is really a shelter to all." Other meaning : "As of noble birth, well-behaved and keeping

1. Cf. :

   Payodharabharākrānte vidyullekhāvirājite/
   Kāntaḥ sarvajanābhīṣṭo bālenduḥkhena labhyate//

2. Cf. SRB No. 1, p. 549 :

   Mahāśayamatisvacchaṁ nīraṁ santāpaśāntaye/
   Khalavāsādatiśrāntaḥ samāśrayata he janāḥ//

3. Ibid, No. 2, p. 549 :

   Yathā satprasavaḥ snigdhaḥ sanmārgavihitasthitiḥ/
   Tathā sarvāśrayaḥ satyamayaṁ me vakuladrumaḥ//

to a righteous path, this one actually is the main prop of my family, a shelter to all." Here, with the *Bindu* or *Anusvāra* of *ya* in *Satyamayaṁ* being dropped, and the following two letters *me* (which is separate) and *va* (which is part of the word Vakula) having been associated with the residue *Satyamaya*, the whole word, thus formed, is *Satyamayameva* (i.e. really only this), which is quite meaningful. In this case, the residual last word, *Kuladrumaḥ*, is to be expounded thus : *Kule druma iva* (i.e. one who is like the main tree in the family or dynasty). This *Bindu*, which is dropped, can form part of a single word : [1]"In whomsoever paramour, this young woman, having besmeared herself with sandal-paste, likeable, decorated with a mark on her forehead, and the breeding-ground of cupid, shall not produce delight?" Other meaning : "In the snakes, whomever, this mountainous tract (of Malaya Mt.), shady (or, full of turmeric or indigo plants), having sandal trees, agreeable (or having Priyaṅgu creepers or the large cardamoms) and having Tilaka trees, shall not generate pleasure ?" When this is not elided, the word *Anaṅgabhūḥ* stands for a damsel, otherwise, the initial *a* being coalesced with the preceding *Eṣā*, the word left is *Nagabhūḥ* (i.e. 'the mountainous tract') standing for the *Malaya* mount. As for the dropping of *Visarga*, in the word *Mahāsuḥ* (i.e. high-souled) in the given verse, it is remarkable that the word left associates with the following word *khāt* (i.e. from the heaven or sky), making a separate word *Mahāsukhāt* (i.e. from the great pleasure), giving a turn in the meaning of the verse : [2]"The lion-hearted *Nahuṣa*, having boarded the chariot of *Brahmā*, on account of the curse of sage *Agastya*, fell from the sky (or, heaven) and took the form of a serpent." (The other way : 'fell down from a great pleasure' instead of 'fell from the sky' and without 'the lion-hearted.').

Again in the following, we see that a whole letter *Na*, being the initial letter of the word *Nadīnaḥ*, is dropped, as

1. SRB. No. 1, p. 549 :
   Suśyāmā candanavatī kāntā tilakabhūṣitā/
   Kasyaiṣā'naṅgabhūḥ prītiṁ bhujaṅgasya karoti na//
2. Ibid. No. 2. p. 549 :
   Agastyasya muneḥ śāpād brahmasyandanamāsthitaḥ//
   Mahāsuḥ khāt paribhraṣto nahuṣaḥ sarpatāṁ gataḥ//

if making a different verse altogether : [1]"Who seeks after the ocean, insipid and having a bad surrounding, though great, highly patient and replete with myriads of gems ?" Other meaning : "Who serves the poor, of dry temperament, and having bad entourage though great, highly patient, and having many good things ?" By placing this letter where it was, the word *Nadīnaḥ* having been expounded *Nadīnāṁ inaḥ*, means 'the lord of the rivers'. This dropping of the letter can be of the middle one, or of the penultimate or last one. For example, in the verse quoted, we get the middle letter of the word *Sugataḥ* (i.e. Lord Buddha) dropped, thus causing a change in the meaning : [2]"Of good habit, of golden complexion and having a face like that of a full moon, to whom does not Lord *Buddha* give pleasure, having been enshrined in the heart ?" (The other way : 'son', replacing 'Lord Buddha'). In that eventuality, the word formed is *Sutaḥ* (i.e. son). Now among the category of the dropping of a letter, there can also be partial dropping or loss of the consonant or vowel. However the dropping of vowel, leaving the consonant associate with the word, is a very rare phenomenon. In the following we find an instance of the dropping of a consonant in the aforesaid manner, where the letter *Bh* in *Bhikṣavaḥ* is lost, consequently causing the rise of a new word *Ikṣavaḥ* (i.e. the surgarcane sticks), thus giving two meanings : [3]"All the beggars are desirous, the chemicals sustaining life (i.e. food and drinks) are dear to all. Those (i.e. beggars) endowed with tolerance, are mostly seen in *Magadha* country." Also : "The sugarcane sticks are exhilarating; the juice is liked by all people. They (i.e. the sugarcane sticks), abundantly sown in the earth, are found mostly in *Magadha* country."

1. SRB, No. 1, p. 549 :
   Mahānapi sudhīro'pi bahuratnayuto'pi san/
   Virasaḥ kuparīvāro nadīnaḥ kena sevyate//
2. Ibid, No. 2, p. 549 :
   Suśīlaḥ svarṇagaurāṅgaḥ pūrṇacandranibhānanaḥ/
   Sugataḥ kasya na prītiṁ tanoti hṛdi saṁsthitaḥ//
3. Ibid, No. 1, p. 550 ;
   Bhikṣavo rucirāḥ sarve rasāḥ sarvajanapriyāḥ/
   Kṣamāyāmabhisaṁpannā dṛśyante magadhe paraṁ//

In this connection, we may deal with the dropping of the place (Sthānacyuta), that is, the changing of the rightful place of words in a sentence. In another way, it can be said that under this category, words like the subject, predicate etc. change their places and the prose order becomes difficult : [1]"God *Śiva* is dependent on equivocators (otherwise, serpents), the moon wanes, the sun is a heat-scorcher, *Brahmā* is sexually incapable (otherwise, peace-loving) and *Indra* is the enemy of his own people : therefore, *Lakṣmī* having ignored these, chose *Viṣṇu* who may protect the worlds !" Among the adjectives, *Dvijihvāśritaḥ*, (i.e. one depending on equivocators) qualifies *Haraḥ*, *Kṣayī* (i.e. one prone to waning) *Candraḥ*, *Tāpakaraḥ* (i.e. one giving heat) *Vivasvān*, *Śāntaḥ* (i.e. one sexually debilitous) *Vidhiḥ* and *Gotraripuḥ* (i.e. foe of one's own kinsmen) *Sudeśaḥ* (or Sureśaḥ ?). This gives the key to the normal prose order. This kind of riddle is similar to, or even identical with, the *Kliṣṭānvaya* type of *Kūṭa*. In the like manner, the dropping or placement of a letter in a word can be alternate. That is, in one and the same word, some letter is dropped and some other letter is kept in its place instead : [2]"Whose the charming damsel, with a face like that of the full moon, and having white *Sārī*, does not brighten heart which is highly inquisitive for love," (The other way : 'The pleasant night, having as its face the full moon and having a clear sky......). Here, a change in the meaning of the verse is effected by dropping the initial letter *Ka* of *Kāminī* (i.e. damsel) and placing letter *Ya* in its position, making the word, *Yāminī* (i.e. the night). Also, certain words like *Pūrṇacandramukhī*, *Nirmalāmbarā* etc. have two meanings, and hence are applicable in both cases. But to illustrate a slightly different variety : [3]"The

1. SRB, No. 2, p. 549 : Haraḥ kṣayī tāpakaraḥ sudeśaḥ
   śānto harirgotraripurvivasvān/
   Candro dvijihvāśrita ityupekṣya
   lakṣmyā vṛtaḥ pātu vidhirjaganti//
2. Ibid, No. 2, p. 550 :
   Pūrṇacandramukhī ramyā kāminī nirmalāmbarā/
   Tanoti kasya na svāntamekāntamadanāturaṁ//
3. Ibid, No. 3, p. 550 :
   Kūjanti kokilāḥ sāle yauvane phullamambujaṁ/
   Kiṁ karotu kuraṅgākṣī vadanena nipīḍitā//

cuckoos chirp on the mango-tree, the lotus is blooming in the waters ; what one, with eyes like those of the deer, would do, when afflicted with cupid ?" Here, we observe that some letter is dropped in some word and some other letter is placed instead in some other word, and again, in the same word, some letter is dropped and in its place, some other letter is kept. For example, in the verse in question, the letter *Ra* of the word *Rasāle* is dropped and letter *Yau* is placed in the word *Vane*, the dropping and placing of both being in the beginning of the words concerned. In the second half, the initial letter *Ma* of the word *Madanena* is dropped, and letter *Va* is placed there making the word *Vadanena* to dupe the reader. In the first half also, two new cogent words, *Sāle* and *Yauvane*, are formed for the same purpose. Actually, the dropping or placing could happen with respect to a half syllable, one syllable and the like, but in anthologies, this is found only in the case of a letter.

Of the riddles (Prahelikās), from amongst the sixteen enumerated and illustrated by *Daṇḍin* and the twentyfour of *Viṣṇudharmottara* of which a few are coincident, many are similar to some of the *Kūṭas* already noticed. Not only this, even some of the figures comprising *Ubhayacitras* might have occurred here and there, in the course of the treatment of *Kūṭa* poetry, as they constitute the foundation of the latter. Among such figures, is [1]the subversion of speech (Vakrokti), as *Kūṭa* itself is, in a way, the subversive (Vakra) style of expression. Among the riddles (Prahelikās), *Samātratā*, *Vikrāntagopitā*, *Muṣitā*, *Kalpitā* and *Vyāmūḍhā* of *Viṣṇudharmottara*, are identical with *Daṇḍin's Samāhitā*, *Vyutkrāntā*, *Pramuṣitā*, *Prakalpitā* and *Samūḍhā*. Besides, both give *Vañcitā*, *Paruṣā*, *Nāmāntaritā*, *Nibhṛtā* and *Samānaśabdā*, and are at one regarding their meanings. Only in the case of *Vañcitā*, is there a different reading as *Vanditā* in the text of *Viṣṇudharmottara*. However, *Parihāsikā* of *Viṣṇudharmottara* seems to be different from the *Parihārikā* of *Daṇḍin*, though looking identical, and although both enumerate *Samānarūpā* and *Saṁkhyātā* in an identical way, they mean differently. Again, *Daṇḍin* mentions

1. Vide Supra, p. 83, Fn. No. 2.

Ekacchannā and *Ubhayacchannā* and also *Viṣṇudharmottara.* It may be noted in this connection that the latter is obscure as to their import, but the former makes it clear. [1]*Saṁkīrṇā* has been defined in *Viṣṇudharmottara* as *Sambhavopetā* and if, here, we interpret the word *Sambhava* as *Saṁkala*, it agrees with the definition given by *Daṇḍin.* [2]Over and above these, *Viṣṇudharmottara* goes on to explain *Gūḍhā*, *Arthakarī*, *Vyabhicāriṇī*, *Naṣṭārthā*, *Naṣṭākṣarā*, *Anyārthatā*, *Arthadā*, and *Leśa.*

Of these, [3]*Samātratā* or [4]*Samāhitā* is almost the same as [5]*Sandhikūṭa.* [6]In *Vañcitā* or *Vanditā* we have certain word or words with a specialised sense as in the [7]case already discussed. [8]*Vikrāntagopitā* or [9]*Vyutkrāntā* is identical with the [10]*Kliṣṭānvayakūṭa* or the [11]*Sthānacyuta.* [12]*Muṣitā* or [13]*Pramuṣitā* is like [14]one previously cited where the meaning is made difficult to understand owing to the use of obsolete words. Moreover, though not [15]*Parihāsikā*, yet [16]*Parihārikā* of *Daṇḍin* resembles the [17]*Samāsamālākūṭa* effected through the power of indication on account of the farfetched sense. [18]*Samānarūpā*, in the view of *Viṣṇudharmottara*, will be like [19]*Yamakakūṭa*, but will be an

1. Vide VD III. II, Vol. II, p. 21.
   Cf. KD III, V. 105, p. 409.
2. Vide VD III, XVI, Vs. 11-14, Vol. I, p. 36
3. Ibid, V. 3, p. 35.
4. Cf. KD III, V. 98, illustr. 108.
5. Vide Supra, p. 74, Fn. No. 2.
6. Cf. VD, Vol. 1, XVI, V. 3, p. 35.
   Cf. KD III, V. 98, illustr. 109.
7. Vide Supra. p, 74, Fn. No. 2.
8. Cf. VD III, Vol I, XVI, V. 4, p. 35.
9. Cf. KD III, V. 99, illustr. 110.
10. Vide Supra, p. 73, Fn. No. 1.
11. Vide Supra, p. 93. Fn. No. 1.
12. Cf. VD III, XVI, V.4, Vol. I, p. 35.
13. Cf. KD III, V, 99, illustr. 111.
14. Vide Supra, p. 72, Fn. No. 3.
15. Vide VD,III. Vol. I, XVI, V. 5, p. 35.
16. Cf. KD III, V. 104, illustr. 120.
17. Vide Supra, p. 71, Fn. No. 3.
18. Cf. VD III, V. 5, Vol. I, XVI, p, 35.
19. Vide Supra, p. 70, Fn. No. 6.

example of [1]*Śleṣakūṭa* if we take the meaning offered by [2]*Daṇḍin*. As for [3]*Paruṣā* and [4]*Saṁkhyātā*, the [5]former consists in words having two meanings at least, of which one based on the secondary sense is at the root eluded by the obvious sense, and the latter is like the [6]*Saṁkhyākūṭa* mostly found in the Vedas. In [7]*Kalpitā* or [8]*Prakalpitā*, the intended meaning is concealed by a different apparent meaning, [9]explained and illustrated earlier. [10]*Nāmāntaritā* and [11]*Nibhṛtā* are like pure riddles exemplified elsewhere, [12]where some reply is to be found but where the query might not be explicitly posed. [13]*Vyāmūḍhā* or [14]*Samūḍhā* depends for its suspense on the concordance of one or more words, and may come under the [15]*Kliṣṭānvayakūṭa*, and there is nothing very peculiar if, in [16]*Gūḍhā*, the intended meaning is obstructed owing to a particular *Bandha* being used in the verse. Likewise, [17]*Naṣṭārthā* is similar to the [18]*Mātrādatta*, where the meaning becomes clear and relevant by putting the missing syllable in the verse, and [19]*Naṣṭākṣarā* and [20]*Anyārthatā* are themselves, similar to each

1. Vide Supra, p. 83, Fn. No. 3.
2. Cf. KD III. V. 100, illustr. 112,
3. Cf. VD III, Vol. I. XVI, V. 6, p. 35.
   Cf. KD III, V. 100, illustr. 113.
4. Cf. VD III, V. 6, Vol. I, XVI, p. 35.
   Vide KD III, V. 101, illustr. 114.
5. Vide Supra, p. 71, Fn. No. 2.
6. Vide Infra, chap. VI; FN. RV. 10, 17-8 etc.
7. Cf. VD III. Vol. I, XVI, V. 7, p. 35.
8. Vide KD III, V. 104, illustr. 115.
9. Vide Supra, p. 71, Fn. No. 2.
10. Cf. VD III, XVI, Vol I, V. 7, p. 35.
    Cf. KD III, V. 102, illustr. 116.
11. Vide VD III, Vol. I, XVI, V. 8, p. 35.
    Cf. KD III, V. 102. illustr. 117.
12. Vide Supra, p. 75, Fn. No. 2.
13. Cf. VD III, Vol. I, XVI, V. 9, p. 35.
14. Vide KD III, V. 103, illustr. 119.
15. Vide Supra, p. 73, Fn. No. 1.
16. Cf. VD III, Vol. I, XVI, 9, p. 35.
17. Ibid, V. 12, p. 36.
18. Vide Supra, p. 90, Fn. No. 2.
19. Cf. VD III, Vol, I, XVI, V. 13, p, 36.
20. Ibid, V. 13, p. 36.

other and may come under the [1]*Akṣaracyuta*. Only, in the former, the meaning is concealed by the dropping of a letter, while in the latter, the meaning becomes quite different due to that dropping.

[2]*Ekacchannā* and [3]*Ubhayacchannā* are also like the said pure riddles, where in the first case, the *Āśrita* is expressed and the *Āśraya* concealed, while in the second, both are concealed. In [4]*Arthakarī*, the obvious meaning is supposed to lead to some other meaning, thereby concealing the intended purport and in [5]*Vyabhicāriṇī* the same effect is achieved through a particular word. Similarly, in [6]*Arthadā*, interpretation of meaning through a particular tense, gives a different sense, and in [7]*Leśa*, only the seed of the meaning is suggested and the rest is to be found. These riddles resemble some given earlier, or else are like the pure ones. Only [8]*Saṁkīrṇā* is different in that it consists of a combination of more than one riddle. To emphasise the point, we quote the instance given by *Daṇḍin* : [9]"If this army (i.e. Alphabet) is not won with *Haya* (i.e. horses, or in case of alphabet : *ha, ya* letters), *Gaja* (i.e. elephants, or otherwise : *Ga, Ja* letters) and *Bhaṭa* (i.e. pedestrian warriors, or in other case : *bha, ṭa* letters), then this our son would remain ignorant of the idea of riches and prestige (or, otherwise, ignorant of even the syllables)!" Here, the effects of both *Nāmāntaritā* and *Vañcitā* are combined.

Among the other chief varieties of literary recreations, prevalent in the middle age, were *Akṣaramuṣṭikā*, *Bindumatī*, *Samasyāpūrti* and *Bhāṣācitras*. [10]*Akṣaramuṣṭikā* is of two types:

1. Vide Supra, p. 92, Fn. No. 1.
2. Vide, VD III, Vol. I, XVI, V. 10, p. 35.
   Cf: KD III, V. 104. illustr, 121.
3. Vide VD III, Vol. I, XVI, V. 10, p. 35.
   Cf: KD III, V. 105, Illustr. 122.
4. Cf: VD III, Vol. I, XVI, V. 10, p, 35.
5. Ibid, V. 11, p. 36
6. Ibid, V. 13, p. 36.
7. Ibid, V. 10, p. 35.
8. Vide KD III, V. 105.
9. Ibid, V. 123 : Sahayā sagajā senā sabhaṭeyaṁ na cejjitā/
   Amātriko'yaṁ mūḍhaḥ syādakṣarajñaśca naḥ sutaḥ//
10. Vide, VKS I-III, p. 34.

one where the concealment of certain letters, like that in the palm of hand, engenders charm either with a view to unravelling some concealed purpose, or effecting brevity in a poetic work, and the other, where the concealment is done with a purpose of effecting privacy. In the first variety, we get the semblance of the thing, or purpose (Sābhāsā). It is also called [1]*Akṣaramudrā*. [2]In the example cited, we find in the first foot the first letters of the signs of Zodiac, in the second their particular appellations owing to their conjunction with the points of eclipse, and in the third and fourth the names of the months. [3]The other variety is called *Bhūtamudrā*, which has several sub-varieties. [4]In SKB, on the other hand, there is an instance where all the four feet of the verse are so arranged, that from every foot we get a four-footed verse consisting of *Murajabandha*.

[5]In the second, on the basis of a given verse, there arises another verse of the same meaning, of which indications are put through dots for the vowels, nasals, *visargas* and juxtaposed consonants, in the same order as they exist in the accru-

1. Ibid, quote-RCPV:
   Gahanaprasannasarvāṁ katipayasūtrāmimāmanantamukhīm/
   Anadhītyākṣaramudrāṁ vādasamudre pariplavate//
2. Ibid : Mevṛmikasiṁkatuvṛdhamakumbhī mūdhasavāsuśakanidhaka-āvyāḥ/
   Phācaivaijye-āśrābhā-ākāmāpaumā caiva//
3. Ibid. quot : Muṣṭiḥ kisalayaṁ caiva cchaṭā cārī patākīkā/
   Patākāṅkuśamudrāśca mudrāvargeṣu saptasu//
   Aṅgulyaścākṣarāṇyeṣāṁ svarāścāṅguliparvasu/
   Saṁyogādakṣaraṁ yuktaṁ bhūtamudrā prakīrtitā//
4. Vide 11, illustr. 361, p 300 :
   Atiḥ atiḥ anma-alaṁ prīdyaradya jadya phadya/
   Melā melā melaṁ melaṁ phasa phasa phasa phasa//
   The verse arising out of the first foot : cf : illustr. 362 :
   Adya me saphalā prītiradya me saphalā ratiḥ/
   Adya me saphalaṁ janma adya me saphalaṁ phalam//
5. Ibid, illustr. 363 :
   Tavāvavādaḥ pratyabdhi patākā pratisaṅgaram/
   Phalaṁ pratyadbhutopāyaṁ yaśāṁsi na tu na kvacit//
   The indications in dots of the accruing verse :
   The verse actually accruing :
   Udadhāvudadhāvājñā saṁyuge saṁyuge jayaḥ/
   Sāhase sāhase siddhiḥ sarvatra tava kīrtayaḥ//

ing verse. [1]In the third, we have some *Samasyā* or problem in a foot or so of a verse, which has to be extended to all the feet in such a way that the verse seems to be an organic and single whole. The charm is all the more enhanced if the problem given is of some [2]paradoxical nature, otherwise it may also constitute some [3]general statement, or some [4]aphorism, or even some [5]onomatopoetic sounds, or some idiom or [6]proverb. When not given as a problem (Samasyā), the last one is called [7]*Ābhāṇaka*. In *Bhāṣācitra*, a verse appears to have been composed in more than one language, giving some suspense to the reader. [8]Sometimes a foot or feet made up of a different language, may be construed in the one generally used, but [9]often it may not. [10]Among the less important ones, are *Pratimālā*,

1. Vide SRB No, 1, pp. 520-524.
2. Ibid : Hīnahatyā dadhātyeva lāghavaṁ mahatāmapi/
   Iti matvā dvipadveṣī mṛgāt siṁhaḥ palāyate//
3. Ibid : Śmaśāneṣvāvāso vasanamibhacarmaiva jarako
   Vṛṣo vāho bhasma draviṇamanugā bhūtanivahāḥ/
   Tathāpyekaḥ śaṁbhustribhuvanamidaṁ rakṣati sadā
   Kriyāsiddhiḥ sattve vasati mahatāṁ nopakara e//
4. Ibid : Nijapatirādyaḥ praṇayī harirdvitīyaḥ karomı kiṁ gopi/
   Śṛṇu sakhi pāṇinisūtraṁ vipratiṣedhe paraṁ kāryam//
5. Ibid : Rāmābhiṣeke madavihvalāyāḥ hastāccyuto hemaghaṭastaruṇyāḥ/
   Sopānamāsādya karoti śabdaṁ ṭhaṭhaṁ ṭhaṭhaṁṭhaṁ ṭhaṭhaṭhaṁ ṭhaṭhaṁṭhaḥ//
6. Ibid :
   Laḍḍūkairdvijakulamadya bhojayitvā dīnāraṁ pratijanamapyanupradāya/
   Yad vīṭīṁ nṛpa na dadāsi tanna yogyaṁ vikrīte kariṇi kimaṅkuśe vivādaḥ//
7. Vide SM No. 30, p. 353 :
   Bahukleśe'lpaphalade kārye bhāvyaṁ na sādaraiḥ/
   Vidārya giriśṛṅgāṇi mūṣakākarṣaṇena kiṁ ?//
8. Cf. : SRB No. 3, p 568 :
   Kamanekatamādānaṁ suratanarajatucchalaṁ tadāsīnam/
   Appatibhānaṁ khamate so'ganikānaṁ naraṁ jetuṁ//
9. Ibid No. 15, p. 570 :
   Haranayanahutāśajvālayā jo jalāyā
   Ratinayanajalaughaiḥ khāka bākī bahāyā/
   Tadapi dahati cittaṁ hāya mai kyā karūṅgī
   Madanaśirasi bhūyaḥ kyā balā āga lāgī//
10. Cf : VKS I-III, p. 29.

Durvācakayoga, *Mlecchitavikalpa*, *Saṁpāṭhya*, *Mānasī*, *Kāvya-kriyā*, *Kriyākalpa*, *Ākīrṇamantra* and *Parakāmohana*, etc.

[1]*Pratimālā* is also known as *Antyākṣarī*, where two teams consisting of one or more individuals, reciprocate in a competition in which one has to recite from memory, a verse beginning with the last letter of the one just recited by the opponent and this course goes on, until in the end, one fails to recite the requisite verse posed by the other team.[2] In *Durvācakayoga*, verses consisting of such words are made to reciprocate in a competition, which either verbally or in sense, or both, is difficult to pronounce or use. Also, a team might throw the challenge to the other team, or else, try to put it in a tight corner by posing a verse which has to be replied to in an *Antyākṣarī* way, by an even more hard-to-pronounce verse. Ordinarily, a team has to recite with clear pronunciation, as many verses as the other has recited, otherwise it does not get through.

The [3]*Mlecchitavikalpa* consists in the various devices prescribed by experts, of making the words comprising a verse difficult to understand, by reversing, in a certain order, the positions of letters. In [4]*Saṁpāṭhya*, one person chosen to initiate recites a book and the other, without hearing it first, recites extempore so that the two voices coincide, accentuating the tone of recitation. Of [5]*Mānasī* there are two varieties, one perceptible and the other imperceptible. In the

1. Ibid, p 32 :
Pratiślokaṁ kramādyatra sandhāyākṣaramantimam/
Paṭhetāṁ ślokamanyonyaṁ pratimāleti socyate/
2. Ibid :
Daṁṣṭrā'grarddhyā prāgyo drākkṣmāmaṁbvantaḥsthāmuccikṣepa/
Devadhruṭ kṣiddhyṛtvik stutyo yuṣmānso'vyātsarpātketuḥ//
3. Cf : VKS I-III, p. 34 :
Dādeḥ kṣāntasya kādeśca svarayorubhayorapi/
Bindūṣmaṇorviparyāsāt durbodhamiti saṁjñitam//
Akau khagau ghaṅau caiva caṭau ñaṇau tapau namau/
Yaśau raṣau lasau ceti mūladevīyamucyate//
Grahanayanavasusametaṁ ṣaḍānanākhyāni sāgarā munayaḥ/
Jvalanāṅgaṁ tukaśṛṅgaṁ durlikhitaṁ gūḍhalekhyamidam//
4. Ibid, p. 35.
5. Ibid.

first, some person, without telling the meaning, jots down a verse in consonants, nasals and aspirates, in due order, composing the poetic designs of lotus etc., and some other person reads it out, having provided the proper syllables, metres and juxtapositions, etc. On the other hand, when it is read out, it belongs to the imperceptible variety and is called *Ākāśamānasī*.

Besides, [1]*Kāvyakriyā* is poetry-writing as a hobby in Sanskrit, Prakrit and *Apabhraṁśa* ; [2]*Kriyākalpa* is the acquisition of the knowledge of rhetoric principles for appreciation of poetry; [3]*Ākīrṇamantra* is talking some secret in some type of code language in a crowded place, and [4]*Parakāmohana* is misleading some person with apparently making clear to him something other than the actual fact. Riddles are of use in effecting these arts. At present these are obsolete, but there was a time when people feverishly talked them, and organised various types of literary circles known as *Sarasvatībhavana*, *Kāvyadevāyatana* and *Vidyāgoṣṭhī* etc.

1. Ibid.
2. Ibid.
3. KD III, V. 97.
4. Ibid :
   Yadrūpamanyarūpeṇa saṁprakāśya hi vañcanaṁ/
   Devetaraprayogābhyāṁ jñeyaṁ tacchalitaṁ yathā//
   Divyaṁ śūrpaṇakhārūpamitarad vāyunandanaḥ/
   Chalitavānabhisṛtya śriyā rāmaṁ ca kīcakam//
   Cf : VKS I-III, p. 35.

CHAPTER V

ARTHACITRA

In the current chapter, our aim is to deal with peculiarity of meaning (Arthacitra). In consonance with what we have established in the introductory chapter, we must again make it clear that we are not going to take all the figures of sense within the ambit of *Arthacitra*, as prescribed by the Sanskrit rhetoricians, as in that case the concept of image (Citra) will suffer. *Dīkṣita* deals in the traditional style with all the figures of sense, capable of creating poetic charm. In spite of very high thinking on some aspects of poetry, Sanskrit Poetics has not been able to evolve a true concept of *Citrakāvya*, or image poetry, or even of *Arthacitra* in the modern sense of the term. Among old rhetoricians, [1]*Ānanda* was the first to come near the concept. He propounded that some sort of picture or image is generated in *Citrakāvya*, but added that it is as if devoid of any life. By life he means the power of suggestion, and there he becomes one with other rhetoricians who have thought of this power of suggestion as the differentia for the three varieties of poetry i.e, suggestive (Vyaṅgya), semi-suggestive or the poetry where the suggestion is subordinate (*Guṇībhūtavyaṅgya*), and the non-suggestive (Citra).

It is our firm conviction that a true image has no opposition with the power of suggestion. On the contrary, sometimes it is found that the latter nourishes and enhances the beauty of the former. But even the most progressive among

1. Cf. DL-III, p. 495 :
Kevalavācyavācakavaicitryamātrāśrayeṇopanibaddhālekhyaprakhyaṁ yadābhāsate taccitram/
DL : Yamakacakrabandhādicitratayā prasiddhameva tattulyārthamevārthacitraṁ mantavyamiti bhāvaḥ/
Ālekhyaprakhyamiti rasādijīvarahitaṁ mukhyapratikṛtirūpaṁ cetyarthaḥ/

Sanskrit rhetoricians, like *Paṇḍitarāja*, will not accept this position. [1]He certainly has taken *Arthacitra* from the lowest order of poetry, and has placed it in the second category, at par with the poetry of subordinate suggestion. In this connection, he has, in his Chef de oeuvre, dubbed unacceptable, in the context of sublime poetry, the views of commentators who have separated the former from the latter. [2]He has criticised the whole thesis propounded and established in the *Citramīmāṁsā*. He does not mean to say that *Citra* variety of poetry is completely bereft of the power of suggestion. As a matter of fact, even from this standpoint, the only reasonable explanation is that here, the figures of speech become prominent and the power of suggestion is of secondary importance. [3]In fact, very seldom is poetry written which has no thoughts and only pictures or images, and the other way round, poetry with no images and only thoughts, is even rarer. On the other hand, there can be poetry only when the thoughts be transmuted into pictures or images, with the help of metaphors and similes, and sensibility be produced in them so that they are only the vehicles of the intellect.

In the evolution of this *Arthacitra*, the similes or the metaphors are of utmost help. [4]According to the indigenous view, simile (Upamā) is the source of all, or most, of the figures of sense. [5]"This one and unique simile," as *Dīkṣita* avers, "appears like the actress, who, by adopting diverse roles and

1. Cf. Vide RG I, p. 20 :
Yattu atādṛśi guṇībhūtavyaṅgyamityādikāvyaprakāśagata-
l akṣaṇe citrānyattvaṁ ṭīkākārairdattaṁ, tanna/
Teṣāṁ guṇībhūtavyaṅgyatāyāścitratāyāśca sarvālaṁkāri-
kasammatattvāt//
2. Cf. CMK V. 2 :
Rasagaṅgādhare citramīmāṁsāyā mayoditā/
Ye doṣāstatra saṁkṣipya kathyante viduṣāṁ mude//
3. KB, p. 118.
4. CM, p. 43 :
Tadidaṁ citraṁ viśvaṁ brahmajñānādivopamājñānāt/
Jñātaṁ bhavatītyādau nirūpyate nikhilabhedasahitā sā//
5. CM, p. 41 :
Upamaikā śailūṣī saṁprāptā citrabhūmikābhedān/
Rañjayati kāvyaraṅge nṛtyantī tadvidāṁ cetaḥ//

dancing on the stage of poetic composition, delights the mind of those who are well-versed in it." At the least, this is capable of giving rise to all the figures of sense based on similes and they are the most important figures from our point of view of image production. So far as the essential feature of simile is concerned, it consists in the delineation of similarity subsisting between two numerically distinct objects. In the light of the western treatment of image, metaphor has this place in relation to the other figures of speech, and in respect of the production of image. But Lewis thinks that image is a broader concept and its field is also wider. [1]The functions of both metaphor and image might seem identical in one sense, but on the basis of his discussion on this topic in his masterpiece, we can assume that the nature of image is definitely subtler. Lewis admits the metaphorical nature of image, but to a certain extent only. In the metaphor, it is not that the feeling of the thing compared and the standard of similitude is destroyed, but in image, the difference between the above disappears into an intensity of feelings. As a matter of fact, in imagery the standard is engendered out of the thing compared, and the latter means not the matter in hand, but the poetic experience begotten of it.

[2]Lewis has not given the name of image to one used only with shallow sentiments for the display of embellishment alone, and has called this a far-fetched conceit. [3]He has also felt that a poet's discriminatory insight, large-heartedness and thoughtfulness, are indispensable in the creation of an exquisite poetic image. [4]He has lauded the natural overflow of poety from images and has disdained the use of images imposed by either tradition or individual. [5]In poetry, metaphor in general has been used as a figure, but there might be certain metaphors having as much depth as images born out of an unconscious mind. It is not irrelevant to point out that it

1. Cf L-P I, p. 18.
2. Ibid, p. 91.
3. Ibid, p. 45.
4. Ibid, p. 121.
5. Ibid, p. 24.

sounds a little strange that [1]Lewis, on the one hand, takes poetic images to the farthest depths of the primordi, and on the other, uses metaphor in sundry measures. It is true that among figures of sense the metaphor is, perhaps, closest to the concept of image, but from the point of view of thoughts and sentiments, that cannot be said to be co-ordinate with the image. In metaphor, the formal relation of identity subsisting between one thing and another is important, [2]while in an image, the very experience is metamorphosed into the envisioning of the object.

This learned theoretician has expressed his opinion, [3]taking into account the profound relation of image with experience, that image, instead of creating a thing or object, visualises it in the context of experience. Thus, the object, focussed in the image, comes as part of a series of relationships, as also part of the nature of metaphor. It originally acts in more than one way and it might suggest a partial intellectual flash of the whole universe. It is as well, the function of every poetic image, that it would indicate the limitless expanse in a limited way. It is most remarkable to find that though the theory of image propounded by Lewis is not so comprehensive and complete as the Indian theory of suggestion, but in the latter there is an unquestionable disregard for the visual element, forming the foundation of image-creation. It is to the credit of *Paṇḍitarāja* that [4]he has stressed the element of enchantment (Ramaṇīyatā) in poetry, and has endowed *Arthacitra* with this visual element. He pulled poetry out of the mire, but unfortunately, even he could not strike at the subtle forms of poetic charm arising out of this visual element in poetry.

In Indian literature, we find a very high order of the perception of image, but it is surprising that in old rhetorics

1. Cf. L-P I, p. 141.
2. Ibid, p. 70
3. Ibid, p. 121.
4. Vide SV-IV, V. 17 :
   Kṣaṇe kṣaṇe yannavatāmupaiti
   Tadeva rūpaṁ ramaṇīyatāyāḥ/

it has been assigned a low position. A true perspective regarding it has not developed in Indian poesy. It ought to have been seen as an independent unit, separated from the figures based on similarity. The uniqueness of both sentiment and form is important in itself. The perception of form or image has its own suggestions and gradations, in which it can be sublime besides being of a lower order. The discernment of an image is an independent business where the suggestion of image through image itself, can be possible from subtle to subtler shades.

In modern Indian criticism, the word *Bimba* has stood for image, but here we shall take it as expressive of reflection through which the standard of similitude is reflected in the object compared, or through which an image is effected. Modern western literary critics have associated this image with almost all the varieties of poetic expressions. They have no predetermined and delimited frontiers of sentiment, figure, or suggestion and it is, therefore, that the form of image which their critique of poetry brings before us, has only a very slight semblance in the *Arthacitra* of Indian poetics. The element of the similitude of form found in *Arthacitra*, would automatically be lost if all the figures of sense were associated with it. [1]In this situation, *Citratva* only denotes *Vicitratva* as we have pinpointed in the foregoing pages. True to the real fact, and in conformity with the western concept of image, we mean by *Citratva* picturesqueness, imagery, etc., and as a necessary corollary, all the figures of sense will not be included in it.

In Sanskrit poetry, for the production of this imagery, [2]there must be, *Bimbapratibimbabhāva* (or *Bimbānubimbabhāva* as it is also called) viz, the relation of the reflected (Bimba) and the reflecting element (Pratibimba) between the

1. KPI. IX, p. 212 : Vaicitryamalaṁkāraḥ/

2. SD-fn X, p. 599 :

Bimbaṁ śarīraṁ pratibimbaṁ tacchāyā, tayorbhāvaḥ ākārapratyākāratulyatvam/ Prativākyaṁ vibhinnasyāpi sādhāraṇadharmasya tulyarūpatayā vākyārthayorupamāsampādakatve..../

thing compared and the standard of comparison. [1]In the thing compared (Upameya) the standard of similitude (Upamāna) is mirrored or focussed, and an image is produced. In technical language, this might also be called tinging (Rañjana) of the former by the latter. In other words, *Upameya* is tinged with the colour of *Upamāna* and becomes one with it. [2]This is often possible through the process of merging of the latter in the former. [3]In the figure metaphor (Rūpaka), there is seldom this merging or identification between the aforesaid two objects. On the other hand, in the majority of cases, the nature or properties of one object are attributed to another. In the former situation, the soul of one object is transmuted or mirrored into the other, while in the latter there is superimposition or placement of the form of one object on to the other, as if from outside. Therefore the identification is intrinsic and complete in the former, whereas, if it is identification, it is exterior and superficial in the latter.

It may sound surprising that the metaphor, which in Aristotle's view is very near the idea of image, which place the simile has been accorded in Indian poetics, is, on the above ground, rejected by [4]*Appaya Dīxit* and some such rhetoricians from the pale of *Bimbapratibimba* relation, as also from the domain of image. But it is a matter of relief that once again, [5]*Paṇḍitarāja* comes to the rescue, and stoutly

1. V-AS, p. 35 :
   Loke hi darpaṇādau bimbāt pratibimbasya bhede'pi madīyamevātra vadanaṁ saṁkrāntamityabhimanyante/
2. Cf. KN, p. 44 :
   Viṣayasya svaśabdollekhanaṁ vināpi viṣayivācakenaiva śabdena grahaṇaṁ viṣayanigaraṇaṁ, tatpūrvakaṁ viṣayasya viṣayirūpatayā'dhyavasānam..../
3. SD X, p. 541 :
   Rūpakaṁ rūpitāropo viṣaye nirapahnave/
   Cf. AS, p. 44 : viṣayiṇā viṣayasya rūpavataḥ karaṇāt rūpakam/
4. Vide A—KN
   Upāttabimbāviśiṣṭaviṣayadharmikāhāryāropaniścayaviṣayībhūtamupamānābhedatādrūpyānyataradrūpakam/
5. Vide RG, II, p. 300 :
   Yadapi rūpake bimbapratibimbabhāvo nāstītyuktaṁ tadapi bhrāntyaiva/

defends the position of *Jayaratha* that this relation is not altogether impossible in regard to the metaphor. The latter has quoted a [1]verse to substantiate his ideas, and *Paṇḍitarāja* has wholeheartedly supported it as an instance of *Bimbapratibimba* relation in metaphor. Here, it must be pointed out, that given *Bimbapratibimba*-relation, if there is one impression throughout a verse there is image. So one unified picture is necessary in an image, though these may have broken images also.

In connection with any discourse on image as identical with *Arthacitra*, it is customary to deal with symbol. [2]In Indian literature, symbols are taken to be the old images, but in western literature, these symbols have developed into images and so they constitute the first phase of the development of thought into imagery. A symbol, through the medium of the manifest indicates the unmanifest but with an image, there is identity of both. This is despite the fact that there also, the movement is from manifest sentiment to unmanifest, and the identified position of both is the equation of two varied actions. With an image, the express meaning might be one, but the symbolical meanings might be many. This is because one image may represent many things. Therefore the perception of the letters used in certain words comprising an image, may symbolise several concepts.

Among the western theoreticians, Baudelairé attached much value to symbols, owing to their particular quality of transporting experience beyond the terrestrial and making it transcendental. He gave it the name of liberating value.' To German philosophers goes the credit of making poetry the means of the mystic revelation of the universe. Sensations were taken to be the only source of experiencing unspeakable truths, and by symbols such experience could be expressed. [3]In the course of critically thinking over such ideas of sym-

1. Quote : V-AS, p. 44 :
Kandarpadvipakarṇakambunalinairdānāmbubhirlāñchitaṁ
Saṁlagnāñjanapuñjakālimakalaṁ gaṇḍopadhānaṁ rateḥ/
Vyomānokahapuṣpapucchamalibhiḥ sañchādyamānodaraṁ
Paśyaitat śaśinaḥ sudhāsahacaraṁ bimbaṁ kalaṅkāyitam //
2. Cf. HK, p. 24.
3. Cf. SSMP, p. 70.

bolism, Remy dé Gourmont laid greatest stress on the visual element and the use of exact, appropriate words in poetry. As a result of this, there was a turn in the second generation of the symbolists away from the indirect subtleties of Baudelairé shrouded in the mystic layers of 'conscious-subconscious.' [1]It is peculiar that Gourmont, alone among the symbolists, stressed the importance of vision in the poetic structure beyond the tangibly visible.

Imagists drew inspiration from the symbolists, and breaking their circle of thoughts, tried to give a new vision of art. The main purpose of an image is the presentation of the experienced object, and the objective of a symbol is fulfilled by the representation of certain ideas. [2]Eliot made the symbol the carrier of both thought and sensation. Thus the idea of the imagist symbol is the result of the equation and synthesis of both the presentation and representation of fact, as well as of thought. From a word expressive of the cognition of an object, is understood also the cognition of the concept innate in that particular object, or attributed to it by the user. Therefore, one side of the word-and-meaning relation is imagist, and the other symbolist, and these two always balance each other. Symbols that are also images are a primary contemporary concern, because the image, as a form of knowledge and an artistic impression, has for several centuries been suspect.

The beauty of the poetic image or the *Arthacitra*, consists in the synthetisation and concretisation of abstract thoughts in poetry. The usefulness of the language of poetry is found in the concrete rather than in the abstract. [3]Those, who, taking inspiration from the art of the abstract, want to establish it in the field of poetry, do not really understand the real nature of language. But with the condensation of ideas there is always the danger of the language lacking the strength to carry the meaning. This might result in ambiguity, which should be avoided.

To sum up, the search after the basic contents of *Arthacitra* started, among other reasons, due to an awakened

1. Cf. SSMP, p. 70.
2. Ibid, p. 111.
3. Ibid.

attitude to discover something in the Indian poetic concept, similar to the modern concept of image (Bimba) in the form of poetic truth. There is, also, the attraction towards poetic utility and structural unity in the formal matter of poetry. In the following verse, a forceful and sublime image has been evolved, underlying the imagination of the poet and it has been taken by *Mammaṭa* as an example of *Arthacitra* in the traditional way—[1]"The *Amarāvatī* looked as if she had closed her eyes because of fear, whose doors *Indra* nervously bolted, having heard him (i.e. Hayagrīva), the giver of prestige (to friend), come out at will from his mansion." The poet has on the basis of conception qua poetic figure (Utprekṣā), evolved a very lively and captivating image of a fear-stricken woman, with her eyes closed, and this the poet has done by expressing the formal imaginative picture of the city whose doors have been bolted.

In the above case, we find an abundant measure of suggestion as well, and doubt occurs regarding the acumen of the seers of poetry like *Mammaṭa*. Though he has created a lifeless, photostat simile here, he did not commit any major mistake, as *Ānanda* and *Abhinava* were his guides. Two questions arise : firstly, whether there is any real relish in such a simile, and secondly if there is, why should it be made to look so impoverished and be placed in a lower category of poetry ? It is clear that Indian thinkers could not probe into the intricacies of this imagist relish. The theory of sentiment in poetry had come, by analogy, from the field of dramaturgy, and had so engrossed the attention of the rhetoricians, that the visual element found in the former was not fully appreciated or evaluated.

None of the old rhetoricians have given time to the discussion of the nature of the image, of a particular sentiment manifesting itself. Whatever discussion there has been, has related only to the peculiarities of the secondary significa-

1. Cf. HV :
   Vinirgataṁ mānadamātmamandirād
   Bhavatyupaśrutya yadṛcchayā'pi yam/
   Sasaṁbhramendradrutapātitārgalā
   Nimīlitākṣīva bhiyā'marāvatī//

tion, founded on some resemblance between the primary and secondary sense of a word (Gauṇī Lakṣaṇā), of the suggested sense through the use of some figure (Alaṁkāradhvani), or of the figures arising out of similarity. Otherwise, it has limited itself to making threadbare the question, whether figures are permanent properties of a particular sentiment, or its temporary phase. When we make an assertion about the beauty of the similes of *Kālidāsa*, it does not denote different varieties and subtleties of formal similitude found in his poetry, nor does it give the idea that a particular simile is sublime because it is conducive to a particular sentiment. To illustrate : [1]"Having reached the mountain, white with snow, which is the source of that river, and whose rocks are fragrant with the musk of the deer sitting there, you, having been seated on its peak and removing the fatigue of the way, would bear the exhilarating beauty comparable to that of the mud dug up (through the horns and clung on to them) by the bull of *Shiva* (lit. three-eyed one)." When the poet writes this piece, it cannot be said that the personal appeal of motive and powerful imagery, would have had its value with the sentiment in separation, and without that suggestion there would not be that appeal.

It would be not only a misadventure, but a poetic fallacy as well, to place this piece of poetry under the lowest category on account of its *Citratva*. This literary appeal is related to a different kind of sensibility. This has a very wide appreciation in Indian Arts, but in poetics it has been ignored because of its nature of engulfing within it all the elements of poetry viz, suggestion, sentiment and figures etc. The greatest proof is the fact that *Citrakāvya*, in the form of different *bandhas*, remained circumscribed to the conception of *Citrālaṁkāra*, and the very basis of *Arthacitra* almost died out. Gradually, even the figures of sound lost their inner appeal and *Citrakāvya* became regarded as a lower order of poetry in Sanskrit literature.

1. Vide MD I, V. 52 :
   Āsīnānāṁ surabhitaśilaṁ nābhigandhairmṛgāṇāṁ
   Tasyā eva prabhavamacalaṁ prāpya gauraṁ tuṣāraiḥ/
   Vakṣyasyadhvaśramavinayane tasya śṛṅge niṣaṇṇaḥ
   Śobhāṁ ramyāṁ trinayanavṛṣotkhātapaṁkopameyām//

Dealing with the figures of sense which generally evoke imagery, we first take up the simile. We have stressed earlier that [1]this is the root of most, if not all, of the figures. Some of the rhetoricians, to name only the representative ones, like *Daṇḍin* among the old, and *Mammaṭa* among the new, have, from different points of view, conceived several varieties of it. [2]The first-mentioned one has classified it on the basis of various forms and grades of similitude, subsisting between the standard and the object of comparison, [3]while the latter has done it from the viewpoint of how this similitude is expressed. It goes without saying that most of these varieties later developed into separate figures. To take but one example, [4]*Daṇḍin's Anyonyopamā* is nothing but the reciprocal simile (*Upameyopamā*) of today. On the other hand, *Mammaṭa's* modus operandi is grammatical, and he has made divisions of similes, as expressed through various primary and secondary suffixes and in compound etc. [5]It is remarkable to see that *Daṇḍin*, also has hinted at these various types of similes. Then there is a classification based on the elision of any one or two or three of the constituent elements of the simile. It is a pleasant surprise to find that [6]J.S. Mill, by way of analysis, though in a different context, has thrown light on the concept of similarity, constituting the vital element of simile. To pause for critical reflection, we find very subtle grades of difference in the various forms and aspects of similarity. A portrait or landscape may resemble the original in different ways and denote a peculiar content. Similarity between two things may be of different degrees. When it exists in the highest degree, it is called identity and the two similar things are said to be identical. This is metaphor. [7]There is equipollence of both difference and similarity between object and the standard of comparison.

1. Vide Supra, p. 103, f.n. 4.
2. Cf. KD II, p. 109.
3. Cf. KPIX, Vs. 1-4, pp. 224-237.
4. Vide KD II, V. 18, p. 116.
5. Ibid—Vs. 57-60, pp. 138-39.
6. Vide M-EE, p. 207.
7. Cf. ECAJ III, Sec III.

On the contrary, [1]when there is a superiority of difference or of similarity, there might be other figures depending on whether the said superiority is in favour of the object of comparison or of the standard. The common properties play a significant role in the evolution of such figures as are based on similarity. In respect of these common properties, where the points of resemblance are more than those of difference, there is some particular figure. When the points of difference are more than those of resemblance, the figure is altogether a different one. Normally, the object of comparison has less properties, and the standard more, but [2]when we find that the former possesses a greater share of these common properties, more poetic charm is generated and the figure produced is dissimilitude (Vyatireka). [3]In the figure simile, of course, there is numerical difference between the standard of comparison and the object so far as their generic features are concerned, but there is also identity through the medium of common properties.

[4]According to *Mammaṭa*, simile consists in the similarity of attributes or common properties between the standard and the object of comparison, provided they are distinct. Therefore, the central interest lies in comparing one object with another, when both possess a common characteristic. Such a comparison may tend to exalt or degrade an object. In communion of the two objects (Sādharmya), through the same properties, lies the charm (Vicchitti) of the figure. When we compare two objects in point of some attributes, we acknowledge perfect equality between the objects, so far as those attributes are concerned. On the other hand, if there is the slightest consciousness of inequality in respect of the said attributes, there cannot be a simile. Here we may point out, that [5]*Paṇḍitarāja* has criticised this definition for failing to embody charming effect (Hṛdyatva) as an essential of a good

1. Cf. ECAJ III. Sec. III.
2. Vide KP' V. 19, p. 266.
3. Cf. ECAJ III, Sec. III.
4. Cf. KP' X, V. 1, p. 222.
5. Cf. RG, II, p. 212.

simile. But *Mammaṭa* does not specify this in the definition of any figure, indicating thereby, that he tacitly admits it as a necessary prerequisite of all figures.

[1]In simile, the *Bimbapratibimba*-relation would be found in cases where the attributes are mentioned separately. [2]Therefore, it follows that it would be absent in the case of an elliptical simile. [3]On the other hand, it is present in the following verse due to the power of reflection in the underlying attributes of ruddiness and pendulousness, found respectively, between one's being besmeared with the red sandal and the summit's having been reddened with the rays of the newly risen sun, and again, between the pearl-necklace being pendent round one's shoulders and a mountain torrent gushing down : [4]"This *Pāṇḍu* king, with pendent pearl-necklace on his shoulders, having been besmeared with the red sandal on the body, looks resplendent like the *Himālaya* mountain with its summit reddened with rays of the newly rising sun and (rendered beautiful) with the streams gushing forth". Here, in the shape of the white-complexioned *Pāṇḍu* king besmeared with the red sandal and with a pearl-necklace hanging down his shoulders, we get a very beautiful picture of a big snow-clad mountain whose peak looks tawny because of the ruddy rays of the rising sun, and where a cascade of water is rushing down. The verse, when read, gives a visual picture and leaves an indelible impression on our mind. This, in turn, augments the poetic charm engendered through the use of simile.

1. Vide KN, p. 4 :
Vastuto bhinnayorapyupamānopameyadharmayoḥ parasparasādṛśyādabhinnayoḥ pṛthagupādānaṁ bimbapratibimbabhāvaḥ/

2. Cf. R-KN, p. 14-15 :
Ata eva dharmaluptāyāmanugāmitāprayuktameva dharmasya śādhāraṇyaṁ na bimbapratibimbabhāvakṛtamapīti/

3. Ibid :
Bimbapratibimbabhāvakṛtasādhāraṇadharmanirdeśasthale śabdopāttānāṁ haricandanabālātapādīnāmeva aruṇimādisādṛśyamādāya bimbapratibimbamādāya....../

4. Vide RV, VI. V. 60 :
Pāṇḍyo'yamaṁsārpitalambahāraḥ kḷptāṅgarāgo hanicandarena/
Ābhāti bālātaparaktasānuḥ sanirjharodgāra ivādrirājaḥ//

About metaphor, we have discussed its potential for evoking an image, which *Paṇḍitarāja* rightly affirms. To attest this, to quote below a verse: [1]"This night *Kāpālika*, white with the besmearing of ashes in the shape of moon-light, taking pleasure in the art of vanishing at will, moves on a tramp from one island to another, carrying bones in the form of stars, (and) holding fragrance of the unfailing collyrium, on the pretext of the black spot in the skull-bowl of the moon." In this instance too, we get an exquisite image of the night in the shape of a female-mendicant of a particular sect. The mendicant has besmerched her body with ashes, and hence is white, while the night is clear because of the full-moon. The former carries bones, has a facility for making herself invisible, is a rover, and keeps the magic collyrium in her skull-bowl, whereas the latter has stars shining in the firmament, disappears with the rise of the sun each day, as if she relishes this hide-and-seek, moves from one hemisphere to another so that there is daytime in the continent of the particular hemisphere she has left, has the moon like the skull-bowl, and in it is the blackspot like the unfailing collyrium of the mendicant

[2]The attributes of the said mendicant are superimposed on those of the night. So there is the *Bimbapratibimba*-relation between 'moonlight' and 'ashes' on the one hand, and between 'stars' and 'bones' on the other. Again, there might be this relation, but in a slightly different way, between 'moon' and the 'skull-bowl', 'blackspot' and the 'magic collyrium'. The virtue of 'taking pleasure at will', and 'moving on a tramp from continent to continent', is common to both, forcing identification between the two. [3]This is an example of metaphor, having identi-

1. Cf. :
   Jyotsnābhasmacchuraṇadhavalā bibhratī tārakāsthi-
   Nyantardhānavyasanarasikā rātrikāpālikīyam/
   Dvīpāddvīpaṁ bhramati dadhatī candramudrākapāle
   Nyastaṁ siddhāñjanaparimalaṁ lāñchanasya cchalena//
2. Vide KN, p. 76 :
   Tatrāpi viṣayaviṣayiṇostadviśeṣaṇānāṁ ca pratyekamevaikyāropaḥ na tu jyotsnādiviśiṣṭarātrirūpaviṣayasya bhasmādiviśiṣṭakāpālikīrūpaviṣayiṇaśca viśiṣṭarūpeṇaikyāropo'sti/
3 Cf. KP X, V. 7, p. 243 :
   Tad rūpakamabhedo ya upamānopameyayoḥ/

fication of two objects, on the basis of identification of the attributes pertaining to both. [1]It is distinguishable from simile, in that no word is used expressive of the similitude between the object and the standard. If in the former, it is similitude that charms us, here it is the undivided superimposition of the attributes. But it must be remembered that in metaphor, this superimposition of the standard on the object of similitude, must be based on similarity alone, and should only be intentional or simulated, and not genuine.

In point of the *Bimbapratibimba*-relation, exemplification qua poetic figure (Dṛṣṭānta), is nearest to the figures dealt with above. [2]This consists in the reflection of the standard and the object of similitude as well as the common attributes binding the two. We may note that this figure is based on similitude in the meanings of the sentences and not of words independently. This similarity must only be suggested and not expressed. Further, what is most important, the attributes pertaining to the matter in hand must only be similar to, and not the same as those relating to the standard. In other words, the attributes must correspond to each other but should not be identical. As we shall deliberate later, this correspondence of attributes between the object and the standard of similitude, constitutes the very life-blood of the *Bimbapratibimba*-relation. [3]One thing that must be noted is that the *Bimbapratibimba*-relation exists not

1. Cf. KD, II, V. 66, p. 141 :
   Upamaiva tirobhūtabhedā rūpakamucyate/
2. Cf. SD X, V. 69, p. 599 :
   Dṛṣṭāntastu sadharmasya vastunaḥ pratibimbanam/

   Cf. KP3 X, V. 16 :
   Eteṣāmupamānopameyasādharmyāṇāṁ sarveṣāṁ pratibimbanaṁ dṛṣṭāntaḥ/

   Cf. KN, p. 68 :
   Yatropamānopameyavākyayorbhinnāveva dharmau bimbapratibimbabhāvena nirdiṣṭau tatra dṛṣṭāntaḥ/
3. Cf. V-AS, p. 96 :
   Ataśca dharmāṇāṁ dharmiṇāṁ ca bimbapratibimbabhāvena nirdeśe 'yamalaṁkāraḥ/

   Cf. MC (Comm) :
   Na tu prativastūpamāyāmiva sādhāraṇadharmasyaiva dviḥ prayogaḥ kintūpameyāderapi/

only between attributes, but through it also between those having attributes. Again, both the matter in hand and the standard are verbally mentioned, and in exemplification through dissimilarity (Vaidharmya), the similitude should be conveyed negatively.

In the verse cited below, there is a positive instance of exemplification through similarity : [1]"Nay the kings be a thousand and one, but the earth is having him only as her lord. The night, though replete with constellations, stars and planets, is really illumined by the moon alone." The beautiful image evolved in the form of night, thronged with the cluster of constellations, stars and planets, and illumined by the moon, corresponds to the picture of the earth possessing thousands of (small) kings, but really having only *Magadharāja* as her lord. The *Bimbapratibimba*-relation exists between 'a host of small kings' and 'a cluster of constellations, stars and planets' on the one hand, and between 'earth' and 'night', *Magadharāja* and 'the moon', as well as between the actions of 'overlording' and 'illumining' on the other hand. Therefore, the underlying idea of the verse is : the kings might be a thousand, but only *Magadharāja* is lord of the earth in the real sense of the term, as unnumbered constellations, stars and planets are not able to illumine the night, even together, which the moon accomplishes alone. Like metaphor, but unlike simile, no word here is expressive of the similitude, and there are two independent sentences, each constituting the object and the standard of comparison.

[2]In these respects, as well as in regard to *Bimbapratibimba*-relation, figure illustration (Nidarśanā) is very close to exemplification. [3]Here we come to a figure wherein similitude

1. Vide RV, VI, V. 22 :
   Kāmaṁ nṛpāḥ santu sahasraśo'nye
   Rājanvatīmāhuranena bhūmiṁ/
   Nakṣatratārāgrahasaṅkulāpi
   Jyotiṣmatī candramasaiva rātriḥ//
2. Vide KP'X, V. 11, p. 253 :
   Nidarśanaṁ dṛṣṭāntakaraṇaṁ/
3. Cf. KN, V. 53, p. 69 :
   Vākyārthayoḥ sadṛśayoraikyāropo nidarśanā/

between two things is conveyed, in a veiled manner, by one thing being described as being the same as the other. Thus two sentences, generally connected by correlatives are used, each containing an idea apparently unconnected with the idea in the other, but for that very reason, suggesting the similarity between the two ideas. The poetic effect, as is evident by the very nature of this figure, can be produced in the body of two sentences, or even one sentence, or a word. [1]Though it is normal for a poet to attribute to the object of similitude the properties of the standard, the poet sometimes produces the same poetical effect, possibly with a greater emphasis, by attributing to latter the properties of the former. [2]This figure always goes with an inner identification of meaning (Ārtha abheda) which is quite exclusive of superimposition as found in metaphor, or supersession of either the object or the standard of comparison occurring in hyperbole. For instance : [3]"On the rise of the sun and setting of the moon, with their rays stretched up like strings, this mountain assumes the grace of a big elephant, with two bells dangling down its two sides."

In some cases above, it has been seen that through images, abstract and intangible things have been given concrete shape, but here there is crystallisation or superconcretisation of the concrete phenomena of nature. The image that is called up is superb. On one side of the *Raivataka* mountain is the rising halo of the sun in the east, and on the other side the setting disc of the moon on the west. The two constellations, both round-shaped, are like two large spherical bells,

1. Vide KN, p. 73 :

   Upamānopameyayoranyatarasminnanyataradharmāropaḥ padārthavṛttirnidarśaneti.../

   Cf. R-KN, p. 97 :

   Tacca dharmiṇi dharmyantaratādātmyāropa-taddharmāropābhyāṁ dvividhamityeva yuktamityasmaddeśikapariśīlitaḥ panthāḥ/

2. Vide RG, II, p. 462 :

   Evañcāropādhyavasāyamārgabahirbhūta ārtha evābhedo nidarśanājīvitaṁ/

3. Cf. SV, V. 20 :

   Udayati vitatordhvaraśmirajjāvahimarucau himadhāmni yāticāstam,
   Vahati girirayaṁ vilambighaṇṭādvayaparivāritavāraṇendralīlām//

dangling on both sides of the elephant. The rays of the rising sun and the setting moon are like the strings tied up on the back of the elephant, on to which the said bells are hanging down. With the movement of the elephant, the bells move. This shows the dynamic character of the said constellations. When the bells move, a tinkling sound is produced. There is no such suggestion in the verse, but we can infer it from the chattering notes of the birds in the morning described. The image becomes all the more pleasing because of its homeliness, as we know that an elephant, with two bells dangling and tinkling on its sides, is a common sight in the countryside, even today.

In other words, to the *Raivataka* mountain is attributed the grace of an elephant, and [1]this juxtaposition, though apparently unconnected, aims at driving at the similarity of the former to the latter. [2]The figure illustration is under the category where a seemingly impossible relation between two objects is established. The *Bimbapratibimba*-relation is between the said mountain with the rising sun and setting moon on its two sides, on the one hand, and an elephant with two bells dangling on either side, on the other. More specifically, it is between the mountain and the elephant, two constellations and two bells, as well as the rays of the constellations and the strings to which the bells are attached. [3]In this figure it must be noted that the similitude exists implicitly in the meanings of grammatically dependent sentences, and the charm lies in juxtaposing two facts having no apparent connection between them.

It has been seen above, that in the *Bimbapratibimba*-relation, attributes, or the object with attributes in one place, are different from those in another, but still they correspond, just as the thing reflected is different from the reflection,

1. Vide RG, II, p. 455 :
   Upāttayorarthayorārthābheda aupamyaparyavasāyī nidarśanā/
2. Cf. KP'X, V. 11, p. 253 :
   Abhavan vastusambandha upamāparikalpakaḥ/
3. Vide KP, 3 X, p. 395 :
   Atrānyalīlodvahanasyānyenāsaṁbhavād vāraṇendralīlāsadṛśīṁ līlāmityupamāyāṁ paryavasānam/

though one corresponds to the other. This is the ideal condition for the production of an image. On the contrary, in the typical comparison (Prativastūpamā), there is traditionally the rather less attributes *Vastuprativastu*-relation. [1]It means the relation of the attributes in one place to those in another, when these attributes are the same but couched in different words. This evokes less poetic charm but its capacity to produce an image cannot be denied. For example, in the following verse, there is a good image : [2]"O daughter of *Vidarbha* king, you, by whom even the king of *Niṣadha* (i.e. *Nala*) is captivated on account of your exalted virtues, are fortunate indeed ! What more praise can be possible than of the moonlight which makes even the ocean tremulous ?"

There is a focussing of similitude between *Damayantī* and 'the moonlight', *Nala* and 'the ocean', as well as between the actions of 'captivating' and 'making tremulous.' [3]From the word *Stuti* (i.e. encomium) in the second sentence constituting the standard, are expressed the noble qualities of the moonlight forming the reflection (Pratibimba) of the high qualities of *Damayantī* (Bimba). Also from the use of the word 'moonlight' for *Damayantī*, is suggested her soothing though powerful virtues, making even *Nala*, with oceanlike gravity, ruffled. From this instance, it must be conceded that in some cases at least, it becomes difficult to judge precisely whether it is the *Bimbapratibimba*-relation or the *Vastuprativastu*-relation. The same attribute, stated in different words, is likely to be mistaken for two corresponding attributes, or vice versa. It must be mentioned here, that this figure, consisting of at least

1. Cf. Candrikā (Comm.) :
Bhinnaśabdabodhyaikadharmagamyaṁ prastutāprastutavākyārthasādṛśyaṁ prativastūpamā/
Cf. KP 2 X, p. 90 :
Dṛṣṭānte tu sākṣāttadvṛttidharmāṁśe'pi....../ dharmasya pṛthakśabdābhyāmupādānaṁ vastuprativastubhāvaḥ/
2. NC, III, V. 116 :
Dhanyāsi vaidarbhi guṇairudarāiryayā samākṛṣyata naiṣadho'pi/
Itaḥ stutiḥ kā khalu candrikāyā yadabdhimapyuttaralīkaroti//
3. V-SD X, p. 598 :
Atra damayantī upameyā candrikā upamānaṁ tayordhīrākarṣaṇameko dharmaḥ/

two mutually independent sentences, implies the similitude inherent in those sentences without any expressive word. Each sentence must embody the attribute, whether constituting the matter in hand (Prakṛta), or the standard of similitude (Aprakṛta), and this similitude may be stated positively or negatively. The chief charm lies solely in the same attribute presenting itself in more than one case. Besides, we do not come across corresponding objects having attributes; they may occur, but the poet does not stress them.

In the figure conception (Utprekṣā), the rhetoricians have not found the *Bimbapratibimba*-relation, or even the *Vastuprativastu*-relation, but [1]with the possibility of similitude, if not actual similitude, it will be amply clear from the verse below that such a thing is not impossible in particular cases : [2]"The moon, with rays as if with fingers holding the braid of hair, like darkness, kisses, as it were, the face of the night having lotuses, like eyes, half-closed." Here there is a very beautiful picture of the moon, in the form of a lover, kissing the face of the night (who is like the beloved), holding her braid of hair. In this verse, the sentiment of love in union is implicit and is emphasised by the fact that night, the beloved, has become enamoured and has half-closed her eyes, while she relishes the pleasure of union with her lover. Actually, the moon is rising in the eventide, dispelling the darkness and consequently, making the lotuses droop, but from this a picture emerges of a lover holding the braid of his beloved's hair with his hand, and kissing her face, as a result of which the latter closes her eyes from overpowering sentiment. The *Bimbapratibimba*-relation might also be found between 'fingers' and 'rays', 'braid of hair' and 'the patches of darkness', and the word *Rajanīmukha* means 'commencement of the night' in one case, and 'the countenance of the beloved night' in the other. Again, 'the evening time has the lotuses

1. Vide KN, p. 35 :
   Anyadharmasambandhanimittenānyasyānyatādātmyasambhāvana-mutprekṣā/
2. Cf. : Aṅgulībhiriva keśasañcayaṁ sannigṛhya timiraṁ marīcibhiḥ/
   Kuḍmalīkṛtasarojalocanaṁ cumbatīva rajanīmukhaṁ śaśī//

half-closed, like eyes' and 'the face of the night-damsel has her eyes, like lotuses, half-closed.'

From the figures exemplification, illustration, and typical comparison, the difference here, is chiefly that there are not two sentences, and there is no correspondence in point of having the *Bimbapratibimba*-relation between the objects. The word expressive of similitude, based on poetical fancy, is used twice. In conception qua poetic figure, we pass on to a figure [1]which has the element of simile in it, but which is more highly poetical than the latter. [2]Moreover, this figure is prominenly leaning towards identification (Abheda), and if hyperbole, in which the object of comparison is swallowed up by the standard, be taken to be the height of poetical effect in the direction of this identification, then the figure conception is, indeed, a milestone on the way. [3]Here the poet's mind is said to be in a state of suspense or incertitude, of course intentional and not actual, and wavering between the standard and the object of similitude, but with a greater bias towards the former.

Among such figures which traditionally have no *Bimba-pratibimba* or even *Vastuprativastu*-relation, but often evoke images, by way of specimen we may take up only model metaphor (Samāsokti) and the figure concealment (Apahnuti), as our aim is only to throw torchlight in this direction, and not to deal with all the figures that flash, or might flash, an image, because as we shall see, image-creation is a different art and calls for a definite, purposive effort on the part of a poet. [4]Of the model metaphor, it can be said that it is a

1. Cf. X, p. 36, KP 2 :
   Sambhāvanā ca ramaṇīyadharmanimittikā grāhyā/
2. Ibid, p. 38 :
   Etāvataivotprekṣāyāṁ sādhyavasānatvavyavahāraḥ prācāmiti bodhyaṁ/
3. V-AS, p. 70 :
   Sambhāvanā hi ekatarapakṣaśithilīkaraṇena pakṣāntaradārḍhyena ca prādurbhavatītyasyāḥ sādhyādhyavasāyatulyakakṣatvaṁ/
4. Cf. SD X, V. 74, p. 612 :
   Samāsoktiḥ samairyatra kāryaliṅgaviśeṣaṇaiḥ/
   Vyavahārasamāropaḥ prastute'nyasya vastunaḥ//

figure based on verbal similitude with the superimposition of the behaviour of one thing over another. It is customary with poets to see in the action of a particular object, the striking reflection of the action of some other object. They describe a particular action in such a way that appreciative people are at once reminded of the corresponding action of the standard, even when the latter is not mentioned, or, if mentioned, not so explicitly. In fact, the charm of the figure lies in so describing the action of the former that the latter is at once suggested. To illustrate these points, we cite a verse : [1]"The autumn, possessing a rainbow in the form of a readymade nail-scratch, and making visible the moon with a black spot because of whitish clouds, generated more glow in the sun."

Here, it is natural for the autumn season to have pale-white clouds and a clear sky, enabling the moon to be visible, and adding more heat to the sun. We also get the behaviour of a beloved, appeasing her paramour with the gift of her white-complexioned breasts under the very nose of her lover, and thus engendering the heat of jealousy in him. The use of the word 'readymade nail-scratch', standing in comparison to the 'rainbow', is the key to this figure. The many-coloured rainbow, with red colour in prominence, on the whitish clouds in the sky, is like a readily given blood-stained nailmark on the white breasts of a damsel. So, on the one hand, there is the picture of an autumnal sky with pale-white clouds, with the moon clear and the sun aglow, and on the other, of a beloved with bloodstained nailmarks on her breasts, caressing her paramour, and thus, making her lover jealous. The former picture constitutes the matter in hand, and

Cf. KN, p. 87 :

Samāsoktāvaprastutavyavahārasamāropaścārutāhetuḥ/ Na tu rūpaka iva prastute'prastutarūpasamāropo'sti/

1. Vide Quote : SD X, p. 619 :

Aindraṁ dhanuḥ pāṇḍupayodhareṇa śaraddadhānārdranakhakṣatābhaṁ/

Prasādayantī sakalaṅkaminduṁ tāpaṁ raverabhyadhikaṁ cakāra//

the latter the standard, and [1]from the description of the former, the latter is suggested or reflected.

But we must be definite about one thing, that the use of any clue, as in the present verse, is never necessary in the model metaphor figure, for the true mirroring of the standard. Had the use of word 'readymade nailscratch' not been made, the behaviour of the lover, the paramour, and the beloved, would still have been suggested. What is most important here is [2]the dexterous use by the poet of beautiful adjectives with double significance, when one meaning applies to the matter in hand which is expressed, and the other to the standard which is suggested. Here adjectives are understood in their wider meaning, and not in the strict grammatical sense. Therefore, this figure borders the double entendre. Again, if there is reflection or correspondence between the two objects, one expressed and the other suggested, then I do not understand why this should not be taken for the *Bimbapratibimba*-relation which the rhetoricians have denied. In the above verse, there is a good piece of suggestion in the use of the word *Ārdra* (i.e. wet) for the nailmark, showing that it is readymade.

[3]Concealment qua poetic figure (Apahnuti) is metaphor supplemented by a denial. If in the metaphor there is superimposition of one thing over another, in concealment this superimposition is backed by denial, to the effect that the matter in hand is not what it is. To adopt mīmāṁsist termi-

1. KP 2, p. 64 :
   Aprakṛtagatavyavahārarūpārthasya vacanaṁ prakṛtavṛttānte āropo vyañjanayā pratipādanamityarthaḥ/
   Cf. P-KP 3, X p. 393 :
   Asyāñca samāsoktau prakṛtavṛttānto 'bhidhayaiva pratīyate'prastutavṛttāntastu vyañjanayā/
2. Vide KN, p. 92 :
   Ata eva śliṣṭaviśeṣaṇāyāmiva sādhāraṇaviśeṣaṇāyāmapyaprastutavyavahārasamāropa ityeva prācīnānāṁ pravādaḥ/
3. Vide AS, p. 63 :
   Apahnavapūrvaka āropaḥ, āropapūrvako'pahnavaḥ chalādiśabdairasatyattvapratipādakairvā 'pahnavanirdeśaḥ/
   Cf. KN, V. 26, p. 28 :
   Śuddhāpahnutiranyasyāropārtho dharmanihnavaḥ/

nology, there is affirmation supported by denial, and it is needless to say that such denial gives emphasis to the affirmation. But the denial must be intentional, and the aim of the denial and assertion may be to convey similitude, pertaining to the word or to the meaning. An example of concealment[1] based on similarity, pertaining to the word, may be cited. [2]"He clung to my feet, prating'; 'was it your lover ?' 'No, my anklet !" Such types give the riddles dealt with earlier. As to the production of image within the purview of this figure, it is a rare thing. For example : [3]"The forest region being devoid of water, the trees having been scorched with the flaming heat of the meridian sun, as if with their tongues outstretched ask for water on the pretext of the flames of the forest fire rising from under the trunks." This is a good image, in the form of very thirsty people with their tongues stretched out, as if asking for water in a waterless region. In this instance, the real fact of the trees having caught fire is concealed by the use of the phrase 'on the pretext of', and instead, the fact of their spreading out tongues for water like thirsty people is established.

Among lesser figures, we find a different sort of mirroring in the figure *Bhāvika*, where there is visualisation of the things, past or future. This may be effected in two ways : either the things being described might have that horror or beauty which makes them seem actually present before our eyes, or because they might have been so vividly delineated due to the extraordinary power of expression of a particular poet. While *Bhāmaha* and *Udbhaṭa* insist on only those cases where the power of evocation rests on the adequacy of the verbal tissue created by the poet, *Mammaṭa* feels inclined to include the former, within this figure. His reason is that the figure is like natural expression (Svabhāvokti), where the beauty is

1. Cf. BK III, V. 21, p. 75 :
   Apahnutirabhīṣṭā ca kiñcidantargatopamā/
2. Vide KN V. 30, p. 32 :
3. Cf. Quote KN, p. 34 :
   Rikteṣu vārikathayā vipinodareṣu madhyāhnajṛmbhitamahātapatāpataptāḥ/
   Skandhāntarotthitadavāgniśikhācchalena jihvāṁ prasārya taravo jalamarthayante//

more or less initially given (Siddha); and since the latter sometimes appears as an evocative figure, as we shall shortly see, this class of evocation of the 'glorious' past or future should be accepted as a poetic figure. There may be some sort of visualisation in this figure, but to me it does not look an imagist one, and so, except under exceptional conditions owing to the superb creative power of a poet, this figure may be rejected.

It has been noted above, that ordinarily, the *Bimbaprati-bimba*-relation is the first criterion of an image, then the *Vastuprativastu*-relation to a lesser degree. But above all, it depends on the calibre of a poet, together with his power of using the words appropriately so as to evoke visual pictures. An instance may be cited : "[1]The damsels having only wallowed in the waters, with effort stroking their fleshy thighs gently, the mass of waves having been broken asunder, spread out on to the shores, driving away the cranes." Here, the traditional figure is the natural description (Svabhāvokti), but the poet has, by dint of his extraordinary skill, evoked an image without the above preconditions being present, and even without the suggestion of any simile. The words used are very powerful in conveying the image. When read out, the stanza immediately creates before us the visual picture of the mass of waves rushing towards the shores of the big pond or river, where cranes have spread out in a network, and where in waist-deep water, beautiful women are bathing their fleshy thighs. With the onrush of the waves the cranes, as if foreseeing trouble, fly away with nervous chattering sounds.

Among Sanskrit poets, *Bhavabhūti* has most of this power of endowing pictorial representation to the expressed sense in a natural way. The examples are copious in his *Uttararāma-carita*. The only thing to stress here is that under such conditions, there is less chance of getting the suggested sense as in the figures of image, where there is the *Bimbapratibimba*-relation, or where there is some simile. But the possibility

1. Cf. KJ, VIII, V. 31 :

Vigāḍhamātre ramaṇībhirambhasi prayatnasaṁvāhitapīvarorubhiḥ/
Vibhidyamānā visasāra sārasānudasya tīreṣu taraṅgasaṁhatīḥ//

cannot be gainsaid altogether, as seen in the following example of *Arthacitra* given by *Paṇḍitarāja*: "[1]The monkeys, sleeping comfortably in the cold season on the summits of the *Sahya* mountains, hot with *Rāma's* fire of separation, are wroth with *Hanūmān*." The context of this verse relates to the arrival of *Hanūmān* with the message of *Sītā* to *Rāma*, who is living at the *Sahya* mountains with his army of monkeys. The poet means to suggest that before *Hanūmān's* coming, *Rāma* was feeling intensely, burning with the fire of separation from *Sītā* and, thus even in the cold season, as the mountains were warmed with that fire, the monkeys were sleeping comfortably. But when *Hanūmān* comes with the message, *Rāma* no longer feels the pangs of separation and the fire dies out, and so the mountain range is as cold as before. As the monkeys are afflicted with the cold, they become angry with *Hanūmān* because ultimately, it was he who made them suffer. [2]The suggestion here, according to *Jagannātha*, is explicit (Jāgarūka).

[3]In the *Bimbapratibimba*-relation, we have seen that there is more poetic charm, or more chance of the poetic image being created as on grounds of different attributes the objects are reflected into each other. But in the *Vastuprativastu*-relation, the properties being the same, though couched in different words, the objects are only coordinate with each other. Even beyond this, if the words used for the object compared and the standard of similitude are identical, there is no mirroring (Bimbana) as in the case of self-comparison (Ananvaya), and the reciprocal simile (Upameyopamā). In these figures, for want of any reflective element, no image can be produced, and repetition of the identical words is, in the most part, the cause of any poetic charm. As for the production of image, even in simile it is not there if the two objects

1. RG I, p. 20 :
Rāghavavirahajvālāsantāpitasahyaśailaśikhareṣu/
Śiśire sukhaṁ śayānāḥ kapayaḥ kupyanti pavanatanayāya//
2. RG, I, p. 23 :
3. PY, p. 366 :
Ekasyārthasya śabdadvayenābhidhānaṁ vastuprativastubhāvaḥ/
Dvayorarthayordvirupādānaṁ bimbapratibimbabhāvaḥ//

are barely compared, there being no magic in description or in the correlation of the common properties. In hyperbole and some other figures also, it is some other quality, like the subversion of the cause-and-effect relation, and not the production of imagery which might be the chief cause of poetic charm.

When a whole picture is generated by one verse, and different words used in it, instead of detracting go to cooperate towards that end, there is a greater chance of image being evolved because it is generally created out of one impression. So, in figures where there are many impressions rather than one, there is no imagery, or even broken images accepted on the authority of western rhetorics. Finally, we can say that an image is a different thing outside the limitation of any particular figure of speech as separate entity, and is the real test of a poet, being more difficult to use or evoke than any of the beautiful figures. What is needed for achieving this feat is a surcharging of the imagery with feelings and emotions. Therefore, to be genuinely evocative, images must be emotive. Emotion, like an oily substance, gives contours in the images. *Arthacitra* constituting these images, to be highest type of poetry, must emerge from the depth of heart. These images when devoid of emotions, become like still-lifes to be hung up on walls. Originally what indigenous rhetoricians might have meant by rejecting *Citrakāvya* as the lowest grade of poetry, is this.

The verses quoted above in support of the thesis in this chapter, are ample proof of the fact. They cannot be torn away from life without being separated from the real imagist properties, from emotions. In this context, we must affirm that even in natural description (Svabhāvokti), where there is no scope for similitude, there are beautiful images when they have an emotive appeal. Here it may be pointed out, that [1]this natural description or poetic naturalism, is one of the two chief figures originally conceived in both eastern and

1. Cf. KD II, V. 363, p. 329 :

Śleṣaḥ sarvāsu puṣṇāti prāyo vakroktiṣu śriyam/
Bhinnaṁ dvidhā svabhāvoktirvakroktiśceti vāṅmayam//

western poetic thought, the other being the [1]deviant expression (Vakrokti), in which almost all figures of ornament were included. This natural description is the most direct form of expression, as opposed to suggestion, and has a direct appeal to the heart, especially, if the images be sparsely strewn. [2]If the moods or emotions are changing, the images in a poem are like a series of mirrors set at different angles, so that as the theme moves on, they are reflected in a number of different aspects.

Here we quote two instances to illustrate changing emotions from *Vālmīki*, the first, as well as one of the greatest, of India's epic poets. In the first we find *Rāma* experiencing the first bitter rains after his separation from *Sītā*. Sometimes he sees in it his own passionate image, sometimes that of an injured person—his own reflection, and at times that of *Sītā* struggling in the hold of *Rāvaṇa*. [3]"The sky, having its wound bound up with smooth rags in the shape of clouds, stained with the vivid tints of the setting sun, having super-white borders and yellowish clouds, appears like a passionate person, breathing in slow wind and besmeared with the red sandal of the eventide. The earth, like *Sītā*, afflicted with scorching heat, though sprinkled with the first rains, sheds tears, having

1. Cf. B-RC I : "A figure of speech is a deviation from the plain and ordinary mode of speaking, for the sake of greater effect : it is an unusual from of speech."
2. Cf. L-PI III, p. 80.
3. Vide VR, KK XXVIII, V.5-12, p. 114-115 :

   Saṁdhyārajotthitaistāmrairanteṣvadhikapāṇḍaraiḥ/
   Snigdhairabhrapaṭacchedairbaddhavraṇamivāmbaram//
   Mandamārutaniḥśvāsaṁ saṁdhyācandanarañjitam/
   Āpāṇḍujaladaṁ bhāti kāmāturamivāmbaram//
   Eṣā gharmaparikliṣṭā navavāripariplutā/
   Sīteva śokasaṁtaptā mahī vāṣpaṁ vimuñcati//
   Meghodaravinirmuktāḥ kahlārasukhaśītalāḥ/
   Śakyamañjalibhiḥ pātuṁ vātāḥ ketakigandhinaḥ//

   — —

   Kaśābhiriva haimībhirvidyudbhiriva tāḍitam/
   Antaḥstanitanirghoṣaṁ savedanamivāmbaram//
   Nīlameghāśritā vidyut sphurantī pratibhāti me/
   Sphurantī rāvaṇasyāṅke vaidehīva tapasvinī//

been tormented with the pangs of separation. The breeze, emerging from the heart of the clouds, is cool as the white lotus and redolent with the fragrance of the *Ketaka* flowers, can be sipped in cupped hands......Whipped by the golden thong of the lightning, the sky, as if in pain, seems to be crying out aloud with thunder. The lightning, leaping out in the black clouds, is, to me, like sorrowful *Sītā*, struggling in the hold of *Rāvaṇa*." The whole picture is charged with emotions, the mood is poignant and *Vālmīki's* profound creative intuition is revealed by the imagery embodying ideally the like emotion.

In the second, *Rāvaṇa* and his hosts camp by the river *Narmadā*. The breath of the river tempers the heat, and the spot is ideal for a halt. *Rāvaṇa* is gratified : [1]"The sun of a thousand rays seems to have changed the world to gold, and in the sky, this orb of day, whose beams were intense, having observed me seated here, has grown as cool as the moon. The wind, cool owing to having contacted the waters of the *Narmadā*, and able to reduce fatigue, blows steadily, diffusing sweet fragrance, as if in fear from me. This *Narmadā*, most excellent among the rivers, and one enhancing amorous pastimes, is like a round damsel, as though because of the waves (generated) due to alligators, fish and birds." The poetic sentiment reflected is the love in union, as against the former, where clearly there is yearning love in separation. In the latter instance, the amorous feelings of *Rāvaṇa* determine the individuality of the river, which, though described by the poet, is seen through the eyes of that hedonist. A purely formal analysis might reveal that the imagery effected here is dependent on an incipient comparison, but is really the resultant rapproachement between two distant realities. In such a case, erotic sentiment becomes the

1. VR, UK XXXI VS. 27-29 :

    Eṣa raśmisahasreṇa jagatkṛtvaiva kāñcanam/
    Tīkṣṇatāpakaraḥ sūryo nabhaso 'rdhaṁ samāśritaḥ//

    Māmāsīnaṁ viditveha candrāyati divākaraḥ/
    Narmadājalaśītaśca sugandhiḥ śramanāśanaḥ//

    Madbhayādanilopyatra vātyeṣa susamāhitaḥ/
    Iyaṁ cāpi saricchreṣṭhā narmadā narmavardhinī//
    Nakramīnavihaṅgormiḥ sabhayevāṅganā sthitā//

unconscious bond of association which annihilates distance.

How beautiful the verses quoted above are, only appreciative people can assess. In *Vālmiki*, we find both wisdom of the heart and grandeur of the imagination. While the latter is responsible for the use of the figures of speech, the former prunes it to propriety. If the figure is an adornment, emotion is the very life. [1]*Ānanda* clarifies that as the putting on or off of even ordinary ornaments suggests to us the mental state of a person, so the use or surrender of figures suggests the poetic emotion or mood. The image emerging from the deepest recesses of the heart is really born with the very first poetic urge, and [2]I am sure this holds good with the imagery of our poet. The surging emotions, stirred in his heart at the sight of the wounded *Krauñca* couple, became concretised in the shape of poetry. He was equally successful in both naturalism and imagery, because he made his heart the sole decider between the two, with the result that both proved ideal for the deeper poetic purpose. *Vālmīki's* mastery in both makes clear to us, that reality of feeling is the most important thing in poetry, and the qualitatively strong tension of the heart determines the mode of the poetic expression.

Besides, we mark above one very important aspect of the production of images, that when there is natural description, or more exactly, description of nature there is generally a high grade of imagery through anthropomorphisation, or the attribution of human forms to the elements of nature. But only poets of very high calibre can arouse such images. In the instance first cited, the hovering dark cloud is anthropomorphised as the ill-intentioned *Rāvaṇa*, and the lightning as the beautiful and chaste *Sītā*, struggling to get out of the cruel clutches of the former. But, there are many instances especially in the works of *Kālidāsa*, where there are no clues to the similes, and in that case, the personification becomes even more charming and life-like. To substantiate this position :

1. Vide DL, II, V.6, p. 204 :

   Tamarthamavalambante ye 'ṅginaṁ te guṇāh smṛtāḥ/ etc.

2. Ibid, I, V.5, p. 85 :

   Krauñcadvandvaviyogotthaḥ śokaḥ ślokatvamāgataḥ/

[1]"That river, having a little water in the form of a stream, might be expressing, on account of her state of separation, O fortunate one, your good fortune through the yellow, worn-out leaves falling from the trees sprung up on her banks; it is (now) left to you to devise the way she sheds her emaciation."

Here the cloud has been given the shape of a lover and the river that of his beloved. It is now one year since the last rainy season that the cloud was away, and during this time the river was as if yearning and tossing in bed, lean and thin. She was yellow with the fallen, yellowish leaves of the nearby trees. But with the onset of the rains, her lover has returned and in no time she will be green and happy, and full of water, which will rush like passion in her veins. The poet adds that the beloved has kept her fidelity intact in separation, and so the lover should congratulate himself and restore her to her original happy position. Here, over and above the exquisite picture of cloud and river and their actions apart, there is a geographical fact in that in summer, rivers generally run short of water, and during the rains, they are filled up. In the instance under review, there is also some element of suggestion.

[2]As above in the case of the suggestion of poetic figures (Alaṁkāradhvani), the evocation of feeling is the sole arbiter. [3]Kathleen Raine refers to the juxtaposition of images being the basis of the poetic figure. This, of course, points to the normal association of images in poetic figures and not in particular to the image that is suggested. Broadly speaking, this is applicable to the field of the expressed image as well. [4]But the

1. MD, I, V. 29 :

   Venūbhūtapratanusalilā 'sāvatītasya sindhuḥ
   Pāṇḍucchāyā taṭaruhatarubhraṁśibhirjīrṇaparṇaiḥ/
   Saubhāgyaṁ te subhaga virahāvasthayā vyañjayantī
   Kārśyaṁ yena tyajati vidhinā sa tvayaivopapādyaḥ//

2. Cf. L-DL, I, p. 52 :

   Rasacarvaṇātmanastṛtīyāṁśasyābhidhābhāvanāṁśadvayottīrṇatvena nirṇayāt, vastvalaṁkāradhvanyo rasadhvaniparyantatvameveti....../

3. Vide K-SR.

4. Ibid.

perpetual images, however intense or refined, lack a dimension without which there is a feeling of claustrophobia. There should be a synthesis of the symbolic and the contemporary. That is, the expressed image as well as the suggested one, should be an objective correlative of the inward feeling.

[1]Old Indian theorists hold that when there is suggestion in image, the suggested image is, as a result, an embellishment (Alaṁkāra) and not embellished (Alaṁkārya), and so it should be relegated to the subordinate position. They demand that in order to qualify as the finest shade of poetry, the centre of gravity in the particular poem should shift to the suggested sense. On the other hand, where the suggested meaning is the embellishment rather than the embellished, the poetic achievement has to be graded lower, as an instance of the poetry of subordinated suggestion. But this is not true. The fact remains that the suggested sense has the force of an accompaniment in music. Poetic naturalism might have been adequate in itself to arouse feeling, but that is not the point. The quality of the suggested image blends with the quality of the literal image, and what is resultant in our experience is a feeling, both unitary and enriching. The exponents of the theory of suggestion themselves first raised suggestion to the pedestal of the supreme poetic value, and then, having moved on further, gave sentiment or feeling that status. In that case, if an enriched feeling is contained in a poem, it should not be relegated to the inferior position simply because the centre of gravity of the particular poem does not lie on the plane of suggested sense, but is found in the stratum of expressed meaning. [2]Even

1. Cf. DL, II, p. 198 :
   Yatra rasasyālaṁkāryatā rasāntaraṁ cāṅgabhūtaṁ nāsti tatra śuddhā evopamādayaḥ/

   Ibid, p. 197 :
   Upamādīnāmalaṁkāratve yādṛśī vārtā tādṛśyeva rasādīnāṁ/ tadavaśyamanyenālaṁkāryeṇa bhavitavyaṁ/ tacca yadyapi vastumātramapi bhavati, tathāpi tasya punarapi vibhāvādirūpatāparyavasānād rasāditātparyameveti sarvatra rasadhvanerevātmabhāvaḥ.
2. Vide DL, II, V. 17, p. 223 :
   Dhvanyātmabhūte śṛṅgāre samīkṣya viniveśitaḥ/
   Rūpakādiralaṁkāravarga eti yathārthatām//

according to *Ānanda*, the figure to suggest the feeling should be born along with the poet's revelation and delineation of it. It will then have to be naturally and easily introduceable, and the poet will not have to pause to make a special effort to effect it.

Lastly, we must in this connection examine the visual capacity and the evocative power of the words themselves, so that when combined in a poetic organism, they might create a unitary, visual impression, called image, given the magic touch of the poet. [1]In fact, Sanskrit poetics have always affirmed that feeling is the soul of poetry, and sound as well as sense, together constitute its body. As such, the concept of the parity of the two implies that sound representing the word-texture might also arouse nuances of feelings. As Sanskrit rhetoricians insist that all literary ornaments should subserve feeling, and [2]as in a verbal figure replacement by a synonym is ruled out, it is clear that word as a phonetic entity functions directly as a poetic cue. [3]Even the analytical findings that soft vocables and vowels suit the erotic sentiment, while consonantal explosives are ideal for the expression of the sentiments of anger and heroism, confirm that our rhetoricians realised that feeling tones could be directly excited by words. [4]Really, the whole basis of the art of literature is that the emotions and feelings directly excited by the words, should intensify our emotions and feelings arising from the contemplation of the meaning.

1. Vide SD, I, V.3, p. 19 :
   Vākyaṁ rasātmakaṁ kāvyam/
   Cf. DL, I, p. 45 :
   Kāvyasya hi lalitocitasannivesácāruṇaḥ śarīrasyevātmā sārarūpatayā sthitaḥ sahṛdayaślāghyo yo 'rthaḥ...
   Ibid, V.8, p. 97 :
   So'rthastadvyaktisāmarthyayogī śabdaśca kaścana/
   Yatnataḥ pratyabhijñeyau tau śabdārthau mahākaveḥ//
2. Vide Supra p. 34.
3. Cf. M-W.
4. Vide W-SME, p. 98.

CHAPTER VI

HISTORY OF CITRAKĀVYA

The history of *Śabdacitra* like chimes, alliterations, and the *Bandhas*, is comparatively recent. In the *Rigveda*, there is no special effort for striking verbal effects [1]except in odd cases. The later *Vedas* might have started the attempt, but it begins from the dawn of classical Sanskrit. The intention of using these verbal juggleries is clear, though not always, even in the early great trio of *Bhāsa*, *Aśvaghoṣa* and *Kālidāsa*. Of *Ubhaya-citra* in the shape of riddles and poetic tricks, the endeavour seems to be more business-like from the beginning, and we see it in the form of [2]riddle hymns in the *Ṛgveda*, of *Brahmodyas* in the *Brāhmaṇas* and the *Upaniṣads*. The Vedic sages perhaps found themselves leaning more towards the attempted use of such *Kūṭas* and riddles, due to reasons such as generating a sense of curiosity or wonder, expressing experiences metaphysical and mystical, and the desire to conceal knowledge from others, which we have pointed out elsewhere.

It is generally acknowledged that poetry begets a sense of curiosity consisting of beautiful sentiments born of appropriately chosen words. That is why that even in the early poets and sages there is a tendency to embellish and endow their works, with art and beauty. Often, to a thrilling effect they resort to the device of the concealment of sense. This serves the twin purpose of engendering suspense in the minds

1. Cf. ṚV, 4-40-5 :

   Haṁsaḥ śuciṣad vasurantarikṣasad
   Hotā vediṣad atithirduroṇasat/
   Nṛṣad varasad ṛtasad vyomasad
   Abjā gojā ṛtajā adrijā ṛtam//

2. Cf. Ibid, 164-33 :

   Dyaurme pitā janitā nābhiratra bandhurme mātā pṛthivī mahīyam/
   Uttānayoścamvoryonirantaratrā pitā duhiturgarbhamādhāt//

of the readers, and of bringing artistry into poetry. Also, the mystical and metaphysical experience being inexpressible, recourse is taken to symbols and metaphors. Even riddles and *Kūṭas* may be used to keep the experience concealed, and thus safe from the hands of the undeserving. Here, the first category, being suggestive, is among the highest type of poetry, but in the second, though the objective of the concealment of sense is not a genuine characteristic of good poetry, yet sometimes, this also arouses a unique sense of curiosity and gives a new meaning with unprecedented pleasure.

[1]Among the said riddle hymns, there are only a few to which the commentators have given the right exposition. In some cases, they have offered corrupt explanations, and there are some still left, of which the meaning is not yet clear, as is explicit from the views expressed by [2]*Yāska* and [3]*Sāyaṇa*. Among such verses, a few spiritual, mystical or philosophical, are called by *Yāska* such relating to the probe of the supreme spirit (Ādhyātmikī), and others all composed beyond our ken (Parokṣakṛtā). Some such hymns are also found in the [4]*Atharvaveda*, and some philosophical ones in [5]the *Upaniṣads* as well. This tradition of occult poetry in the old Vedic books can best be called pragmatic and mystic. Often symbols are used, and in that case, they may be called symbolic tricks (Pratīkakūṭa) in the modern sense of the term. It is not beyond our jurisdiction to mention here, that such poetry has also been written sometimes with a view to safeguarding the confidential nature of religious thoughts and actions. [6]Even today, this idea is prevalent among the *Tāntric* and *Vaiṣṇava* sects of Bengal and the *Pāñcarātras*.

There is also a ritual aspect of some sacrificial stanzas which are like riddles in the shape of a questionnaire. On the

1. Vide W-HIL I, p. 117: "The hymn ṚV 1.164 contains a large number of such riddles, most of which, unfortunately, we cannot understand."
2. Vide Y-NN VII, p. 132.
3. P-HSR : SP, p. 11.
4. Vide Infra., p. 139, Fn. No. 1.
5. Vide Infra., p. 139, Fn. No. 2.
6. Cf. ST1.19 : Deyaṁ śiṣyāya śāntāya viṣṇubhaktiratāya ca/
   Cf. PR 4, 7-5 : Gopanīyaṁ gopanīyaṁ gopanīyaṁ prayatnataḥ/

occasions of big sacrifices, the officiating priest (Ṛtvik), or any other sacerdotal personage, puts these questions to the kings and ministers present. Here also, symbolical and even mystical language is used, and the symbols are often taken in the shape of numerals from the universe of nature. The earth, the sky, the sun, the moon, the atmospheric region, the cloud and its genesis through the process of evaporation, the rains, the solstices, the year, the seasons, the month, the days and nights etc. form the chief contents of the symbolical expressions. Understanding their sense was thought to be the highest touchstone of literary sensibility. For example, in the following verse, the year is being described as a wheel with twelve peripheries in the shape of months, three hubs as important seasons, and three hundred and sixty spikes as days : [1]"Who knows that only wheel with twelve peripheries and three hubs ? There are also three hundred and sixty moving spikes fixed to it."

To take one now in a purely enigmatic style : [2]"The dark night has begotten a white (i.e. fair-complexioned) child. The reddish baby has together (with mother) mounted the firmament." Obviously, the description is of the sun's rising in the eastern horizon in the morning, as if from the womb of the black night. The sun, at the time, is like a white, lustrous, palpable and reddish baby. The seeming contradiction lies in *Kṛṣṇā* (i.e. Draupadī) giving birth to *Arjuna* (who was one of her five *Pāṇḍava* husbands). These two words should be taken here, as adjectives, and not as substantive proper names. In the same style, the verse below strikes more wonder and curiosity : [3]"One having only one leg is speedier than one having two, the two-legged than the tripod; the quadruped comes at the call of the two-legged, beholding and waiting upon the flock." Here the ram, having one leg, is suggested as the symbol for the god of wind. Some also explain it as the

1. ṚV-1, 164.48 :
   Dvādaśa pradhayaścakramekaṁ trīṇi nabhyāni ka u tacciketa/
   Tasmintsākaṁ triśatā na śaṁkavo 'rpitāḥ ṣaṣṭirna calā calāsaḥ//
2. Ibid : I.164-2 : Kṛṣṇāyāḥ putro 'rjuno rātryā vatso ajāyata/
   Saha dyāmadhirohati ruho ruroha rohitaḥ//
3. Ibid : 10, 117-8 :
   Ekapād bhūyo dvipado vi cakrame dvipāt tripādamabhyeti paścāt/
   Catuṣpadeti dvipadāmabhisvare saṁpaśyan paṅktīrupatiṣṭhamānaḥ//

sun, having a wheel or halo. The two-legged is, of course, man and the three-legged, an old man with a supporting stick. The four-legged stands here for a dog, though it may generally denote any animal with four legs.

To give one more such verse which, depending on the magic of numbers, inspires awe in the description of a great god with four horns, three legs, two heads and seven hands : [1]"This bull has four horns, three legs, two heads and seven hands. Having been tied threefold, it bellows. This great god has come among the mortals." At first sight the verse seems contradictory and meaningless, but [2]*Sāyaṇa* has given several meanings of which we put forth only two, one relating to the description of the sacrificial fire, and the other connected with the sun. In regard to the first one, the four horns mean either the four *Vedas*, or the priests of the same number, the three legs stand for the three *Soma*-extracting ceremonies to be performed in the morning, noon and evening, the two heads are *Brahmaudana* and *Pravargya*, and seven hands denote the seven vedic metres (i.e. Triṣṭup, Jagatī, Uṣṇig, Gāyatrī, Paṃktī, Anuṣṭup and Bṛhatī). It is bound thrice by *Mantras*, *Brāhmaṇas* and the *Kalpas*, and is called a bull because it bears or rains the fruits of the sacrifice, and roars in melodies produced by the songs of *Sāman* and *Yajus*.

As for the second meaning, the said number of horns, legs, heads and hands symbolise the same number of directions, Vedas, day and night, and the rays. The three places are earth, the atmospheric region and the sky. That rains, and so it is called the bull. It is noteworthy that [3]*Patañjali* has explained this in relation to the supreme power of words (Śabdabrahman) having four horns in the four types of words (i,e. Nouns, verbs, prepositions and indeclinables), three legs in the three tenses (i.e. present, past and the future), two heads in the word and the meaning, seven hands in the seven case-endings, tied at three places, the bosom, the throat and

1. ṚV : 4.58.3 :
   Catvāri śṛṅgāstrayo'sya pādā dve śīrṣe sapta hastāso 'sya/
   Tridhā baddho vṛṣabho roravīti mahādevo martyān āviveśa//
2. Ibid : ed. MM, vol. II, 4.5.58-3, p. 492.
3. Vide P-MB, 1.1.1, p. 13.

the head. Now we add one verse from the famous *Kuntātapa* hymn of the *Atharvaveda*, reflecting the paradox of ritual mysticism bordering on the philosophical : [1]"The mouth of the spoon is downward and the bottom upward ; there are seven seers on its sides, and the eighth one is speech." The spoon stands for the skull (or, head) in whose various parts live the five breathing winds (Pañcaprāṇavāyu), the energising agents. The sense-organs reside close to them, among which is speech-power, the giver of intuition.

From the *Upaniṣads*, amongst many philosophical riddles the one quoted is the most familiar and homely : [2]"Two birds, who are mutual cooperators, are friends, sitting on the same tree ; one of them eats up the delicious *pippal* fruits, (or, berries) and the other, eating nothing, simply waits (lit. shines forth). The two birds are the individual soul and the supreme soul, mutually cooperating in a relation of the restrained and the restrainer (or, ruler and ruled), and are friends on account of a similar supreme spirit, and staying on the same tree of the body corporeal, or the universe. Only the individual soul consumes or experiences the fruits of actions in this universe, and not the supreme soul.

To turn towards the exposition of *Arthacitra* in Vedic literature, it is important to note that sensibilities and sentiments befitting the expression of true poetry developed in the pre-historic past. There is good poetry in the *Rigveda* due to the anthropomorphisation of the elements of nature, in the forms of divinities. However, poetry with embellishment does appear at times. The Vedic sage describes the wild fire devouring the heath and shrubs as like a barber shaving the earth : [3]"The fire, having been fanned by the wind, has spread in the forests and is razoring the sprouting hair of the Earth." Some of the verses from the hymns to *Agni* are marvellous and

1. Vide AV-10.8, 9 :
   Arvāgvilaścamasa ūrdhvaṁ budhnastasmin yaśo nihitaṁ viśvarūpam/
   Tasyāsata ṛṣayaḥ saptatīre vāgaṣṭamī saṁvidāneti//
2. Cf. MK, 3.1-1 :
   Dvā suparṇā sayujā sakhāyā samānaṁ vṛkṣaṁ pariṣasvajāte/
   Tayoranyaḥ pippalaṁ svādvattyanaśnannanyo 'bhicākaśīti//
3. Vide RV-1. 65.8 :
   Yad vātajūto vanā vyasthādagnirha dāti romā pṛthivyāḥ/

create real images. To take one more example : [1]"The fire is swallowing up the forests with its sharp fangs (i.e. with swirls of the fire). It is clearing them and is uprooting them in such a way, as if a warrior was uprooting enemies."

It is not unusual to get such word-pictures. Sometimes, the [2]sage distinguishes the poetic speech from the ordinary, as "one sieves the barley powder." Elsewhere, [3]he prays the Almighty to ward off the cares "that are consuming him as rats eat weavers' threads". Here there is a unique instance of the concretisation of an abstract, intangible idea. [4]Again in one verse the supreme spirit is described as "a swan seated in the midst of light." It is to be noted here that in classical literature, the word *Haṁsa*, often in a mystical context, stands for the supreme being. Among the hymns of the *Ṛgveda*, those relating to *Uṣas* are accepted to be the most beautiful. In this connection, we cannot but quote [5]one full verse to show its imagist value : "Like a dancer, she enrobes herself with embroidered garments; she bares her bosom, as the cow yields her udder; creating light for all the world of life, *Uṣas* has laid open the darkness, as cows their stalls."

After the *Vedas*, it was from the *Mahābhārata* that the *Kūṭa* style of poetry flourished. [6]There is a story there of how it began. When there was a problem of writing the first script of this epic at the dictation of *Vyāsa*, the work was entrusted to *Gaṇeśa*, and the latter accepted it, but on the condition that his pen would never stop. In order to get out of this quandary,

1. ṚV : 1, 143.5 :
   Agnirjambhaistigitairatti bharvati yodho na śatrūn sa vanānyañjate/
2. Ibid : 10.71.7 :
   Saktumiva titaunā punanto yatra dhīrā manasā vācamakrata/
   Atrā sakhāyaḥ sakhyāni jānate bhadraiṣāṁ lakṣmīrnihitādhi vāci//
3. Ibid : 10, 33.3 :
   Mūṣo na śiśnā vyadanti mādhyaḥ stotāraṁ te śatakrato/
   Sakṛt su no maghavannindra mṛlayā 'dhā piteva no bhava//
4. Vide Supra p. 135, Fn. No. 1.
5. Cf. ṚV, 1.92, 4 :
   Adhipeśāṁsi vapate nṛtūrivāporṇute vakṣa usrevā barjahaṁ/
   Jyotirviśvasmai bhuvanāya kṛṇvatī gāvo na vrajaṁ vyuṣā āvartamaḥ//
6. Vide MB-AP I, V. 116 :
   Yasmin pratijñayā prāha munirdvaipāyanastvidam/
   Granthagranthiṁ tadā cakre munirgūḍhaṁ kutūhalāt//

the poet asked *Gaṇeśa* not to write anything which he did not understand, and he began to create knots and *Kūṭas*, so that while the script-God was engaged in understanding them, he moved on further. *Vyāsa* says that he began to devise difficult knots in the midst of his work, as an exciting pastime (Kutūhala). The use of *Kutūhalādhyāyī* in *Agni-Purāṇa*, on which there is a separate chapter, points to that direction.

In the *Mahābhārata*, we find a full-fledged use of alliterations, puns, and chimes, together with such *Kūṭas*. So, there was a clear attempt to display pedantic skill in poetry, although in the epic itself, this trend is very limited, except in the places where it is required. For instance, in the *Ādiparvan*, *Vidura* hints in this very occult language to *Yudhiṣṭhira*, the plot of *Duryodhana* to burn the *Pāṇḍavas* to ashes in the lac-house built in *Vāraṇāvata* : [1]"That rogue would set that house on fire; he is a dreadful foe; you can guard yourself only when you run away through the subterranean passage." Here the word *Kakṣaghna* stands for *Purocana*, who had been set for the purpose. Again, *śiśira* is fire, the destroyer and *Śiśiraghna* is also for the abovesaid crafty man who was to destroy the lac-house with the help of fire, and *Mahākakṣa* means 'arch enemy'. Moreover, the reason for speaking in this *Kūṭa* style is put in a beautiful *Kūṭa*, itself based on pun and chimes : [2]"The knowing one, easily understanding the local dialects of the village-folk, spoke those words to the person who himself used to understand those dialects. People, not understanding those dialects, could not understand those words; only people understanding those could understand them." The word *Prājña* here has three meanings : wise, village-fool and one difficult to understand, and the word *Pralāpajña*, two meanings : the person who knows the dialects of the village folk, and one prattling like an uncultured person.

So there are many varieties of riddles and *Kūṭas* found

1. MB : 145-3 :
   Kakṣaghnaḥ śiśiraghnaśca mahākakṣe vilaukasaḥ/
   Na daheditі cātmānaṁ yo rakṣati sa jīvati//
2. Ibid : 145-20 :
   Prājñaḥ prājñapralāpajñaḥ pralāpajñamidaṁ vacaḥ/
   Prājñaṁ prājñaḥ pralāpajñaṁ pralāpajno vaco 'bravīt//

in the epic, some even mystical, and some very occult. [1]One philosophical-mystical one resembles one found in the [2]*Īśopaniṣad,* based on chimes, and [3]an occult sort, explained, among many others, by [4]*Dr. V.S. Agrawal,* is similar to one quoted in the body of this thesis elsewhere. One such occult verse, taken by the said scholar, suggests in a peculiar way some metaphysical symbols : [5]"An ox with humpback, a parrot with bent beak, the blissful heaven, an eye-sore, a heavenly tree or its flowers giving ichorous saturation, dancing, especially of a peacock, something persecuting, especially *Bhairava* and the roundball sweets of the mouth—these eight whomsoever bite becomes frantic, loses sense and (ultimately) perishes". [6]According to *Sarvajñanārāyaṇa,* corroborating on the authority of *Devabodha,* these eight respectively symbolise eight mental deformations, namely, desire, anger, greed, illusion, vanity, conceit, spite and egotism.

In yet another interesting verse, some inauspicious signs are described which began to appear just before the *Mahābhārata* war : [7]"The small babies in the houses of the commonfolk, who are still in the sucklings' chamber, sing and dance,

1. MB : 5 46-9 :
   Pūrṇāt pūrṇānyuddharanti pūrṇāt pūrṇāni cakrire/
   Haranti pūrṇāt pūrṇāni pūrṇamevāvaśiṣyate//
2. Cf. Is-1 :
   Pūrṇamadaḥ pūrṇamidaṁ pūrṇāt pūrṇamaducyate/
   Pūrṇasya pūrṇamādāya pūrṇamevāvaśiṣyate//
3. Vide MB : AK, 18.7 :
   Jalecaraḥ kāñcanayaṣṭisaṁstho vyāttānanaḥ sarvatimipramāthī/
   Vitrāsayan rājati vāhamukhye sālvasya senāpramukhe dhvajāgryaḥ//
4. Vide KNPP : MKKS, 1962 :
5. Vide MB : UP : 94.38-39 :
   Kākudīkaṁ śukaṁ nākamakṣisantarjanaṁ tathā
   Santānaṁ nartanaṁ ghoramāsyamodakamastakam/
   Etairviddhā sarva eva maraṇaṁ yānti mānavāḥ/
   Unmattāśca viceṣṭante naṣṭasaṁjñā vicetasaḥ//
6. Cf. : Kāmakopau mohalobhau madamānau tathaiva ca/
   Mātsaryāhaṁkṛtī caiva kramādeta udāhṛtaḥ//
7. Vide MB : BP, 3.8 :
   Pṛthag janasya kuḍakāḥ stanapāḥ stanaveśmani/
   Nṛtyanti parigāyanti vedayanto mahad bhayam//

foreboding great fear." *Dr. Belvelkar* takes *Kuḍaka* as a reading of *Kuḍika*='small water-vessel' or, as *Kaḍava* or *Kuḍapa*='a grain-measuring small vessel.' Similarly he takes *Stanapa* as *Tanapa* and *Stanaveśma*, as *Stenaveśma*. [1]*Dr. Agrawal* thinks all these are corrupt and derives *Kuḍaka* meaning 'small baby' from the Skt. *Kuṭika*, and correlates it with the Panjabi *Kuḍi* or *Kuḍa*. He also takes *Stanapa* as qualifying it. Of the two, this seems to be the better.

After the *Mahābhārata*, [2]there are some mystical and paradoxical verses in *Bhāgavatapurāṇa*, some of them resembling those based on a number already quoted. Skipping then we come to *Bhāravi*, the representative of a periodic change wrought with the change in literary taste. As a result of a high sensibility among readers for poetry and art, a vast literature of the type was produced in the middle age. It was an art to write riddles and *Kūṭas* in poetry and a marvel to compose *Citrabandhas*. [3]This art was at par with, for example, gardening as a means of recreation, inspired by the desire of striking awe-producing and suspense-giving expressions. Here, skill and pedantry were required. In fact, social life was happy, and the poets generally thought of amusing their patrons with the help of this artistry. Therefore, from an Indian point of view, the highest objective of poetry is not only imitation of life, as Aristotle would have it, but is also amusement and pleasure.

Bhāravi could be said to be almost the progenitor of this style of poetry, but he does not always involve in *Le jeux de mots* (i.e. verbal jugglery), which is found only in the 5th and 15th cantos of his work. [4]In the 5th canto, the poet has got entangled in the vortex of alliterations and chimes. Many of the forms and varieties of chimes have been illustrated here Vide verses 5, 7, 9, 11, 13, 20, 23 etc.) of which the detail is

1. Vide : KNPP : MKKS : 1962 :
2. Cf. BP, 11 13-32 :

   Dve asya bīje śatamūlastrināla̤ḥ pañcaskandhaḥ pañcarasaprasūtiḥ/
   Daśaikaśākho dvisuparṇanīḍastrivalkalo dviphalo 'rkapraviṣṭaḥ//

3. Cf VKS, I,III 16, p. 29.
4. Cf. KJ, p. 73.

not needed in this chapter. [1]Canto 15th describes battle-scenes illustrating various kinds of *Śabdacitra* and the *Bandhas*, and some of the verses have been taken in the present work, as examples in the chapter of *Śabdacitra*. Some of the verses are made up of only one or two letters, some have no labial or such other letters, and moreover, there are different varieties of chimes culminating in *Samudgaka*, *Ardhabhrama* and *Sarvatobhadra*.

Later, *Bhaṭṭi* has used alliterations with various intensity, and also some chimes in the 10th canto of his epic. *Bhaṭṭikāvya* actually is the symbol of the dual objective of the poet, of showing skill in pedantry as well as accentuating the readers' curiosity. But after *Bhāravi*, *Māgha* alone is the real artist with a leaning more towards the use of double entendre, and in this, at least, he is certainly superior to his famed predecessor, though his poetry is more artificial or affected. In the 6th canto of *Śiśupālavadha*, the six seasons make their advent at the *Raivataka* mountain, and the poet has described their beauty in alliterations. From the point of view of this figure, *Māgha's* setting of words is very charming.

[2]In the 16th canto, the messenger of *Śiśupāla* comes and gives message to *Krisna* in a punning style, meaning that either *Krisna* should bow down to the suzerainty of *Śiśupāla*, or should be prepared to fight battles. [3]In the 19th canto, *Māgha* delineates battle-scenes, taking resort to *Citrakāvya*. Here various *Citrabandhas* have been used, but as their discussion is out of our scope, we only quote a verse having three meanings, to show the height of paranomasia : [4]"*Hari*, the pleasure-giver to the proud *Balarāma* (or, destroyer of *Bali*, the king of demons and giver of pain to the gods—in respect of *Indra*; or, at whose rising all the ailments are gone and who gives new vigour to good people—with regard to the sun), the salvager of the Earth (or, the destroyer of poison—in regard to *Indra*; or, the dryer

1. Cf. KJ, p. 254.
2. Cf. SV, p. 271.
3. Cf. Ibid, p. 419.
4. Cf. Ibid, V. 116 :

   Sadāmadabalaprāyaḥ samuddhataraso babhau/
   Pratītavikramaḥ śrīmān harirharirivāparaḥ//

of waters—with respect to the sun), the measurer of the three worlds with three steps (or one of famous valour—on the side of *Indra*; or one renowned for his movement in the sky—in relation to the sun), and one having *Lakṣmī* with him (or one having riches—in regard to *Indra*; or one having lustre or splendour—as regards the sun) looked like a second *Indra* or the sun." It can be seen that *Māgha* is very adept in the use of puns. These are sometimes dependent on other figures, but pure puns are also used profusely (Cf. 3. 57, 5.45 etc). Sometimes these puns are so involved, that there is no understanding of the sense, without alterations in case-terminations to suit two meanings on two sides (Vibhaktivipariṇāma).

After *Māgha*, among big poets who have used *Citrakāvya* only sparsely and have not written any separate work in this variety of poetry, *Śrī Harṣa* stands out prominently. He appears to be very familiar with the most subtle types of *Śabdacitra*, as is evident from the verse quoted here to show the contrast in the relish of the poetic sentiment : [1]"O one with pupils in your eyes like emeralds, by way of the pretext of pouring forth heavy drops of tears, is known your immense skill at using *Binducyutaka* (i.e. a variety of riddles), for undoubtedly, you yourself make the *Saṁsāra* (i.e, the world) *Sasāra* (i.e. endowed with the very quintessence) !" It is queer to find that instead of evoking emotions, even on such a delicate spot, this poet goes on to brandish the sword of his pedantry. His *Nala*, in spite of seeing his beloved weeping profusely, keeps himself weighed down with heavy artifice : weeping *Damayantī* seems to him to shed, as if in one day, all the drops or dots by way of shedding drops of tears, so that the word *Saṁsāra* will also have its dot removed. The effect here is of a beauty which the discerning can appreciate, despite a setback in the emotive portrayal. *Nala's Damayantī* is weeping, but it seems even her weeping is beautiful because through her 'weeping' existence, she endows the world with life and essence.

1. Vide NC, IX, V 104 :

   Cakāsti binducyutakāticāturī
   Ghanāśrubinduśrutikaitavāt tava /
   Masāratārākṣi sasāramātmanā
   Tanoṣi saṁsāramasaṁśayaṁ yataḥ //

Śrī Harṣa does not use the chimes and *Bandhas* feverishly in the manner in which *Bhāravi* and *Māgha* indulge. He is a master of the beautiful subversions of speech, like the one quoted, and also of puns. In the 13th canto of his *Naiṣadhacarita*, there is a height of paranomasia when, in a [1]single verse, he is able to give five broad meanings, or, taking the suggested ones, even more, by describing the five *Nalas*, one real, and the rest, four gods impersonating *Nala*. First, the gods are described separately, and in each case there is a suggestion through the change of voice (Kāku), that the particular god be avoided. To take the first meaning in respect of *Indra* : "O scholarly woman, this god who is not the master of the terrestrial region (i.e. who is lord of heavenly regions), who has the weapon hurling down with its onslaught onto the mountain, who is the master of the eastern quarters, shattering the mountains, and who has more powers (as compared with that of human beings), who is not as weak as the *Nala* grass (rather, who is very strong) choosing whom you would get gambols in the *Nandana* forest etc. and long life, why is he not decided upon and chosen ? If you leave him, the elder brother of *Viṣṇu*, who would then be your fiance/or your desired-one, viz, only your foe, or the one would be your choice, who is to be tamed by wind, or who is to be pacified by water (Agni) !"

The reason to leave him is being sounded; "Are you not choosing him as he is not *Nala*, the protector-god of the earthly region ? Or, not that he is not the husband of *Śacī*, the breath of life ? Or, as he is not your *Nala*, the mighty one, but only looks like *Nala* ! Or, as he looks weak like the *Nala* grass, so he is not your *Nala* ! If you leave him, then your choice would be one sailing in the ocean of happiness and comforts ! Or are you not making him up and choosing him, as only *Nala* is your life-force, the king of *Naiṣadha* ? Then, is it not an advantage in leaving one whose prowess is put to doubt by the demons (i.e. Indra) ?"

1. Vide : Ibid : V. 34 :
   Devaḥ patirviduṣi naiṣadharājagatyā nirṇīyate na kimu na vriyate bhavatyā /
   Nāyaṁ nalaḥ khalu tavātimahānalābho yadyenamujjhasi varaḥ kataraḥ paraste //

In point of *Agni* : "One who is known by the speed (or gait) of the ram, his carrier, or of the mountainlike ram, or of the ram on this earth (i. e. Agni), the master (owing to protecting the three worlds by way of helping the kitchen), or one whose carrier is the ram, who is the shelter of the *Āgneyī* direction (i.e. the master of it), the god who is not *Nala* but having the appearance of *Nala*, and who is more resplendent than him, why should not he (Agni) be decided upon and chosen ? If you shun him, then who else is the better one, or who else is to be your choice—rather your enemy !" *Damayantī* is sounded that she should leave him : "You would not decide upon him and choose him because he is not *Nala*, the mighty one, rather one only having his appearance and whose glamour is proved towards the grass *Nala* only (viz, not towards the demons !). You whose only alternative is the king of *Niṣadha*, should not choose and decide upon this *Agni* !"

In the case of *Yama*, the meaning would be: "One who is endowed with the gait of the buffalo, hurling away with hoofs the hills and mountains, the master, (being in the shape of Dharma) or the master of the southern quarters having access to his buffalo there, the powerful, the occult (on account of being in the shape of Dharma), the god, why do you not choose and decide upon him ? If you leave him, no advantage would accrue to you (rather loss !). Except him, nobody would be a better husband ! He is not *Nala* but one from whom you could have the profit of a very long lease of life, who has too much of honour, and who is, in respect of splendour, like *Agni*, or if you leave him, who would be your staunchest enemy (or he himself !) ? Or one who moves in the waters (i.e. Varuṇa) would be your choice !" Suggestion to leave him: "you are not choosing and deciding upon him as he is lord of the southern quarters and he is not *Nala*, but one whose prowess is darkened on account of the demons—only he appears as *Nala*. If you leave him, then your choice would be *Nala*, the ocean of bliss."

In relation to *Varuṇa*: "One who is the lord of the life-force of all the animate and inanimate beings (i.e. water), who is the mainstay of one who is the nourisher (of the universe) and the birthless (i.e. Viṣṇu), and who has a great halo like

Nala and hence appears like him, who is without the glimmer of *Agni* (i.e. opponent), the highly honoured one, why do you not decide upon him and choose him ? If you eliminate him, then who superior would be your suitor or your fiance would be your foe. If you leave him, the devotee of *Viṣṇu,* then no profit would accrue to you (rather loss !)". The idea of leaving him is thus sounded: "He is the lord of the northern quarters and none else. So, if you brush him aside, then you get abundant life, because in that case your husband would be *Nala,* the ocean of pleasure."

Lastly, *Sarasvatī* points to the real *Nala* and asks her, without any ambiguity, to choose him: "This, the overlord, with knowledge, is the king of *Naiṣadha,* the human *Nala* (not the god in his guise !), the lord of the terrestrial region or the king of *Niṣadha* who is the only option for you, or through the signs (like falling of the eyelids etc.) of those born on the terrestrial plains (i.e. human beings), the one who is not god (but a human being on the other hand !), this one who is, on account of great beauty, cupid on the earthly region, why do you not decide upon him and choose him, as you would be getting (in this way) the great *Viṣṇu,* or you would be getting long lease of life ? If you leave him, then who would be your choice, or there would be great misfortune for you or, there would be no profit (rather loss !) or whose choice would be a better one ?"

In the said canto, the poet gets an opportunity of double entendre; up to the verse which has been explained, most have two or three meanings. [1]*Śrī Harṣa* has clearly told that at certain places he has, with endeavour, placed knots in his work. [2]It is important to note that he also uses the word *Granthagranthi* for these intellectual knots. Even ordinarily,

1. Vide : Ibid. XXII, 151 :

   Granthagranthiriha kvacitkvacidapi nyāsi prayatnānmayā
   Prājñammanyamanā haṭhena paṭhitī māsmin khalaḥ khelatu /
   Sraddhārāddhaguruślathīkṛtadṛḍhagranthiḥ samāsādaya-
   Tvetat kāvyarasormimajjanasukhavyāsajjanaṁ sajjanaḥ //

2. Cf. Supra P. 140, Fn. No. 6.

his poems are difficult owing to the inculcation of philosophical ideas, and due to the drawing of symbols and similes from their domain. *Subandhu*, perhaps, in the same conceited style, also favours puns, and he promises to give them in every letter. He has used them in pure form as both *Sabhaṅga* and *Abhaṅga*, and has based on it other figures with seeming contradiction and computation. Ordinarily, we also get chimes and alliterations in his work, as also in the works of *Daṇḍin* and *Bāṇa*.

The former has devoted almost the whole of seventh chapter of his *Daśakumāracarita* to *Niroṣṭhyakāvya* where *Mantragupta*, having been bitten by his beloved in the lip, is naturally made to eliminate labial latters in his speech. Besides, *Setubandha* of *Pravarasena* and *Ajiyasantithaya* (Pkt) of *Nandīṣeṇa* also contain a few glimpses of *Citrakāvya*, though *Nalacampū* of *Trivikramabhaṭṭa* is replete. In this connection, we may mention the name of *Avantivarmā*, the Kashmir king, who took a keen interest in the development of this type of poetry, and patronised *Śivasvāmī*, *Ratnākara* and *Ānandavardhana*. The first one wrote *Kapphiṇābhyudaya* and the second *Haravijaya*. The latter is an epic in fifty cantos, of which the forty-third, forty-sixth, and forty-eighth ones, are devoted to *Citrakāvya*. The third one, *Ānandavardhana*, though a prominent theorist of *Dhvani* school, has composed *Devīśataka* consisting of the poetic designs of net and quiver, besides the usual ones. Here the wheel-design with thirty-two spikes is a wonder to watch.

Thus far, we had been treating *Citrakāvya* found mostly in stray verses. Now to deal with it in the shape of integral compositions (Prabandhakāvyas). They are, broadly, of two types : the poems of chimes (Yamakakāvyas), having different varieties of chimes used throughout, so that words, feet, or hemistich, or even whole verses are repeated, having different meanings, and the poems of puns (Śleṣakāvyas), having the same set of words, giving more than one meaning in the verses throughout the composition. Among the latter, are some where the same verse gives two different meanings, thus narrating two different tales (Dvisandhānakāvya), relating three different tales side by side on the basis of three meanings in each verse (Trisandhānakāvya), and such others. Besides, there is a poem having no nasals (Niranunāsikakāvya) and there might be even one having no labials (Niroṣṭhyakāvya), one having no dentals (Nirdantyakāvya) etc. There is also a poem in which throughout, the first half of the verse is repeated backwards in the second half (Vilomakāvya). In fact, these are over and above the regular poems, delineating particular designs (Citrabandhakāvyas), of which there are certain ones which comprise only a particular variety of *Bandha*. Moreover, there is a poem consisting of deviant expressions (Vakroktikāvya), and one comprising tricky compositions (Vyājoktikāvya), besides the dyglot poems consisting of verses that can be read in two or even more languages.

Among these, to take first the chiming poems. Here the first important one we find, is *Kīcakavadhaṁ* of *Nītivarman*. [1]*Premacandra*, in his commentary on *Kāvyādarśa*, cites it as a rare instance opening with benediction. It has been a favourite of the Pandits of Bengal. It dates, perhaps, to the earlier part of the nineth century A.D. The poem describes, in five cantos, the episode of *Kīcaka's* assault on *Draupadī* and his final finish by *Bhīm*a. The poet draws his material from the *Virāṭaparvan* of the *Mahābhārata*, but only in parts, to suit his purpose, so that he makes up the story in his own way. In the history of *Śabdacitra*, this poem marks an important phase of development. Perhaps, it was written to illustrate the extent to which chimes might be used as accessories in the [2]delineation of the semblance of *Kīcaka's* erotic sentiment.

About the patron of the poet, nothing is clearly known, but [3]from an eulogy at the end of the first canto, it appears that he might have been a king of *Kaliṅga* and it was, perhaps,

1. Vide KD with MP (comm.) I, p. 17.
2. Vide DL II. p. 222 :
   Yattu rasavanti kānicid yamakādīni dṛśyante tatra rasādīnāmaṅgatā yamakādīnāmaṅgitaiva / Rasābhāse cāṅgatvamapyaviruddham /
3. Vide KV, V. 21 p. 10.

for his delectation that *Nītivarman* has written this interesting *tour de force*. Actually, more than a chiming poem, this can be called a punning-chiming poem (Śleṣayamakakāvya) because, though there are mostly chimes throughout the book, in the third canto, paranomasia is interspersed with chimes of one particular variety in the long speech of *Draupadī* to the *Pāṇḍava* brothers. Considerable skill is displayed in managing these verbal tricks, and some of them are very good and not in the least laboured, like those of *Nalodaya*.

The last named is a short poem, consisting of four cantos. It describes the life of *Nala*. There are about fifteen commentaries on this book. The authorship is generally attributed to *Kālidāsa*. [1]*Rāmarṣi*, on the other hand, in his commentary on this poem, ascribes it to *Ravideva*, the son of *Nārāyaṇa*. But [2]*Viṣṇu*, another commentator, mentions its author as one *Vāsudeva*, son of *Ravi*.

The author, quite ostensibly in this poem, wants to display his poetic dexterity in manipulating the most varied and artificial metres, together with all the elaborate tricks of style. He purposively makes use of chimes in order to achieve pedantic effects in poetry, a tendency exhibited in the later *kāvyas*. But it is quite uncommon that he introduces rhyme even in the middle, and at the end, of the metrical lines. It goes without saying that this brings sonorous and soothing melody in the otherwise artificial, and hackneyed poetry. As for the real epic material, it is scanty, no doubt, and the narration is full of long descriptions and lyrical exuberances.

Among some important but comparatively small poems of this variety, are the *Rākṣasakāvya*, *Saurikathodaya* and *Tripuradahana*. The first one is attributed to *Kālidāsa* as well as to

1. Cf. :

   Iti vṛddhavyāsātmajamiśrarāmarṣidādhīcyaviracitāyāṁ ravidevaviracitamahākāvyanalodayaṭīkāyāṁ yamakabodhinyāṁ nalarājyaprāptirnāma caturtha āśvāsaḥ /

2. Cf :

   Iti nalodaye vāsudevakṛte caturthaḥ parichhedaḥ /
   Ravitanubhūyamitāyāḥ kṛtergatiśśabdacitrabhūyamitāyāḥ /
   Janahāsāyamitāyā dhiyaśca vivṛtā mayādhunā yamitāyāḥ //

Vararuci, and is a short poem of twenty verses in an enigmatic style, full of alliterations. It is a description of the sylvan scene effected through the mouth of a person moving about with his spouse in the forest region. The second one, on the contrary, narrates the life of *Śrī Kṛṣṇa* right from his birth to the conquest of *Bāraṇāsura*, on the basis of *Harivaṁśa*. The third one describes the story of the destruction of the three cities by *Śiva*. We have six extant commentaries on *Rākṣasakāvya*, and one each on the latter two. Comparatively speaking, *Yudhiṣṭhira-vijaya* might be chronologically a bit earlier, and is a bigger poem in eight divisions in *Āryā* metre. It might have been composed at the time and under the patronage of king *Kulaśekhara* because his name is mentioned as the reigning king. The real source of the poem, so far as story goes, is the *Mahābhārata* but the poet, to suit his purpose, singles out the episode from the hunting expeditions of the *Pāṇḍavas*, to the coronation of *Yudhiṣṭhira* after the great war. One *Sokkanātha* has written a commentary on it.

Then there is one *Caturviṁśatikā*, a panegyric consisting of four groups of verses. The first group is in praise of the twenty-four *Tīrthaṅkaras*, the second of all the *Jinas*, the third eulogises the Jain doctrine, and the fourth various deities. Here it is noteworthy, that the writer *Śobhana* was a Jain, having complete faith in Jain philosophy, and was popularly known as *Śobhanamuni*. He lived in 10th century A.D. in the court of *Dhārā*. It is, also, a chiming poem (Yamakakāvya) and the verses, here, are so constructed, that the second line agrees, to the letter, to the fourth line, but with different meanings.

[1]At about the same time, lived *Śrīvatsāṅka*, son of *Rāma* alias *Vedavyāsa* and a pupil of *Rāmānuja*. He came from a wealthy family, but he later abandoned all, and lived as a mendicant. His memory, it is said, was supernatural. He was a great poet and his verses are fluent with lay fancies as well as the sanctities of theological allusions. His *Vaikuṇṭhastava* describes the glory of *Viṣṇu* in *Vaikuṇṭha*, his *Atimānuṣastava* the

1. Vide SAHṚD. (SJ, Madras) XVII, 65, 89, 113, 130.

great deeds of the same god in his various incarnations, and his *Sundarabāhustava* the grace and purposes of the idolic forms of the said god. Likewise, his *Varadarājastava* relates to the description of the particular merit of *Varadarāja* of *Kāñcī*, and *Śrīstava* delineates the qualities of *Lakṣmī*. These five, together, are called *Pañcastavī*. Quite extraordinarily, his son, *Parāśara* B*haṭṭa*, also became a great poet in this style. He wrote *Viṣṇusahasranāmabhāṣya* and *Śrīraṅgarājastava*. There are commentaries, one anonymous and another by *Veṅkaṭācārya*. Among his minor works, are *Śrīguṇaratnakoṣa*, *Kṣamāṣodaṣī*, *Taniślokī* and *Aṣṭaślokī*, *Caṇḍamāruta*, *Vedāntavidyāvijaya*, *Sadvidyāvijaya*, *Vedāntadeśikavaibhavaprakāśikā*, *Parāśaravijaya* and *Yamakaratnākara*. From amongst these, *Parāśaravijaya* relates to his own history, and *Yamakaratnākara* is a very important poem of chiming variety, in *Āryā* metre, on *Śrī Kriṣṇa*, followed by his own commentary. In the last one, in certain verses, the first hemistich is repeated in the second, proving the highest poetic skill of the poet in matter of chimes. He lived about the beginning of 12th century A.D.

In chronological order, *Dharmaghoṣa* comes next. He was a sage and died in 1301 A.D. He wrote verses capable of even four different meanings. His *Yamakastuti* is wellknown on which *Somatilaka* wrote a commentary. Among his other works are, *Śrīśayamakaśataka* and *Acyutalīlā*. After him, *Manaṅka*, the poet, wrote his *Yamaka* poems, *Bṛndāvana* and *Meghābhyudaya*. He calls himself a king in his gloss on the *Gītagovinda* and is quoted by *Rāymukuṭa* in his commentary on *Amarakoṣa*. Then there is *Rāmalīlāmṛta* of *Kṛṣṇamohana*, having an almost identical theme.

Of *Ānandatīrtha*, the writer of thirty-seven books, at least one of this style *Yamakabhārata* is very important. He is known by various names and was born in 1198 A.D. His early life displayed miracles of divine powers, and by twenty-five, he became versed in all the sciences and the *Vedas*. Later, he renounced family life and became an ascetic. He became the famous founder of the *Dvaita* school of Philosophy, and has written profusely and most authoritatively on the subject. His *Yamakabhārata* is the epitome of his mastery of language, and narrates the *Mahābhārata* story in verses, full of chimes.

There are a few commentaries on it but all anonymous. He also wrote some *Stotras* which, though not meant to display his poetic art, nevertheless do give some hints of it. They are *Āryāstotra*, *Gurustotra*, *Kriṣṇastuti* and *Dvādaśastotra*. Again *Bhāgavatatātparyanirṇaya*, *Bhāratatātparyanirṇaya*, *Kriṣṇakarṇāmṛtamahārṇava*, *Śaṅkaravijaya* and *Śaṅkarācāryāvatārakathā*, are also attributed to him.

Among the poems of puns (Śleṣakāvyas), the lesser ones are *Śleṣacūḍāmaṇi* of *Śrīnivāsa*, *Śleṣollāsa* of *Śivaprasāda*, *Śl ṣacampūrāmāyaṇa* of *Veṅkaṭācārya* and *Śleṣacintāmaṇi* of *Cidambara*. Again, *Rāmāṣṭaprāsa* of *Rāmabhadra*, *Prāsabhārata* of *Sūryanārāyaṇa*, *Citraratnākara* of *Cakrakavi*, *Viśeṣaṇarāmāyaṇa* of *Vīrarāghava* and *Citrakāvya* of *Somakuñjara* also abound in puns, though not like the previous ones, and hence might come under this category. Among the more important *Śleṣakāvyas*, are *Sandhyākaranandin's* *Rāmacarita* (or, Rāmapālacarita) and *Ānandakāvya*. The former depicts at once, the story of *Rāma* and the history of poet's patron king *Rāmapāla* of Bengal, who regained his ancestral kingdom which had been usurped by *Bhīma*. This king ruled between 1104 A. D. and 1130 A.D. Thus, among *Sandhānakāvyas*, *Rāghavayādavapāṇḍavīya* has verses of three meanings, relating three different tales, and *Pañcakalyāṇacampū* deals similarly with five different stories. Here we may note that in the style of abovesaid *Rāghavayādavapāṇḍavīya* we have under this category *Yādavarāghavīya*, *Rāghavanaiṣadhīya*, *Rāghavapāṇḍavīya* etc. Moving on further, *Saptasandhānakāvya* depicts the lives of seven great men. To crown all, one *Somaprabha* has a *Śatārthī-Kāvya* to his credit, where a verse gives hundred different meanings. The composition of the *Suratotsava* of *Someśvaradeva*, *Pādukāsāhasra* of *Veṅkaṭadeśika* and *Sāgaracandra's* *Mantrādhirājakalpa*, also belong roughly to this period.

Moreover, there are also some poems having verses depicting different designs (Bandhakāvyas), illustrating lotus, sword etc. One such poem is the *Lakṣmīsāhasram* of *Veṅkaṭādhvarin*, where there are many poetic designs, such as those of the window, eagle and the *Gaticitras*. In *Veṅkaṭeśvara's* *Citrabandharāmāyaṇa*, there are highly ingenious designs like bracelet, umbrella etc. *Kamalamālikāstotra* of *Veṅkaṭācārya*, son of *Nṛsiṁha*, is another feat of alliterative ingenuity, a garland of lotuses in praise of *Lakṣmī*. It is also accompanied by a commentary. In this class the bracelet-design (Kaṅkaṇabandha) is the most difficult. The narrative is formed here by rewriting a verse, for instance, of thirty-two letters, backward and forward, from a particular starting-point, and making sixty-four verses in all. So, there is *Kaṅkaṇabandharāmāyaṇa*, describing the whole story of the *Rāmāyaṇa*. The author of this poem was one *Kriṣṇamūrti*, son of *Gaurī* and *Sarvagna*, who probably lived in the 19th century A.D.

The idea of the bracelet-design was improved by *Carla Bhāṣyakāra Śāstrī* in a similar composition. He probably lived in the *Agraharam* of *Kakaraparti* in the *Kriṣṇa* district. In his *Kaṅkaṇabandharāmāyaṇa*, he interprets each verse so formed in two ways, by shifting the compounds so that in effect, there results from one single verse a poem of one hundred and twenty-eight verses in all. In *Veṅkaṭeśa's Rāmacandrodaya,* the 26th canto contains *Bandhas* and there is also *Kaṅkaṇabandha*. The poet was the son of *Śrīnivāsa* belonging to the family of *Veṅkaṭādhvarin*, and was born near *Kāñcī* in 1595 A.D. His *Rāmacandrodaya* is a long poem of 30 cantos, describing the story of *Rāma* and was composed in *Benaras* in 1635 A.D. The work bears a commentary by the author himself, who composed his other such poem, *Rāmayamakārṇava* in 1656 A.D., depicting the same theme in *Yamaka* style. Also, there is a poem entitled *Rāmacandrodaya* by *Gopālarāy* or *Gopālasvāmi*, son of *Jīnavallī*, who might have flourished in the second half of 18th century A.D. This also gives the history of *Rāma* in *Yamaka* form. The author himself has written a commentary on it. To this period or sometime earlier, also roughly belong, among famous *Citrakāvyas*, the *Rasikarañjana* of *Rāmacandra*, *Caitanyacaritāmṛta* of *Kavikarṇapūra* and the *Stavamālā* of *Rūpagosvāmin*.

Veṇkaṭeśvara's Rāmāyaṇasaṁgraha composed in 1866 A.D. in 30 cantos in prose and verse, is another important poem. The poet has arranged the letters of the verses so as to form four more poems out of the particular letters combined and read together from the verses. It is, therefore, described as *Catuścitragarbha*. The poet has embedded his own name and description in one of such verses in *Bālakāṇḍa*. He was son of

Viśvanātha and *Kāmābā* and lived, probably, nearabout *Vizianagaram* about the middle of 19th century A.D. He was a poetic genius of rare merit in modern times, and has left an instance of poetic composition at once graceful and unique, a combination of acrobatics of surprising ingenuity.

There is, then, a varied sort of such poems. *Rāmakrisṇaviloma* of *Daivata Śrī Sūryakavi* has the first half of each verse repeated backwards in the second half, and thus, in the two, the stories of *Rāma* and *Kriṣṇa* have been related. In *Nārāyaṇa's Niranunāsikacampū*, *Śūrpaṇakhā* complains to *Rāvaṇa* of *Rāma's* assault, and because her nose has been cut, the poet aptly eliminates all nasals which she could not, perhaps, have pronounced. Like this, we have no *Niroṣṭhyakāvya* or *Nirdantyakāvya* having the elimination of labial or dental or such letters, but in certain books on rhetorics, or even in some poems of classical poets, we might come across such individual examples in verses. To mark a different sort, the poem *Gaurīvivāha* is formed by the regular combination of the first letter of the verses of the different *Kāṇḍas*, from *Ayodhyā* to *Yuddha*, and describes the marriage of *Gauri*, the spouse of *Śiva*. In *Śrīraṅgādikṣetramāhātmya*, there are regular combinations of the first letter in the second foot of the verses, from *Kāṇḍas* ranging as above. Here, thirteen shrines are described with their theological history. On the other hand, we have a regular combination of the first letters of the third foot of the verses from the same *Kāṇḍas*, in the same order, in *Bhagavadavatāracarita*, describing the various incarnations of *Viṣṇu*. When the regular combination is taken of the first letter of the fourth foot of the verses of the same *Kāṇḍas* like above, there results a poem describing the marriage of *Draupadī*. This has been entitled *Draupadīkalyāṇa*.Above all, a combination of the first letters of each of the verses only in *Bālakāṇḍa*, marks *Rāmakavacakāvya*. Thus, we have these five extant poems produced out of the *Rāmāyaṇa* in an ingenious way.

There are, even poems representing the clever subversion of speech (vakrokti), and some types of riddles where the omission of a syllable, a letter etc., or the concealment thereof, makes a lot of difference in the meaning of the constituent verses. On the former variety, there are *Ratnākara's Vakroktipañcāśikā*, *Rambhāśukasaṁvāda*, *Lakṣmīsarasvatīsaṁvāda* and the *Girijākamalāvivāda*. In the latter class, comes *Kriyāgopanarāmāyaṇa* or the *Candrakalāvilāsa* as it is called. *Kṛṣṇakavi*, son of *Raghunātha Dīkṣita* wrote this poem, consisting of fourteen cantos, based on the story of *Rāmāyaṇa*. Here, in all the verses, the verb is concealed in such a way that it is not clearly known to exist. Then, there are dyglot poems, consisting of verses that can be read in any two or more languages, giving as many meanings. *Śrīnivāsa Kavisārvabhauma* has written *Kṛṣṇarājajayotkarṣa* in prose and verse in such a way, that with an alteration in punctuation, the work becomes *Sanskrit* or *Kanarese*. He has also, to his credit, *Kriṣṇarājaprabhāvodaya*, a poem on his patron *Kriṣṇa Rāja Udeyar, a Mahārājā* of Mysore of the last century.

Then, there are some *Kāvyas* of *Citra* style of some general nature. *Vidagdhamukhamaṇḍana* of *Dharmadāsa* is one such book, a collection in four chapters of enigmatical verses on different topics. There are commentaries on it by *Tārācandra*, *Śivarājadhānī* and others, one among them being anonymous. *Viśveśvara's Kavīndrakarṇābharaṇa* is a similar work. The *Vāgbhūṣaṇa* of *Rāmacandra* is a group of periphrastic and curiously composed verses in praise of various deities. Perhaps, he lived in the *Pāṇḍya* country on the banks of *Tāmraparṇī*. *Durghaṭakāvya* is a highly artificial poem, consisting of eighty verses in praise of various gods, with an anonymous commentary. One poem of this name is attributed to *Kālidāsa* as well. By an unknown author calling himself *Kavirākṣasa*, is the poem, *Kavirākṣasīyam*, comprising of one hundred verses of involved meaning. [1]There is a fanciful reason given for this peculiar name. There are three commentaries on it, of which one is by *Nāganarāya*, and the other two are anonymous.

Nāgarāja is a different person from the above and has a poem *Bhāvaśataka* to his name, consisting of 101 verses of which some are in *Prākrit*, and in each of them, a certain person is

1. Cf:

> Sākṣareṣu bhavatīha jagatyāṁ sarva eva hṛdi matsarayuktaḥ /
> Sākṣaraṁ kavijaneṣu tamenaṁ loka eṣa kavirākṣasamāha //

represented to be doing a certain thing in a certain condition, and the reason why he or she does that act, or the minor sense of the verse, is meant to be found out by the reader himself. It is, however, also given at the end of every verse. The poet, himself, is spoken of at the end of the body of his poem, as a king who was the ornament of the *Ṭoka* race. He was the son of *Jalāpa* and grandson of *Vidyādhara*. There is also a poem of this name by *Veṇkaṭācārya* and *Bhāvavilāsa* by *Rudrakavi* and *Bhāvamañjarī* by *Rāma*, son of *Kriṣṇagopāla*. Similarly, there are three books named *Camatkāracandrikā* and the three writers are *Kavikarṇapūra*, *Narottamadāsa* and *Viśveśvara*. On the line of *Vakroktipañcāśikā* there is *Vyājoktiśataka* of *Trivikrama*, and *Sītārāmīya* (also called Śabdodāharaṇa) of *Bhāskarasūri*, son of *Rāmasvāmī Dīkṣita*, narrating the story of *Rāma* and is meant to illustrate grammatical forms like *Bhaṭṭikāvya*. *Sabhyābharaṇa*, on the other hand, is an anthology with double meanings, in nine chapters, by *Rāmacandra Bhaṭṭa*. The last verse interlaces the last *Sūtra* of *Pāṇini* with ingenuity. The poet was a great grammarian. There is a commentary on it by *Govinda*. On the same line, is *Sarvasena's Harivijaya*, a poem with double entendre, describing the victory of *Hari* but the difference is that it also illustrates the movements in chess.

Before touching the current century, I think it proper to give a very brief resumè of the contribution in this field of the *Jaina Ācāryas*, in addition to a few I have mentioned by the way. They have contributed in a big way to the development and growth of this literature. In the 7th century A.D., *Sāmantabhadra*, alias *Śāntivarmā*, wrote *Jinaśataka* or the *Stutividyā*, as it is also called, and *Devanandī* composed *Siddhipriyastotra*. Then, *Mahāpurāṇa* of *Jinasenasūri* deserves our notice among works of 8th century A.D. The work is divided into chapters named *Parvan* of which the poet himself wrote 52 and the rest were taken up and completed after his death by his disciple *Guṇabhadrasūri*. Among the Jain poets who specialised in this branch of poetry during the period from 10th to 12th centuries A.D., *Jinavallabhasūri* stands out, and he has written four books, namely, *Dharmaśikṣāprakaraṇa*, *Saṁghapaṭṭaka*, *Praśnaśataka* and *Citrakāvyasāra*.

In the 13th century A.D., *Sarvajinastavana* of *Dharmaghoṣasūri* is an important work. In the next century, *Jinaprabhasūri* and *Jayatilakasūri* have written one book each, viz, *Vīrastavana* (Citrastava) and *Caturhārāvalīcitrastava* respectively, and *Kulamaṇḍanasūri* has to his credit two works, namely, *Vīrajinastava* and *Pañcajinahārastava*. Sometime later, lived *Munisundarasūri* and *Udayamāṇikyagaṇi*, who, respectively, composed *Tridaśataraṅgiṇī* and *Candraprabhastavana*. In the 16th century, there are three prominent *Jainas*, *Jinasūri*, *Udayadharmagaṇi* and *Samayasundaragaṇi*. They have, in respective order, bequeathed to posterity, *Priyaṅkaranṛpakathā*, *Mahāvīrastavana* and *Harabandhastavana*. Later there are some remarkable *Bandhakāvyas* in the 17th century A.D., like *Īsvaraśataka* of *Avatārakavi*, *Lodrapurapārśvanāthapraśasti* of *Hemavijayagaṇi*, *Vijñaptipatra* of *Udayavijaya*, *Ānandalekha* of *Vinayavijayagaṇi* and *Citrabandhastotra* of *Guṇabhadra*. Specially in the last three, some new poetic designs are available, such as those of the trident, mirror, pitcher, conchshell, necklace, fish, chariot and coconut etc.

Coming to the 20th century A.D., we find *Dayānandadigvijaya* of *Akhilānanda Śarmā*, *Citropahāra* of *Devī Prasād Śukla*, and *Devīnāmavilāsa* of *Maheśvarācārya* alias *Sahib Kaul*. *Alivilāsasaṁlāpa* of *Gaṅgādhara Śāstrī*, though it has very few verses of *Citra* style, is quite an important work. Among the new books of this century, are *Lakṣmīśvaropāyanam* of *Dvirephakavi*, *Kāmeśvarapratāpodayam* of *Pt. Jīvanātka Jhā*, *Ugravaṁśapraśastiḥ* of *Upendra Ṭhākur*, *Karamāhākulapraśastiḥ* and *Khaṇḍavalākulapraśastiḥ* of *Bakhsī Mukund Sharmā* and *Rādhāpariṇayam* of *Kaviśekhara Badrīnātha Jhā*, to note only a few. The *Lakṣmīśvaropāyanam* deals with the exalted character of *Mahārāja Lakṣmīśvara Singh* of *Darbhaṅgā* in North Bihar. The poet seems to have acquired a good command over the Sanskrit language and has, in a very lucid and beautiful style, depicted his theme. He has also very successfully attempted some *Bandhas*. *Kāmeśvarapratāpodayam* gives in chaste, though skilful language, the short life-sketch of *Mahārāja Sir Kāmeśvara Singh Bahādur*, the son of the abovementioned *Mahārāja* of *Darbhaṅgā*. Its writer, *Pt. Jhā*, is the Headmaster, Sanskrit School, Janakapur

(Nepal). The dynastic panegyrics (Kulapraśastis), also relate to the Darbhaṅgā lineage of *Mahārājas*. The author of these panegyrics was a great scholar, having mastered various branches of Sanskrit, and belonged to the village *Ḍhaṅgā-Haripur* in the district of *Darbhagṅā*.

To sketch the history of *Arthacitra*, we have to be brief, as we have shown earlier that by *Citrakāvya*, people have generally meant only the verbal part of it, and *Arthacitra*, according to them, included all the figures of sense. In the sense understood and taken here, *Arthacitra*, the true picturesque poetry surcharged with emotions, gets its scanty glimpses here and there, as we have illustrated in the chapter on the subject. Here we have taken only a few illustrations to show variety. Among old works, *Vālmīki's Rāmāyaṇa* is superb in point of imageries. The illustrations already cited, are sufficient to prove their worth. Later, coming to *Kālidāsa*, we quote one verse from his *Kumārasambhavam* to show his mastery, as well as his uncommon psychological insight, in the use of imagery : [1]"Having seen him, *Pārvatī*, tremulous and perspiring, lifted her leg to step but did not move like a river which is agitated because of a rock blocking its way".

The picture here is of *Pārvatī*, lifting her leg to go away, at the indecorous and slighting behaviour of the *Brahmacārī* but mentally retracing her step the next moment, and not liking to go at the latter's unravelling of his form as *Śiva*. She was undergoing all the penitence for this moment. The sentiment of love struck her, and the sudden change of form made her more nervous. The imagery presented is the most appropriate, that of a river trying to move ahead but incapable of doing so, due to the stumbling-block on its path. Under such state, *Pārvatī* stands personified as a river, trembling and sweating in its surging waves. To take now one example from *Bhāravi*, as it is not possible to touch all the poets who might

1. Cf. KS V., V. 85 :

Taṁ vīkṣya vepathumatī sarasāṅgayaṣṭirnikṣepaṇāya padamuddhṛtamudvahantī /
Mārgācalavyatikarākuliteva sindhuḥ śailādhirājatanayā na yayau na tasthau //

have evolved beautiful images in their poetry : [1]"The world, unsatiated, beheld night when the moon rose (in the sky), and the spell of darkness not greatly broken, like the newly wed wife with her face beaming with the tearing away of the silken veil, but with bashfulness, very much athwart."

Here, too, the image has been evoked in an exquisite way because of the simile which is aptly drawn. There is some degree of romantic tenor in the meeting time of day and night. The day is departing and the night is coming with a glamour of her own. The beaming disc of the moon is like the mirthful face of a newly married wife, about whom there is some mystery of darkness still. It is, no doubt, the mystery of the poetry of *Bhāravi* itself, which sometimes wears the embellished silken veil, but does give its true appearance through it. In his own words, [2]"There should not be any ambiguity in the use of words. There should not be any tautologous use or repetition, and the desirability of sense should never be trampled upon."

1. Vide KJ, IX, V. 24 :
   Udgatendumavibhinnatamisrāṁ paśyati sma rajanīmavitṛptaḥ /
   Vyaṁśukasphuṭamukhīmatijihmāṁ vrīḍayā navavadhūmīva lokaḥ //
2. Vide KJ, II, V. 27 :
   Sphuṭatā na padairapākṛtā na ca na svīkṛtamarthagauravam /
   Racitā pṛthagarthatā girāṁ na ca sāmarthyamapohitaṁ kvacit //

CHAPTER VII

CONCLUSION

The question we are concerned with before giving our conclusions on the subject, is whether, finally, we mean by *Citra* 'peculiarity' or 'image', as we have shown earlier [1]that this denotes both. Discussing the nature and sub-varieties of *Citrakāvya*, we have generally, taken the former sense with regard to the figures of sound (Śabdacitra), and those both of sound and sense (Ubhayacitra). So far as the sense 'image' goes, it is applicable to all but *Ubhayacitra*, because, it is impossible to have images relating to both sound and sense in the same verse. Perhaps this was the trouble which compelled certain rhetoricians to accept only two sub-varieties. But this, *per se*, does not solve our problem, as in that case, so-called dual figures of sound and sense (Ubhayacitra) would have to be included in that of sound only (Śabdacitra), in which case, we should have to cast its constituents outside the realm of *Citrakāvya*, which would be an improbable proposition.

As a matter of fact, we have ample proof to show that [2]the idea of image in the sense of *Citra* is quite customary and old, [3]because in other contexts we find words like *Dhūlicitra*, *Bhāvacitra* etc. in our literature used on the same line. The meaning of peculiarity might have been imported only later, with a view to including the figures pertaining both to sound and sense (Ubhayacitra) in *Citrakāvya*. The riddles, poetic tricks etc., which constitute this sub-variety, did not deserve to be included in any higher category of poetry. Indeed,

1. Supra p. 24.
2. Vide ML I : 900, 901 :
   Sādṛśyaṁ likhyate yattu darpaṇe pratibimbavat /
   Taccitraṁ viddhamityāhurviśvakarmādayo budhāḥ //
3. Ibid : 902, 903 :
   Śṛṅgārādiraso yatra darśanādeva gamyate /
   Bhāvacitraṁ tadākhyātaṁ cittakautukakārakam //

Arthacitra meant the image of sense, and [1]in the various poetic designs (Bandhas) constituting the figures of sound, we get underlying pictures. By stretching the imagination, we may, ultimately, get some such sense even out of the dual figures, as we find some pattern of reading and obtaining the real meaning. Or, as is possible with regard to the simple riddles, the answers might have to be found, with the drawing of pictures of the idea which underlay the verses, but this is nothing more than a farfetched idea. Here we have not bothered much about the peculiarity pertaining to sound (Śabdacitra) or that pertaining to both sound and sense (Ubhayacitra), except in an academic sense. What we are vitally concerned with is *Arthacitra* and its imagist character cannot be gainsaid. We start with it as an axiom, so to say, as we try to bring this sub-variety in line with even best poetry from our Indian standard of judgment.

We have seen how almost all our rhetoricians have touched upon the subject, some deeply, and how vast is this variety of literature in the Sanskrit language which has a wide reading and appreciation even today. We have also witnessed that the literature is still active, and the best of our poets have attempted it. The chime (Yamaka) [2]which is called by certain rhetoricians the veritable tumour in the neck of poesy, has been used even by [3]*Kālidāsa* with credit, so that it is no impediment in the realisation of sentiment. [4]Of poetic tricks (Kūṭas) or riddles, we generally, ascribe the origin to the *Mahābhārata* and even [5]the aforesaid great poet has

1. Vide Appendix No. II.
2. Vide KP[3] IX, p. 344 :

   Tadetat kāvye gaḍubhūtamiti nāsya lakṣaṇaṁ kṛtam /
3. Vide RV IX, V. 28 :

   Kisalayaprasavo'pi vilāsināṁ madayitā dayitāśravaṇārpitaḥ /

   Ibid , V. 33 :

   Amadayat sahakāralatāmanaḥ sakalikākalikāmajitāmapi /
4. Supra, p. 140.
5. Cf. RV VII, V. 40 :

   Matsyadhvajā vāyuvaśād vidīrṇairmukhaiḥ pravṛddhadhvajinīrajāṁsi /

   Babhuḥ pibantaḥ paramārthamatsyāḥ paryāvilānīva navodakāni //

used them. The same story is true regarding the use of the poetic designs (Bandhas). The question arises whether all this was of inferior stuff and hence useless ? It certainly was not. The effort to use these exacted much poetic skill and aroused much of interest and curiosity in the reader. This was in a sophisticated society and it must be admitted that they touched the head, rather than the heart, and were a sort of intellectual exercise. This reached a climax in the composing of [1]verses consisting of identical letters or having even a lakh verses in each of them, let alone verses having manifold meanings.

In Sanskrit poetics, there has been a [2]school advocating the importance of figures of speech in the context of poetry and propounding even verbal jugglery as an important condition for any sort of poetry. This school consisted mainly of the trio, namely, *Bhāmaha*, *Daṇḍin* and *Vāmana* and emphasised more the art of poetry, rather than the content. To them, a writer might have abundant poetic materials based on his personal experience, might have thoughts, sentiments, sensibilities and rich imagination but the poetic work will not be accomplished unless there be proper expression of all these. The materials have to be given an organised form, keeping in view the principles, style, personal likes and dislikes, beauty and effectiveness. The choice of words, flexibility of sentences, their construction, rhythm and cadence—all these are very closely allied with the personality of the writer. In poetry, the form has greater appeal than the intellectual and sensual content. The realism, born of the proper use of the appropriate

1. Supra p. 33.
2. Cf. BK I, V. 13, p. 7 :

   Na kāntamapi nirbhūṣaṁ vibhāti vanitāmukham /

   Ibid, V, V. 3, p. 107 :

   Svādukāvyarasonmiśraṁ śāstramapyupayuñjate /

   Vide KSV 3.2.14, p. 95 :

   Dīptarasatvaṁ kāntiḥ /

   Cf RK XV, V. 21, p. 417 :

   Ete rasā rasavato ramayanti puṁsām /

   Cf. ST[2] X, 4. 2 :

   Lakṣmīriva ṛte tyāgānna vāṇī bhāti nīrasā /

words, and mutual concomitance of the word and the sense, is the true mirror of the poets' creative abilities.

Thus, verbal peculiarity in poetry might not be the only medium of pleasure that awakens the sentiments and sensibilities dormant within the reader. Suspense might be taken to be the original and fundamental human chord which, when struck, paves way for the creation of poetic beauty. According [1]to the advocates of the *Rasa* school, on the contrary, it is the illumination of sentiments which chiefly generates pleasure in poetry, and this is the most widely held view. But this does not mean that poetry of *Citra* type is always devoid of suggestion and sentiment. Also, it cannot be denied completely that there is some element in poetry in general, which produces suspense or curiosity in the reader. It is true that the sense of curiosity or enlightened pleasure is also begotten on account of a poet's skill coupled with his aesthetic sentiments, [2]although that sentiment is not, generally, of much value and does not exist at the time of the realisation of sentiment. Even from the suggestionist (Rasavādī) point of view, the poetic beauty which does not enlighten or enthral the sentiments, might generate curiosity owing to the poets' flight of imagination, or even due to his intellectual capacity through which the reader may derive some pleasure of the intellect in resolving any intellectual knot or problem.

Thus, there is a general lack of interest in the above sort of images, chiefly [3]verbal, because of its incapacity to arouse

1. Cf AŚ, p. 6 :
   Alaṁkārastu śobhāyai rasa ātmā paraṁ manaḥ /
   Cf. RG I, p. 25 :
   Evaṁ pañcātmake dhvanau paramaramaṇīyatayā rasadhvanistadātmā /
   Cf L—DL, p. 27 :
   Tena rasa eva vastuta ātmā / Vastvalaṁkāradhvanī tu rasaṁ prati paryavasyete /
2. Vide, KP[1] IV, p. 36 :
   Tatkālavigalitaparimitapramātṛbhāvavaśonmiṣitavedyāntarasamparkaśūnyaparimitabhāvena pramātrā..../
3. Cf. CM, P. 40 :
   Śabdacitrasya prāyo nīrasatvānnātyantaṁ tadādriyante kavayaḥ, na vā tatra vicāraṇīyamatīvopalabhyata iti /

the greatest emotional response. But in *Arthacitra* with images with depth of meaning, even the highest type of poetry may be realised. This has a direct appeal to the visual sense, as in a drama, and so enables one to have a firm grasp of the sentiment. It depends for its existence on the figures of sense, mostly those having *Bimbapratibimba*-or, *Vastuprativastu*-relation, given the peculiar poetic gift of the particular poet. Naturally, it goes without saying that image-creation generally, goes with the figures of similitude. But although the image evoked in such figures hinges on the appropriateness and compactness of the similitude as in the case of our greatest poet, yet [1]true images cannot emerge from a comparison of two or more distant realities. In fact, no image is produced by comparing two disproportionate realities. On the contrary, a striking image, one new to the mind, is evoked by bringing into relation, that which the inner spirit alone has seized. So, image is a pure creation of the spirit. Shelley held the view that the image is created when [2]the "film of familiarity; is purged from our inward sight." When image-creation is accomplished, it compels us to feel that which we perceive and to imagine that which we know.

As a matter of fact, what goes with the name of *Citrakāvya* in Sanskrit literature is the [3]old, decadent symbolism of western literature and there is nothing like imagism in its crystallised form in our own literature, which the western poetic thought has developed. The symbol and the image form a vicious circle. In western literature, what was image a few decades ago, is now only a symbol in its old form and is discarded, having given place to a new image. It might be, a few centuries hence, that the discarded symbol is again endowed with new aesthetic value and will emerge as a new image. But I am pained to relate that there is no such deve-

1. Cf Reverdy Quot : H-CEL, pp. 98-99.
2. Cf S-LPC, p. 156.
3. Vide Intro., B-HS :

   'The movement with which we are concerned has already spent most of its force......'

lopment of thought in our literature. [1]Lotus, for example, was an independent unit of image here centuries ago, and continues to be so, even today. In the hoary past when it might have come before the poet for the first time, as a standard of similitude, then it would have presented itself with its sprightliness, perfume and colour. It bore so much similarity with the beautiful face of a damsel that it later stood for it. In that event, the import of lotus would come within the ambit of the suggestion of sense.

But in course of time, with the appearance of new sense-perceptions, the old context of new and fresh sensations might go and then, lotus would stand for lotus and nothing else. We have seen earlier that with *Arthacitra* we might even get some tinge of suggestion, but there could be a very beautiful image even in case of direct expression. [2]Between the denotation of sense and its indication, there is not always much distance and so the latter is said to be only the tail of the former. *Bhaṭṭa Nāyaka*, however, thinks that indication is only the extension of denotation. Actually, in the images the layers of meanings unfold themselves later, but their sensibilities start working from the beginning. This is the communicability of literature in the true sense of the term. It acts as a clue to the mode of expression, peculiar to literature, and goes on giving new meanings.

According to *Bhaṭṭa Tauta* description (Varṇana) enshrines vision (Darśana). I think this is the earliest philosophical seed of the concept of *Citra* in poetry. Even ordinarily, only that poet or writer is the most successful who has a miraculous power of description in making the things described visible to the readers' minds' eye. It is through the process of perfect sensuous concretisation, where the direct power of words is brought into full play, that the meanings are given vent to. Among all our senses, the visual has the

1. Vide HK. p. 25.
2. Vide L—DL, I, p. 151 :

   Tathaiva cāmukhyatayā saṅketagrahaṇamapi tatrāstītyabhidhā-pucchabhūtaiva lakṣaṇā /

   Cf. Quot : KP[1] II, p. 14 :

   Abhidheyāvinābhūtapratītirlakṣaṇocyate /

most appeal. It is also most fertile in that it stores up images and can translate them back in the poetic association. Thus it plays an important part in the perception, retention and creative handling of images. The poet is, as it were, a seer who perceives and observes with his intellect, and in course of his composition there is the spontaneous [1]welling up of images without which there can be no poetry. These images are the units of impressions that the poet has gathered, and he arranges them." [2]A work of art, understood dynamically, is the process of arranging images."

[3]The poetic myths engendered by the collective mind enlightening mankind for centuries, are now dying out and poetic images are taking their place. The image can be better termed as the myth of the individual. This marks quite a different direction, or dimension of poetic depth. Its initial nature influences the poetic expression, having stayed behind the individual experience and memory, and comes into light through the medium of the personal vision of the poet. Only a critic, endowed with acumen, can evaluate its vital importance. [4]Jung has, on the basis of the two layers of conciousness, imagined two types of literary creations at the basis of image-creation. Lewis, on that basis but from a different angle of vision, has taken cognizance of a separate existence of aesthetic experience, where we get an indication of a separate element, weaving the impact of the unconscious, with the aroused skill of the poet.

This exists, both, in the poet and the conscious reader, and it is due to this that the imagery of a poet is properly directed. [5]In this connection, Mr. Herbert Read has also made a psychological probe and has thought of an inner organising energy, managing the form of the artistic poetry. In his opinion, "there is a certain art of poetry which arises, we do not quite know how, from the music of vowels and consonants,

1. Cf. M-QW, p. 46.
2. Vide E-FS, Tr. L, p. 25.
3. Vide L-PI, I, p. 32.
4. Ibid : VI, Quot. Jung, p. 143.
   Cf J-MS, pp. 179-180.
5. Vide H-CEL, p. 60.

the sound and association of words, the surprise of images and metaphors......" [1]Lewis, having taken inspiration from Read, has made a psycho-analysis of the process of image-creation. There is much truth in it. The figures of speech make the roots of imagery go deeper. It has inner as well as primeval bearing on the nature of poetic experience.

[2]It is a central theme of Lewis that 'an image does not image itself.' This means that no image is complete in itself. Rather, it helps in the determination of the form of poetry. Even a poet does not move without having predetermined the sense and nature of the particular image. In some other context, the learned critic has expressed the idea that [3]a whole poem be one whole image. As a matter of fact, the first phase of image-creation is a poet's positive identification with the inspiration of this art and if [4]the imagery of the poem, when developed, is meaningless, then the communion of the poet's creative faculty with his experience is loose. In that case, sentiment evoked does not give the highest bliss equal to one begotten of the attainment of the supreme soul.

In a poem there are varied things like emotions, images and the overall texture of the extended poetic tissue. But a unity underlies all these, for there is an inner congruence among all the constituent elements. So the creative impulse is one, but its successive realisations are many which are manifested as it evolves and expands to the various levels. The poetic analysis involves an endeavour that brings in its train emotional experience and its objectification through the workmanship. Emotional inspiration marks the first phase in the poetic creation, and is autonomous. Some images seem to emerge from the unconscious along with it. They are, of course, very natural. In the later phase, we can safely introduce the critical intellect without basically affecting the quality of the poem as a product of inspiration, and then, a poet may press into service some other useful images discovered

1. Vide L-PI, VI quot. APP, p. 143.
2. Ibid : IV, p. 91
3. Ibid : VI, p. 149.
4. Ibid : III, pp. 65, 67.

by his probing intellect. When intellect is secondary to emotion, it subserves the latter and does not mar the total effect of the poem by making it an intellectual exercise. This is because, in this case, the intellect becomes poetically stirred and reflects the emotional experience.

Like the image, metaphor, being more basic, at least, to the western poetic thought, also might be emotive. There it connotes something more than what it stands for in Sanskrit poetics. [1]Trends come and go, diction alters, musical fashions change, even elemental subject-matter may change almost out of recognition, but metaphor remains the life-principle of poetry, the poets' chief test and glory. [2]It engulfs all—sense, feeling, thought and meaning, and moves towards a self-determinate form. It is, really, this metaphor which gives the idea of image a new face-lift but the latter, in its own right, remains the true goal of the poet. One of its chief features is this that it unravels truth insofar as it takes high flights of imagination and probes into the higher relations and makes it easy to be grasped. Lewis holds that emotional logic is the element by which is accomplished the mutual weaving together of images and the unification of their various parts. Every part contributes its bit in the elemental relation thus established. [3]Moreover, there has been a stress on congruity in the said weaving together of images in view of the importance of the association of the factors that influence the reflection of poetic truth. The recurrent forms of rhythm are also of importance. This idea is very near the western concept of 'the fusion of meaning.'

But the use of image brings in its train certain handicaps, the greatest being the verbal complications and occultness. Because of the vigilance of the individual consciousness, all images are not such as are possible of being grasped by every one. Bertrand Russel, while contemplating on the general nature of language, says : [4]"Images, in fact, act as symbols

1. Ibid : I, p. 17.
2. Cf. W-RP, pp. 159-160.
3. Vide L-PI, III, p. 74.
4. Vide R-EMT, p. 241.

just as words do." Thus he has actually hinted at the accomplishment of the work of symbolisation through the medium of images. He has also pointed out how deep is the relation of images with the process of sensation, and how much sensation the perceptible experience evokes. [1]Here, what is important to note, is this that the sensations are generally rounded out by spontaneous images or expectations of their usual accompaniments in any perceptive experience. [2]In this respect, the sensory core has higher inferential value than the rest. We have just referred to the difficulty of occultness in the use of imagery, but to some it can be justified because of the unavoidable leap of sense from denotative to connotative. By way of expressing through symbolic images the ambiguity of the positive reactions of mankind, we take for granted, without any clear social objectives, their conscious, mystic personality and the disdain for intellectualism. [3]Ostensibly, we find in image poetry only an endeavour of seeking similitude, unfamiliar and somewhat away from tradition, for the familiar phenomena of nature. In this way, there is novelty, of course, in the emergence of the visual element and, that, more than offsets the hackneyed effort, if any.

With regard to the theme of such poetry, the western imagist movement has given some new ideas among which are non-traditional nature of contents, preciseness of meaning, clear and straight expression and semi-ocular discernment of the visual element. All these are to purge the language and protect it from prosaicness. In imagism, concentration is the keynote and should form the very essence of poetry. The poetry which is endowed with occult, ambiguous, mystic and dark meanings is the representative of the decadent symbolism we have referred to. On the other hand, the imagist poetry is characterised by clear, definite and artistic expressions. Thus direct, imagist commissioning of poetic matter in appropriate and rhythmic language is the true index of poetic art.

1. Vide R-EMT, p. 120.
2. Ibid, p. 122.
3. Vide J-MS, p. 180 : 'The experience that furnishes the material for artistic expression is no longer familiar. It is a strange something that derives its existence from the hinterland of mans' mind....'

When the great theory of suggestion was being established, the Indian poetic thinking, in spite of some serious lapses, had reached the apex of development. We have seen that *Citra* was placed in the last category of poetry and was thought bereft of the suggestive element, but the discussion has not been resolved. [1]It has been sought to establish that there is nothing which would not generate any type of disposition or state of mind. Naturally, there would be no variety of poetry which would not engender or suggest sentiment, primary or ancillary emotions. In this context, as a result, image poetry (*Citrakāvya*) can only then be possible when these aforesaid elements are not desired and *Citratva* alone be intended, devoid of suggestion which is impossible.

The things of this world are the revealer of some sentiment, and sentiment itself is a state of mind which, if the thing concerned is not capable of producing, then it cannot be the subject of a poet. If, on the contrary, it be accepted that there is no harm in the absence of poetry if the poet himself is its subject, then, it is not coherent because what we call image poetry is itself the subject of a poet's imagination. Now, moving in a different way, there must be some understanding of sense from such poetry, from which some object must be denoted and any object is, necessarily, in the form of a condition producing a state of mind or body (Vibhāva) which, perforce, awakens any particular emotion. Therefore, if the subject matter of a *Citrakāvya* be within the realm of the poet, which, I am sure, it will be, then that must produce delight which is impossible without the arousing of some sentiment. It may be pointed out in this connection that

1. Vide DL, III, p. 495 :

Yatra tu rasādīnāmaviṣayatvaṁ sa kāvyaprakāro na saṁbhavatyeva / Yasmādavastusaṁsparśitā kāvyasya nopapadyate / Vastu ca sarvameva jagadgatamavaśyaṁ kasyacid rasasya bhāvasya vā'ṅgatvaṁ pratipadyate antato vibhāvatvena / Cittavṛttiviśeṣā hi rasādayaḥ, na ca tadasti vastu kiñcid yanna cittavṛttiviśeṣamupajanayati tadanutpādane vā kaviviṣayataiva tasya na syāt kaviviṣayaśca citratayā kaścinnirūpyate/

[1]*Abhinava* has called all these the legend of *Vāsuki* but they are, really, hard facts which cannot be ignored.

In this connection, it is of interest to note that relaxation in the very theory of suggestion which *Ānanda* propounds so enthusiastically, is perceptible in the undercurrents of discussion in *Dhvanyāloka* itself. [2]When the poetic sense is defined first, two of its subdivisions, the expressed and the suggested, are given without any necessary implication that the latter is superior to the former. [3]The subtle shift in the doctrine came later, rather unconsciously. Again, in the very beginning, the author held that the suggested sense was itself the soul of poetry but [4]later, he had to change his position and rethink the issue. No doubt, rather than weakening the position, this has in a classical way, balanced it, but the fresh enthusiasm in the enunciation of a new theory might have tended to obscure this balance among the rhetoricians of posterity.

It is beyond any shadow of doubt that *Dhvanikāra* gives primacy to sentiment and when, indeed, sentiment is the primary thing, it is of secondary importance whether its evocation is direct or through suggestion or, whether the centre of gravity of a particular poem lies on the plane of the suggested sense. These are only the matters of detail. [5]Here, even with the poetry of subordinate suggestion the author goes on to make

1. Vide L-DL, III, p. 496 :
   Anyasya vāsukivṛttāntatulyasyehābhidhānāyogāt kavesced gocaro nūnamamunā prītirjanayitavyā sā cāvaśyaṁ vibhāvānubhāvavyabhicāriparyavasāyinīti bhāvaḥ /
2. Ibid, I, V. 2, p. 43 :
   Vācyapratīyamānākhyau tasya bhedāvubhau smṛtau /
3. Ibid, V. 4, p. 48 :
   Pratīyamānaṁ punaranyadeva vastvasti vāṇīṣu mahākavīnām /
   Yat tatprasiddhāvayavātiriktaṁ vibhāti lāvaṇyamivāṅganāsu //
4. Ibid, p. 78 :
   Tṛtīyastu rasādilakṣaṇaḥ prabhedo vācyasāmarthyākṣiptaḥ prakāśate, na tu sākṣācchabdavyāpāraviṣaya iti vācyād vibhinna eva /
5. Vide L-DL, III, p. 474 :
   Tadayaṁ dhvaniniṣyandarūpo dvitīyo'pi mahākaviviṣayo'tiramaṇīyo lakṣaṇīyaḥ sahṛdayaiḥ / Sarvathā nāstyeva sahṛdayahṛdayahāriṇaḥ kāvyasya sa prakāro yatra na pratīyamānārthasaṁsparśena saubhāgyam /

the concession that it be treated at par with the poetry of pure suggestion, to the extent it realises the poetic sentiment.' This, to my mind, is a very important recognition because it tends to serve as a bridge to span the gulf that separates the specialised poetry of suggestion from poetry in general. So, in the ultimate analysis [1]what is and should be suggested, is the sentiment (Rasa). Whether it is evoked through predominantly direct expression when suggested elements are subordinate, or through wholly indirect means, that is, through suggestion, becomes a matter of taste.

Thus, the theory of suggestion cannot establish that pictorial poetry, or for that matter, material image, can never evoke feeling. Let us take here the case of the suggested material image (Vastudhvani). In fact, there was a lacuna in the very theory of suggestion in that it did not accede to the suggestion of the material image the capability of resolving itself, finally, into the suggestion of feeling. However [2]*Abhinava* very remarkably spans it and propounds that the suggested material image may produce the desired sentiment. Here also, we may mark the miraculous leap in the theory, from image to emotion. If the image can evoke emotion or the sentiment, it goes without saying that the expressed image has no less the capacity to do so, than the suggested image, and it all depends on whether the image, direct or suggested, is correlative of the objective phenomena. Actually, poetic naturalism or the pictorial poetry dispensed with suggestion, according to the theorists, and therefore one can understand why they were not happy about it. But as we have seen above, they could not give weight to their case.

Ānandavardhana must have been fascinated by the basic

1. Ibid : V. 37. p. 475 :

   Mukhyā mahākavigirāmalaṁkṛtibhṛtāmapi /
   Pratīyamānacchāyaiṣā bhūṣā lajjeva yoṣitām //

   Ibid : V. 40, p. 483 .

   Prakāro'yaṁ guṇībhūtavyaṅgyo'pi dhvanirūpatām /
   Dhatte rasāditātparyaparyālocanayā punaḥ //

2. Cf. L-DL, I, p. 52 :

   Yadūce bhaṭṭanāyakena—'aṁśatvaṁ na rūpatā' iti, tadvastvalaṁkāradhvanyoreva yadi nāmopālambhaḥ, rasadhvanistu tenaivātmatayāṅgīkṛtaḥ / etc.

miracle in this type of emotive, imagist poetry. At the root of it, we get a stimulus which senses evoke and which is concrete. [1]But this leads, in turn, to the generation of emotion where the material entity culminates in the immaterial reality. It is difficult to follow, in this quantal leap, every phase of the transition as a continuous processs, but it gives a romantic thrill of its own. Under the spell of this fascination, *Ānanda* extended this concept to the inner poetic fabric. This fabric consists in a linguistic texture, woven out of words which are phonetic entities. Semantically, it is, on the contrary, also a web of meanings. The contours of the expressed sense of a linguistic construction can be precisely fixed because language has certain basic postulates for manipulating the communication of meaning.

What is important in poetry is the objectivity of its poetic value which can be assessed by anchoring it on to the interaction working between the object and the subject. Finally, the result is achieved after a very subtle equation which is subjective experience of the said value and object. Unless the object and the resultant poetic relish are thus equated, the poetic art, especially the imagist one, may either degenerate into a sensational theme, or may lapse into a sort of private fantasy and autosuggestion, without any profound relation to the objective reality.

Therefore, the aesthetic apprehension constituting a visual focus, involves the selecting and ordering of the perceptible elements together with their indicative meanings in a 'unified ideal of relations.' This ordering is done by 'imagic interplay' between the image-forming power of the perceiver and the image-offering character of the object. This, in effect, is what *Abhinava* also asserts. The profound significance of objects is a reality, irrespective of whether it is being imaginatively apprehended by anybody, but, certainly, it is to be the experienced reality of a subject. The subject has, thus, to discover the deeper stratum of the object through intuition. [2]In the exer-

1. Vide V-SD, III p. 87 : Ādye vibhāvādisamūhālambanasya savikalpakatvāt / Antye tu jñānajanyatvena nirvikalpakatvābhāvāt, jñānajanyajñānasyaiva nirvikalpakatvāt /
2. Cf. C-PP, I, p. 62.

cise of his image-forming power, the poet finds new relations of things being established and determined by a harmonic or complementary association governed by meaning [1]beyond the access of logic or the laws of causality.

This can be said to be the generalisation of the particular sentiment which is indispensable for its evolution. This, in poetry, happens to materialise between the poet and his object on the one hand, and between reader and the poetic merchandise on the other. There is a complete identification of the poet with his object in the flood of emotions and only then he is able to produce such poetry which enchants the reader. Here, we may point out that [2]the painful images, born of a tragic situation which the poet portrays, are the most moving ones. They, within the vision, are immediately known and felt intimately. The images, whatever their nature, become 'distanced' like the objects in a far-stretching landscape 'estranged by beauty.' Again, so far as the memory of a poet is concerned, it comes from his personal experience and later, undergoes separation from the concrete experience with the extrusion of the personal aspects.

In this context of the generalisation of sentiment called purgation of feeling in western poetic parlance, sorrow, for example, in a tragic circumstance, remains sorrow. But its meaning to the spirit is profoundly altered [3]under such a situation which the reader relishes as the highest type of spiritual bliss. [4]This, in technical language, is called modulation of meaning, and requires the subtly precise 'distancing' of experience and its 'filtering.' As the process cannot start in 'overdistanced' experience which remains either unconsidered or only theoretically considered, the distance has to be reduced, but this reduction has to be halted at a critical point. So, 'the utmost decrease of distance without its disappearance' is the prerequisite. This distancing means keeping at the minimum

1. Cf. KP[1] I, V. 1 : Niyatikṛtaniyamarahitām.../
2. Cf. B-DAP, V, II, p. 116.
3. Cf. RG I, p. 31 :

   Aśrupātādayo'pi tattadānandānubhavasvābhāvyānnatu duḥkhāt //

4. Cf. B-PD.

distance experience and sensibility, without bringing them too close to each other. This, I may point out, is necessary for the accomplishment of aesthetic relish, especially, in image poetry.

Therefore art, here, is not so much the creation of spontaneous inspiration as of the poetic intelligence. There is no contradiction between this and the feeling. It is consciousness at its subtlest, based on rich, emotional reactivity, but capable of mobilising that reactivity for precise realisation of the poetic sentiment. So the poetry may be inspirational or intellectual, purely suggestive or only pictorially suggestive, but consciousness is, always, at its root. [1]The creative moment is like 'a reverie in which the agent, like the object, is conscious consciousness.' That is, if the resources of the unconscious like the free association of images, are fully tapped, a supremely alert and wakeful consciousness keeps careful supervision over all these processes. The will has to come up to the surface. Once the material is thus available, the will rejects and selects and moulds. [2]Poetic creation needs the maximum consciousness possible.

But this consciousness is not to be equated with merely analytical intelligence, for it is at the same time, both poetically sensitive and critically analytical. Intelligence, as ordinarily understood, cannot create. Poetic consciousness, on the contrary, is intelligence and sensibility combined, functioning as a unified power of the personality. The objective is the concretisation of feeling which is the supreme object of poetry, even in the Indian tradition. Thus, image is a very especialised and indispensable quality of poetry which comes out of that concretisation of feeling. Even pure poetry is called poetry merely on the strength of these images.

In western rhetorics, [3]Lewis has linked the production of images to the depths of the unconscious. Here, he has been influenced by the psychological analysis of Jung. Below the layer of the conscious, in the wave of unconscious energy,

1. Vide P-LQ, pp. 144-145.
2. Cf. P-O, I, p. 1481.
3. Vide L-PI, II, p. 39.

swim the 'primordia' images or archetypes. [1]Jung has dubbed these as psychic residues of countless homogeneous experiences. In these are found not only the individual experiences, but also an amalgam of hereditory experiences. Again, consciousness flowing beneath the materialistic universe makes the images animistic and, [2]according to Lewis, this animism lies at the root of all poetic images. In this way, personification and pathetic fallacy, are both remnants of the primeval animism and the imagist consciousness also manifests itself after having reacted in its association.

In Sanskrit poetics, [3]the suggestion, which is the life of poetry of any variety, has been described by *Mammaṭa*, as the sonic waves coming out of the echoes of the ringing bell. In the creative activity, this idea is just parallel to that of the layer-after-layer of consciousness, having been accumulated in the serene, meditative mind of the poet. Here we get a sort of chemical process taking place between emotions and their different forms and aspects. This poetic analysis is characteristic of the Indian theory of suggestion, original and profound. There might be some thoughtful and sentiment-provoking poems with the self-surrender of the poet as their subject-matter, which cannot be fully understood on the basis of their western imagist analysis, but which might be comprehended on the application of the theory of suggestion. From the point of view of essentiality, this theory offers no opposition to the imagist theory as, [4]Lewis also understands various poetic impressions as "impressions of a hundred sorts, sensuous, lively, lovely and many-hued" forming the image in the ring-after-ring fashion.

1. Ibid, VI, quot. Bodkin on Jung, p. 141.
2. Vide L-PI, IV, 107.
3. Cf. KP1 IV, p. 50 :

   Ghaṇṭāyāṁ vādyamānāyāṁ pradhānaśabdapratītyanantaraṁ yaḥ kṣodīyānaparo'nuraṇanānusvānādipadābhidheyaḥ śabdaviśeṣaḥ pratīyate /

   Cf. R-SKB :

   Tena sahṛdayahṛdayaṅgamādarthāt kāṁsyatālānusvānanyāyena tādṛśamarthāntaramavagamyate sā gatiriti..../
4. Vide L-PI, III, p. 68.

[1]The creation of poetry begins from an impression and a drop of the river of experience is crystallised in the form of an image. The second stage of the process of creation is of effortless, condensed concentration of mind like that of a *Yogī*. Here, as [2]Yeats contemplates, the action both of will and intellect is at a standstill, and the images come in a dashing wave. In Indian terminology this state of poetic creation is more or less like the perfect absorption of the mind in the course of penitence, which, [3]according to the said critic, is like 'a state of trance.' [4]Lewis, on the other hand, has termed this as 'the suspension of intellect.' In the third stage, a poet's creative consciousness is awakened, and then related to the focussing of the inner form of the poem by the method of assimilation and elimination.

In such a state of poetic creation, both subject and object are metamorphosed into quite different forms, ready for a unique confrontation. It has been seen above how the subject poet undergoes the transformation, and is, in the creative moment, quite a different being. His mind, which receives the object, is no longer one behaving in the worldly fashion, and the object too, no longer belongs to the material, external world. It is the perfect awareness of this very subtle nature of poetic experience, which makes [5]*Viśvanātha* affirm that it belongs to the interface between embodiment and transcendence, or the 'bonded-liberated state'. If, then, the mind is now in a state of serene self-possession, the serenity is not to be confused with a withdrawn deadness. [6]Mallarmé has a remarkable passage, reading like an elaboration of [7]the Indian concept of the melting of heart (Druti) in poetic experience ; "The

1. Ibid.
2. Ibid : III, quot. Yeats, p. 69.
3. Vide Y-R : CY, p. 209.
4. Cf. L-PI, III. p. 69.
5. Vide SD, III, V. 23+, p. 179 :

   Yuktaviyuktadaśāyāmavasthito yaḥ śamaḥ sa eva yataḥ /
   Rasatāmeti tadasmin sañcāryādeḥ sthitiśca na viruddhā /

6. Vide M-OC. p, 262.
7. Cf. SD, III, V. 8, p. 77 :

   Aśrupātādayastadvad drutatvāccetaso matāḥ /

teardrop of exquisite relish" that makes its appearance in intense poetic experience, belongs with "the highest summit of serenity where beauty ravishes our spirit."

This poetic state can only be experienced by one's own self, but a western poet-critic who has, perhaps, passed through the process, has been able to describe this very touchingly: [1]"The happy, liberating touch of non-objectivity drew me out into the 'desert' where only feeling is real......From the suprematist point of view, the appearances of natural objects are, in themselves, meaningless; the essential thing is feeling, in itself and completely, independent of the context in which it has been evoked." Abstract art is as valid as respresentational art, because the spirit can relish both in a plenitude of presentation. Again, in both, the suggestions might be latent which can be revealed in the poetic moment and both are creations of imagination. Here the question arises whether auto-suggestion can work up the feeling. In fact it does, but it cannot create art which can communicate the experience to another, as we have pointed out earlier. So far as the object is concerned, its form has to lose all suggestions of organic shape in order to become universal. When, on the other hand, the poetic object is universalised, the poetry gains a sort of universal appeal which, in turn, makes it great. Here, we may point out that psychoanalysts like Jung think that poetry, to be great, must be based upon, and nourished by, the universal experiences of mankind which, in a way, are manifestations of the collective unconscious, of which the contents are called archetypes. These are images impressed upon the mind which might be revealed in the poetic creations, investing them with a universality, all their own.

Besides, the poetic image has, as [2]Whalley has pointed out, a subtle feature in that it is a feeling-vector. According to him, [3]"feeling is centrifugal, vectorial, outward moving and pointing insistently outside the self in which it is generated." Thus, not only is it the vehicle for a 'charge' of feel-

1. Vide AA, pp. 452-453.
2. Vide W-PP, 141.
3. Ibid, p. 68.

ing but it also has a directional character, seeking to move in a certain direction. [1]Whalley confines himself chiefly to the emergence of these vectorial characteristics in the rhythmic pattern, but [2]Lewis, on the contrary, has pointed out the tendency of images to be congruent with one another and, thus form a distinctive pattern. This is necessary for the wholeness of a poem, otherwise the total effect would be marred by being merely a series of stabbing, meaningless flashes. Thus, the poem must have, among its parts, a relationship which underlies all reality.

Again, [3]Whalley means to suggest that the self is the anterior reality, for, it is in this that the feelings are generated. This resembles the *Pūrva-Koṭi* of *Bhoja*. The centrifugal radiation of feelings penetrating into the world, is the middle phase, but the process does not stop here. [4]The fulcrum for feeling is the self, the central point of departure and return. This return constitutes the *Uttarakoṭi* of *Bhoja*. Further, we find that Shelley comes half way to *Bhoja's* insight and he derives all poetry, nay, all creation, from love and [5]defines love as "a going out of our own nature and an identification of ourselves with the beautiful which exists in thought, in action or person, not our own." This, the according to *Bhoja*, is middle phase. In the climactic phase, what is 'not our own', gets assimilated into our being and, the love, now, is the love of the self, thus enriched.

[6]Sanskrit poetry does not have the unexpressed sense to be darkly gathered. Nor does our theory of poetics regard it as indeterminate. It is bound up by means of definite links with the expressed sense without which its existence is not possible. But it is wrapped up in such a way that it is possible only for those who are initiated in the poetic hieroglyphics, to comprehend it in its subtlety. Even the knowledge

1. Vide W-PP.
2. Vide L-PI, III, p. 65.
3. Vide W-PP,
4. Ibid.
5. Vide S-DP, p. 38,
6. Cf. De : HSP, p. 174.

of grammar and lexicon does not help. But men of taste and literary instinct, quickly can follow it. It is the province of the connoisseur (Sahṛdaya) who, as expert in discerning the intricate mess of veiled words and sense, gets into the aesthetic relish of deeper significance.

But, if we link the moments of perception, that would only give lyrical sequences but not a complex structure which, we should always keep in mind, is not sought for its own sake as an absolute pattern. A faithful mirroring of the interaction between sensibility and reality, will, necessarily, have to be complex. It is because the world stimulates desires in sensibility that mature into motivations and actions which, in turn, impinge on reality and change its pattern. It is these changed patterns that confront the sensibility later, and generate fresh emotive reactions which will be related to the original reactions in meaningful ways, with fulfilment or frustration.

[1]As regards the relationship between two images, Mallarmé said that the poet must be careful, because from between the two good images a third element, clear and fusible, will be distilled and caught by our imagination. It is this third image, distilled out of the fusion of the two that charms us more. [2]Imagination here does not play any mean role, but ultimately, experience is the main thing. It is the experience which is the taking-off ground. The more solid this basis, the stronger and deeper the poet's understanding of reality and the further the leap. Thus, poetry is double: it is plastic, representing 'the pure objectivity of the image' and it is musical representing 'the inner mood.' So, if Mallarmé dismissed Parnassian poetry which was plastic, three-dimensional and sculpturesque, it was not because of its inherent defects, but because of his failure to notice that the Parnassian image is a perfectly expressive objective correlative.

To sum up, the most important point which has emerged after this discussion is that pictorialism and direct expression can never be condemned as unpoetic in themselves. The

1. Vide M-CP, p. 134.
2. Cf. S-CAP. p. 74.

test should be whether or not, the mental image is also an emotional image. In tragic situations, we generally have a more emotional ordering of experience, and hence, there is more chance of the image being emotional. When we look into the great epic of *Vālmīki*, we find the wonderful contours of the magnificent ordering of experience, achieved in his aesthetic creation. He refined the first lyrical impulse [1]he received through the sudden and tragic demise of the *Krauñca* bird, and [2]wove out an epic pattern of incidents, accentuating the incidence of tragedy, genetically related to the action and interaction of characters.

The impulse was profound but, nonetheless, it was still a raw intensity of the experience of separation which drove the poet to poesy. The human experience which imbibes the tragic pain, does not shed the latter. Only when it is analysed and dissected, it loses some of its power to blunt the poetic sensibility. Thus, the insulated, initial experience of the first poet could not have borne the heavy load of lyrical emotions without running the risk of degenerating into sentimentality. But his superb imagination stood him in good stead and bridged the gulf between emotions and reality in poetry, giving it an all-embracing vision of life.

So, in the light of what we have discussed here, regarding *Citra* and the image, let us now examine the [3]definition of this variety of poetry propounded by *Ānandavardhana*. We see that it falls to the ground because it is too narrow. *Citrakāvya*, in the sense we take here, especially *Arthacitra*, might not aim at the evocation of feeling and sentiment but at least, sometimes, it is evocative. From another point of view, we can hold that every poetry or, for that matter, any literature, aims at such evocation of feeling; it is quite a different thing that it is not able to achieve it. As regards the second

1. Vide Supra p. 131.
2. Cf. L-DL, p. 85 :
   Yaḥ śokaḥ sthāyibhāvo nirapekṣabhāvatvād vipralambhaśṛṅgārocitaratisthāyibhāvādanya eva, sa eva tathābhūtavibhāvatadutthākrandādyanubhāvacarvaṇayā hṛdayasaṁvādatanmayībhavanakramādāsvādyamānatāṁ pratipannaḥ..../
3. Vide Supra p. 102, Fn. No. 1.

clause, that it does not exploit the special illuminating power of suggestion, we can say that it stands thrashed. As for the third clause, we shall take it only in a broader perspective. The *Citra* or image does, basically, depend on the striking expression and meaning, but let me ask what variety of poetry or literature does not ? So far as its looking like a picture is concerned, I don't think there is any harm in it, if it possesses other essential features of good poetry. I think it does so. It evokes feeling and sentiment and is also suggestive. So, it has got only the additional virtue of picturesqueness. Besides, we have also seen that a subject poet passes through a 'trance-like state' like the producer of the highest grade of poetry according to Indian tradition. It is proof that the said poetry has come out of the fire-ordeal, safe and genuine.

So poetry in this clever definition does not descend to the pictorial level merely because it lacks suggestion. Earlier this defect alone would have been sufficient to condemn it. But now, it must also show the defect or failure to evoke emotion. *Viśvanātha* accepts this position and so does [1]*Abhinavagupta* when he defines pictorial poetry as that which merely imitates genuine poetry, the latter which enshrines feelings. Here embarrassing questions can be asked. Since suggestion and feeling are independent variables, what is the status of poetry which uses suggestion but is not emotive in quality ? What is the status of poetry which is pictorial, and which does not use suggestion, but which incarnates feeling ? The questions are legitimate because the theory has had to admit the independence of the two variables. In the reformulation of theory, feeling regains its prime status and suggestion becomes the technique of its evocation. [2]That is the final

1. Vide L-DL, III, p. 495 :

   Rasādijīvarahitam...../

   Ibid, p. 496 :

   Naiva tatra rasapratītirasti yathā pākānabhijñasūdaviracite māṁsapākaviśeṣe /

2. Cf. DL, II, V. 3 p. 175 :

   Dhvanerātmāṅgibhāvena bhāsamāno vyavasthitaḥ /

   Ibid, V. 4, p. 180 :

   Rasādiparatā yatra sa dhvanerviṣayo mataḥ /

result of *Ānandavardhana's* synthesis.

If, again, feeling is the prime value, why should suggestion be the invariable tachnique ? Does the theory dare to assert that the pictorial image cannot arouse emotion ? It cannot, because *Abhinavagupta* says that the suggested image is really an emotional image. Again, can the theory claim that only the suggested image has this power and not the directly expressed image ? It cannot. For one thing, there is all the weight of the luminous clarification of the emotive power of poetic naturalism. Secondly, even in the poetry of suggestion, does not the image acquire its emotive power because it is an objective correlative, and not because it has been suggested instead of directly expressed ? If suggestion, as such, is the principle of evoking emotion, all suggested imagery would be invariably emotive or, in other words, every suggestive poetry would invariably be genuine poetry. Success, then, would stand guaranteed for any poet in this field as it would be impossible for him to write bad poetry, if only he had the sense to resort to the technique of suggestion !

APPENDIX I

The symbolist movement took its roots in western poetry in the last quarter of the 19th century. Its exponents were Baudelairé, Paul Valéry, Mallarmé, Rainer Maria Rilke, Stefan George and Alexander Blok. In the second wave, when Imagism made its appearance, there came three Englishmen : T.E. Hulme, F.S. Flint and Richard Aldington, and three Americans : Ezra Pound, H.D. (Hilda Dolittle) and Amy Lowell. Among the most modern protagonists are W.B. Yeats, T.S. Eliot, Auden, Spencer and Lewis.

Baudelairé had a keen sense for neopsychology and had much faith in symbols on account of their virtue of purging the experience of its terrestrial quality and giving it a transcendental tone. Valéry felt that the chief task of symbolism was to take back from music what poets had lost to it. He also thought that whenever people talked of philosophy in poetry there was a case of their having been uneasily wedded. He gave supreme importance to words and their rhythm because in his opinion it was they who provided the images and evoked the most appropriate associations.

Mallarmé was most influential among the pioneers. He gave foremost value to the condensation of images in poetry. To him, the machinery of similes and comparisons stood obsolete and there was need for the identification of things with objects. Poetry should not be informative alone but suggestive and evocative as well. It should not name things but create their atmosphere. Thus to add mystery to poetry by suggestion was a noble ideal. Mallarmé certainly created a new mysticism of art. He expressed it disjointedly in words of Heraclitean darkness and power. But he was not merely content to suggest. He, like Valéry, had a profound faith in the musical effects in poetry. He thought poetry was an inevitable part of music and believed that one was almost analogous to the other. Poetry, to him, was a dream, a music of the spheres, a harmony audible to the spiritual ear. The unheard song and the silent word had a glory about them which he tried to convey to others. They also symbolised the poetic ecstasy and had much meaning for him.

Rilke, on the contrary, purported to attempt a harmonisation between two different kinds of poetry which spring from the fulness born of living in the imagination and yielding to every impression which itself in turn comes from the eager quest for sensations. Stefan George held that the worth of poetry is decided not by the meaning but by form. According to him, the essence of poetry is like that of a dream. A very deep insight of the poet or an equally profound impression upon him might be reflected in a poem but they are no guarantee for its goodness unless both are transposed into a sort of music composed of joy and tranquillity. That explains why every poem is something unreal. Beauty is not at the beginning nor at the end; it is just the climax. The true poetic art is that which breathes new life into a poem, partly wakeful and partly sleepy. George wished to bridge the gulf between art and reality. Blok, on the other hand, with his mystical temperament came more and more to find symbolical importance in things and to interpret ordinary happenings as instances of mysterious divine laws. Hulme noted that the importance of similisation in poetry is foremost because there the denotative or direct sense is not so significant as the indicative or the suggestive. If the expression in a poem is simple and commonplace, it loses the desirable effect. Therefore ideas of similitude are indispensable there, otherwise we would have no sentiment in it, no poetic effect, no originality. We may also point out in this connection that Flint is generally known as the precursor of imagism in western poetry. In his opinion, the concretisation of things or ideas which is the life of poetry, is easily manageable within the limits of a small poem like a lyric or a sonnet. In order to give a concrete shape to ideas he thought that the use of such appropriate words as are capable of doing it, is imperative.

The last two poets are very important from the point of view of the development of imagist ideas, as intellectual impulse actually came from the former, while the latter contributed to the technical teaching. But it was Ezra Pound who gave a new definition to image and a new direction to the movement. In this he was surely influenced by the views of Jacob Epstein and Wyndham Lewis who were pioneers of the vorticist movement, but he also influenced such people as Yeats and Eliot. First, he defined an image as that which presents an intellectual and emotional complex in an instant of time. He used the word 'complex' rather in the technical sense employed by such neopsychologists as Hart. Subsequently, he changed his definition and replaced the word 'complex' by 'vortex' or 'clusters' consisting of fused ideas and endowed with energy. Satirising the word 'energy', J. Isaacs wrote that had Pound not lost interest in that exposition of 'image', it would surely have become an atom bomb one day. It is interesting to note here that the vorticists had named their journal 'Blast' !

Yeats held that barring story-telling or portraiture, all art including poetry-writing is symbolic and at the same time purposive and that its purpose is identical with that of the medieval talisman made up of complex colour and form, a part of the divine essence, as it were. In this connection he makes a distinction between two kinds of symbolism : symbolism of sounds and symbolism of ideas. Under the first head he visualises among all sounds, colours, and forms of poetry a beautiful and musical relation, independently and together, making one unit each and because of preordained energies and long associations, evoking one emotion out of many whom he calls the foot-steps of certain disembodied powers over our hearts. Under the second head he speaks of the intellectual symbols that evoke ideas either singly or, those mixed with emotions and eked in respect of pure ideas, more visibly through the mind but in regard to emotions, more invisibly beyond the threshold of sleep, that is, in dreams. As a matter of fact, Yeats, through symbolism found a way to create an extremely lively and concrete poetry about himself. He worked hard to rid his verse of all vagueness and looseness. Thus what he lost in mystery, he gained in power.

According to Eliot, a symbol carries both sensation and thought. Thus the idea embodied in an imagist symbol results from synthesising presentation of fact and representation of thought. True, a word imparts the knowledge of a particular thing, but in it is also ingrained its concept attributed by the user. Naturally, one side of it is imagist and the other symbolist, always balancing each other. Among the various types of images, Auden is very fond of the functional image and there he succeeds too, to a great extent, not because he is a didactic poet able through it to press home his moral but because he has grasp on a wide contemporary situation and has an insight into its patterns which enable him to create powerful themes capable of vivifying and relating his images. Lewis, on the contrary, has breathed a new life into the idea of symbolist imagism when it was sinking into an obsolete form. With Freud and Dr. Jung, he has brought it to the plane of the unconscious and subjected it to psycho-analysis. We are not going to speak more of him because while dealing with *Arthacitra* and the impact of the modern concept of the collective unconscious, we incorporated and utilised his poetic credo.

The French imagist movement chiefly started between 1860 and 1890 as a result of the reactions of naturalism and as second wave of romanticism. It raised with thundering voice the question of poetic expression and the innateness of factual realisation which influenced not only the whole bulk of European but also American literature. This imagist movement is taken to be the re-exposition of the field of poetry. In the manifesto of 1913 (3rd edition), musical clauses were to take the place of metronymic verses. In 1908 Mr. Hulme established one poets' club and edited a paper where one of his poem entitled 'Autumn' was published which was later adjudged as the first important imagist poem. Here for moon we find the image 'red-faced farmer' and the stars were 'with white faces like town children.'

Another member of the club, Edward Storev, in a collection of poems entitled 'Mirrors of Illusion' published one that very year entitled 'Image' consisting of only three lines :

Forsaken lovers,
Burning to a chaste white moon,
Upon strange pyres of loneliness and draught.

Actually, there would not have been any revolution in poetry had this poem not been written after the French symbolist poetry because in Rimbaud's 'The sleeper in the valley' there is greater and more powerful imagery : 'The whole valley bubbled with sunbeams like a bear-glass.' But the American soil didn't prove congenial to the imagist movement and so it couldn't last there long with meagre resources, though it had by then given flow to the general stream of creativeness. Thus Karl Sandberg's famous poem 'Letters to Dead Imagists' sums up conclusion of this era.

In a special number of 'The Egoist', Flint, one of the champions of Hulme, published a brief resumè of the activities of the movement where he admitted on his group the clear influence of French symbolist poetry. According to J.M. Brinin, this influence brought in the field of poetry the effect of purgation. Between 1912 and 1922 thousands of imagist poems were published in collections. During this time, Pound was the most important figure and his association with several countries like Ireland, England, France and Italy increased the extent of his influence outside America to European continent.

He went to Ireland for lessons from Yeats but instead, in a way, taught the latter. The shadow of his influence on Eliot was even larger and most of his poetic concepts originated in the latter's imagist ideas. The new generation of Auden-Spencer-Lewis owes much debt to the generation of Yeats-Pound-Eliot in the field of rhetorics and literary principles, and the rise of imagist symbol in their poetry is ample proof of the fact that we get in their works the aggregate consciousness of symbolism and imagism.

SELECT BIBLIOGRAPHY

A : SANSKRIT

1. Atharvavedasaṁhitā.
2. Aitareya Brāhmaṇa.
3. Alaṁkāraratnākara : Śobhākaramitra.
4. Alaṁkārasarvasva (with "Vimarśiṇī" of Jayaratha) : Ruyyaka.
5. Alaṁkāraśekhara : Keśavamiśra.
6. Alaṁkārakaustubha : Kavikarṇapūra.
7. Amarakośa.
8. Bhāgavatapurāṇa.
9. Candrāloka : Jayadeva.
10. Citramīmāṁsā (with "Khaṇḍana" of Jagannātha) : Appaya Dīkṣita.
11. Dhvanyāloka (with "Locana" of Abhinavagupta and "Bālapriyā" comm.) : Ānandavardhana.
12. Ekāvalī : Vidyādhara.
13. Hayagrīvavadha.
14. Handbook to the Study of Ṛgveda with Sāyaṇa's Preface.
15. Īśopaniṣad.
16. Kāmasūtra : Vātsyāyana.
17. Kuṭṭanīmata : Dāmodaragupta.
18. Kāvyādarśa (with "Mālinya-prońchanī" of Premacandra) : Daṇḍin.
19. Kāvyālaṁkāra : Bhāmaha.
20. Kāvyālaṃkārasārasaṁgraha : Udbhaṭa.
21. Kāvyālaṃkāra : Rudraṭa.
22. Kāvyālaṁkārasūtravṛtti : Vāmana.
23. Kāvyānuśāsana : Hemacandra.

24. Kāvyaprakāśa (with "Udyota" of Nāgeśa Bhaṭṭa, "Pradīpa" of Govinda Ṭhakkura and the "Prabhā" of Baidyanātha Tatsat) : Mammaṭa.
25. Kuvalayānanda (with "Rasikarañjanī" of Gaṅgādhara Vājapeyin and "Alaṁkāracandrikā" of Vaidyanātha Tatsat) : Dīkṣita.
26. Kāvyamīmāṁsā : Rājaśekhara.
27. Kumārasambhava : Kālidāsa.
28. Kādambarī : Bāṇa.
29. Kīcakavadha.
30. Mānasollāsa.
31. Meghadūta : Kālidāsa.
32. Mahābhārata : Vyāsa.
33. Muṇḍakopaniṣad.
34. Nirukta and Nighaṇṭu : Yāska.
35. Naiṣadhīyacarita : Śrī Harṣa.
36. Pāñcarātra.
37. Pratāparudrīyayaśobhūṣaṇa : Vidyānātha.
38. Ṛgvedasaṁhitā.
39. Rāmāyaṇa : Vālmīki.
40. Rasagaṅgādhara : Jagannātha.
41. Raghuvaṁśa : Kālidāsa.
42. Sāhityadarpaṇa (with "Locana" and "Vijñapriyā" comm) : Viśvanātha.
43. Sarasvatīkaṇṭhābharaṇa : Bhoja.
44. Śṛṅgāraprakāśa : Bhoja.
45. Sammohanatantra.
46. Subhāṣitaratnabhāṇḍāgāra (Anthology).
47. Śārṅgadharapaddhati (do).
48. Sūktimuktāvalī (do).
49. Śiśupālavadha : Māgha.
50. Śabdakalpadruma (Lexicon).
51. Sahṛdaya (Journal).
52. Viṣṇudharmottarapurāṇa.
53. Vākyapadīya : Bhartṛhari.
54. Vakroktijīvita : Kuntaka.
55. Vṛttivārttika : Appaya Dīkṣita.
56. Vācaspatyam (Lexicon).

B: *ENGLISH*

1. An Exposition of the Citramīmāṁsā of Appaya Dīkṣita and its Appraisal of Jagannātha's Criticism : Dr. M. Jhā.
2. Aesthetic : Croce.
3. A Call to Order : Cocteau.
4. An Enquiry into Meaning and Truth : Russel.
5. A Defence of Poetry : Shelley.
6. A History of Indian Literature, Vol. I : Winternitz.
7. Crisis in Poetry : Mallarmé.
8. Countries of the Mind : Middleton Murry.
9. Commonsense About Poetry : Strong.
10. Collected Essays in Literary Criticism : Read.
11. Distance as an Aesthetic Principle (Article) : Bullough.
12. Early Essays : What is Poetry ? : Mill.
13. Film Sense : Eisenstein.
14. History of Sanskrit Poetics : P. V. Kāṇe.
15. Kāvya-Prakāśa of Mammaṭa : Eng. Tr. by Dr. Gaṅgānātha Jhā.
16. Letter to Louise Colet : Flaubert.
17. Lettres a Quelques-uns : Valéry.
18. Modern Man in Search of a Soul : Jung.
19. Oeuvres Complètes : Baudelaire.
20. Oeuvres Complètes : Mallarmé.
21. Oeuvres, vol. I : Valéry.
22. Poetic Process : Whalley.
23. Positions et Propositions vol. I : Claudel.
24. Psychical Distance (Article) : Bullough.
25. Rhetoric and Composition I : Bain.
26. Reveries : Over Childhood and Youth : Yeats.
27. Symbolism : Its Meaning and Effect : Whitehead.
28. Shakespeare's Imagery and What it tells us : Spurgeon.
29. Senses and Sensibility in Modern Poetry : William Van O' Corner.
30. Shelley's Literary and Philosophical Criticisms : Shawcross.
31. Sanskrit-English Dictionary : Monier-Williams.
32. Sanskrit Poetics : Kriṣṇa Caitanya.
33. The Heritage of Symbolism : Bowra.

34. The Music of Poetry : Eliot.
35. The Symbol of the Rose (Article) : Raine.
36. The Poetic Image : Lewis.
37. The Poetic Mind : Prescott.
38. The Principles of Literary Criticism : Richards.
39. Vie de Mallarmé : Mondor.
40. Vedic Index of Names and Subjects vol. II : Macdonell.
41. Words, Words (Article) : Montague.

C : *HINDI*

1. Ādhunika Hindī Kāvya Mé Citravidhāna : Dr. R. Y. Singh.
2. Bhāratīya Sāhityaśāstra : Baldeva Upādhyāya.
3. Hindī Sāhitya Mé Kāvyarūpōn Ké Prayoga : Dr. S. D. Avatare.
4. Kūṭakāvya : Eka Adhyayana : Dr. R. Sharmā.
5. Kāvya aur Kalpanā : R. K. Pāṇḍey.
6. Kāvya Mé Abhivyañjanāvāda : L. N. Sudhānsu.
7. Kāśī Nāgarī Pracāriṇī Patrikā (Journal).

APPENDIX II

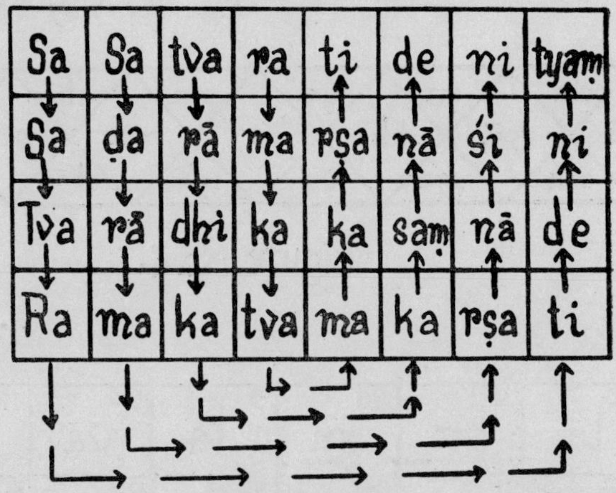

Figure No.1.

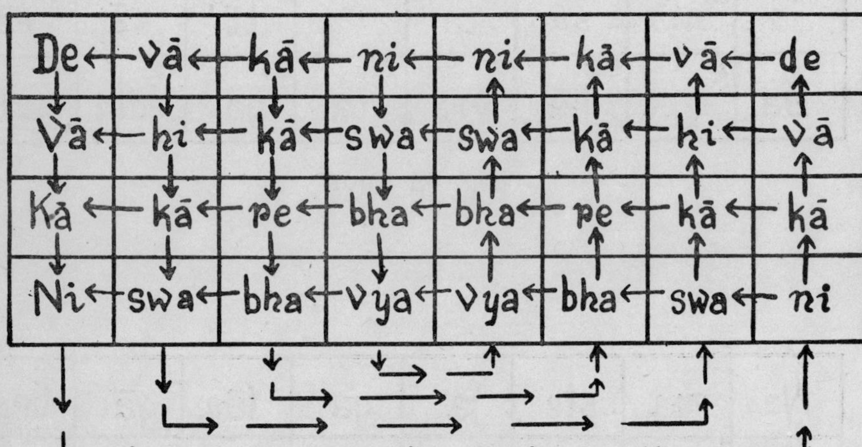

Figure No.2.

Figure No.3.

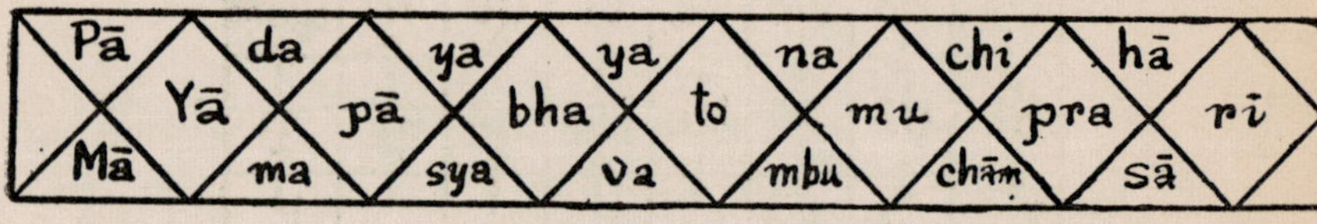

Figure No. 4.

1 Bā	30 lā	9 su	20 kā	3 la	24 vā	11 lā	26 kā
16 kāṃ	19 ti	2 lā	29 la	10 ka	27 lā	4 li	23 tā
31 Sa	8 swā	17 su	14 ta	21 ṿa	6 tī	25 sā	12 rā
18 Da	15 rpi	32 kā	7 vra	28 ta	13 ga	22 rdhi	5 ta

Figure No. 5.

Na	ma	ste	ja	ga	tāṃ	gā	tra
Sa	dā	na	ṿa	ku	la	kṣa	ya
Sa	ma	ste	ja	sa	tāṃ	nā	tra
Mu	dā	ma	va	na	la	kṣa	ya

Figure No. 6.

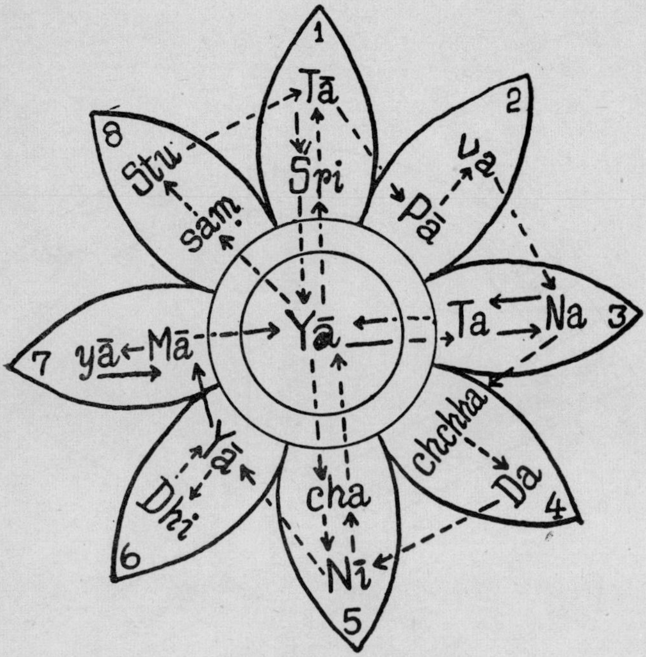

Figure No.7.

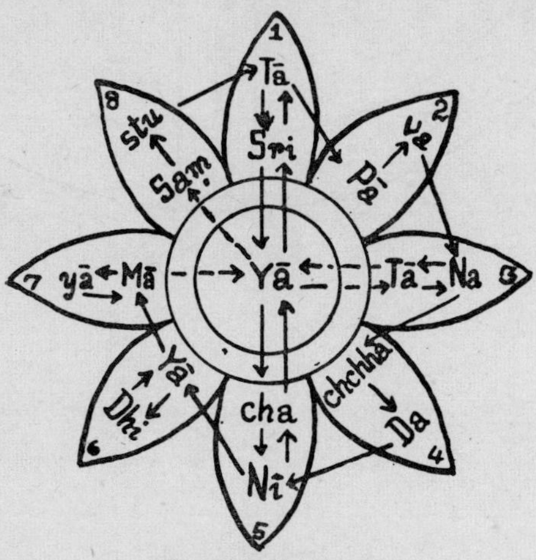

Figure No.8.

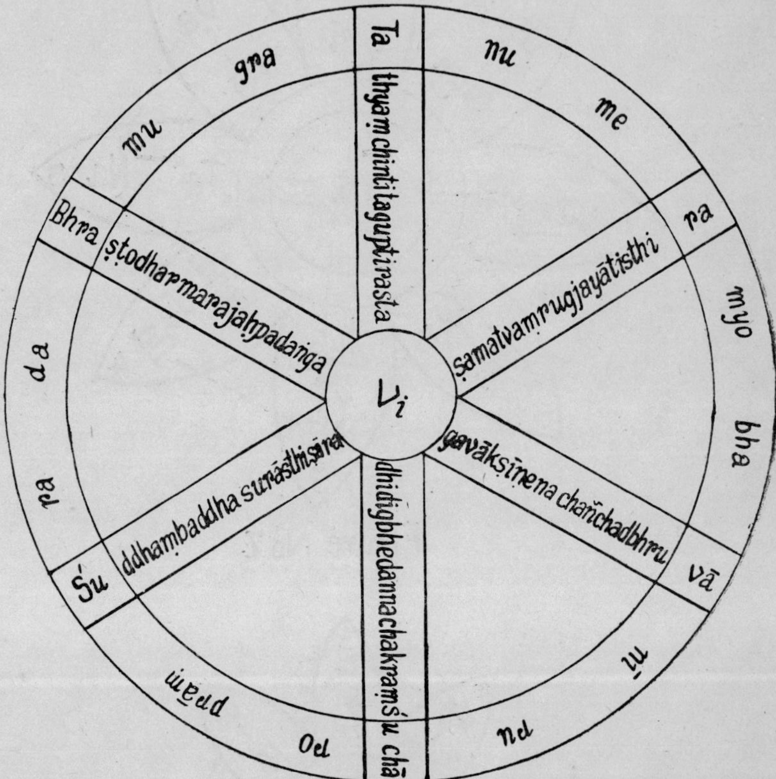
Ta
thyaṃchintitaguptinasta
mu
me
ra
myo
bha
vā
ni
na
chā
Bhra
ṣṭodharmarajaḥpadaṅga
gra
mu
da
ra
Śu
ddhaṃbaddha surāsthiṣira
ṣamatvaṃrugjayātisthi
gavākṣiṇena chañchadbhru
dhitigbhedamnachakraṃśu
Vi

Figure No.9.

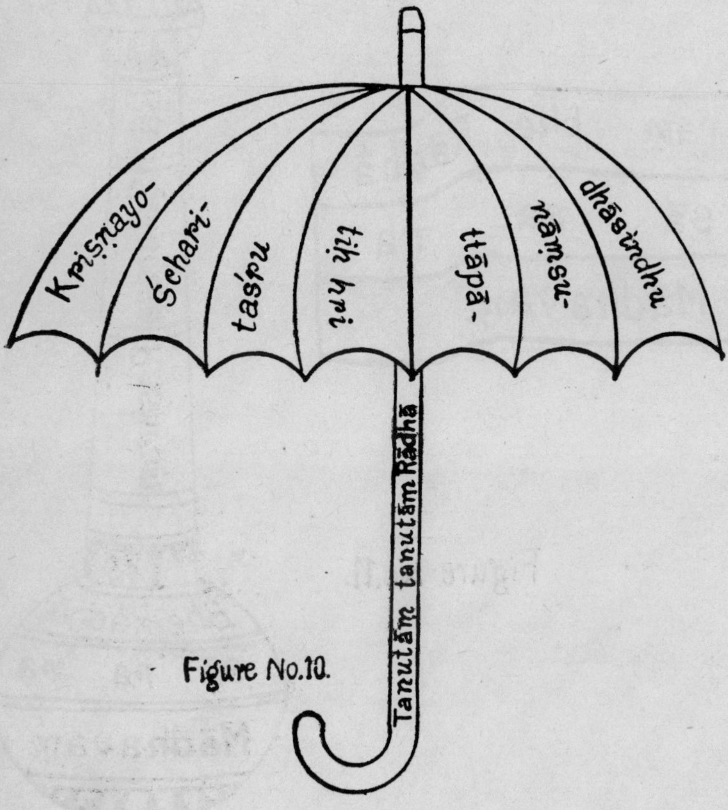
Krisṇayo-
Śchari-
taśpu
tih hri
ttāpā-
nāṃsu-
dhāsindhu
Tanutām tanutām Rādhā

Figure No.10.

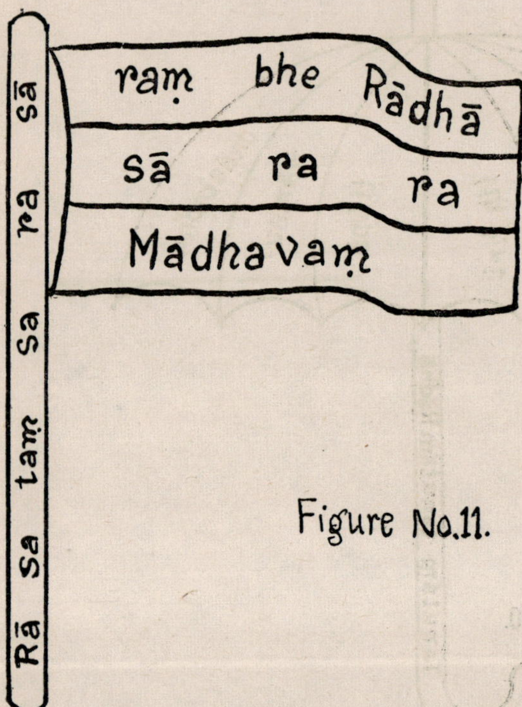

Figure No.11.

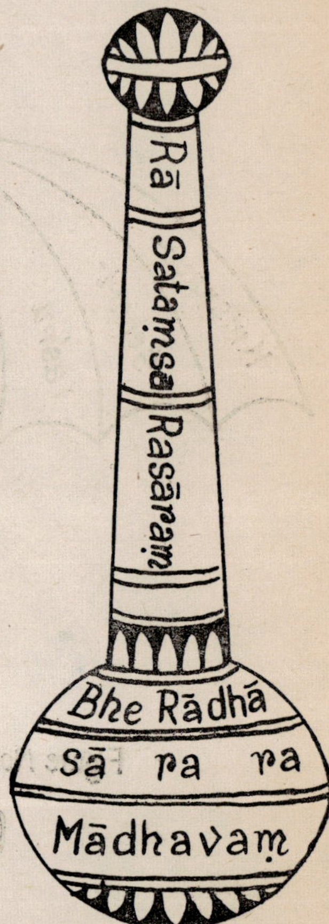

Figure No.12.

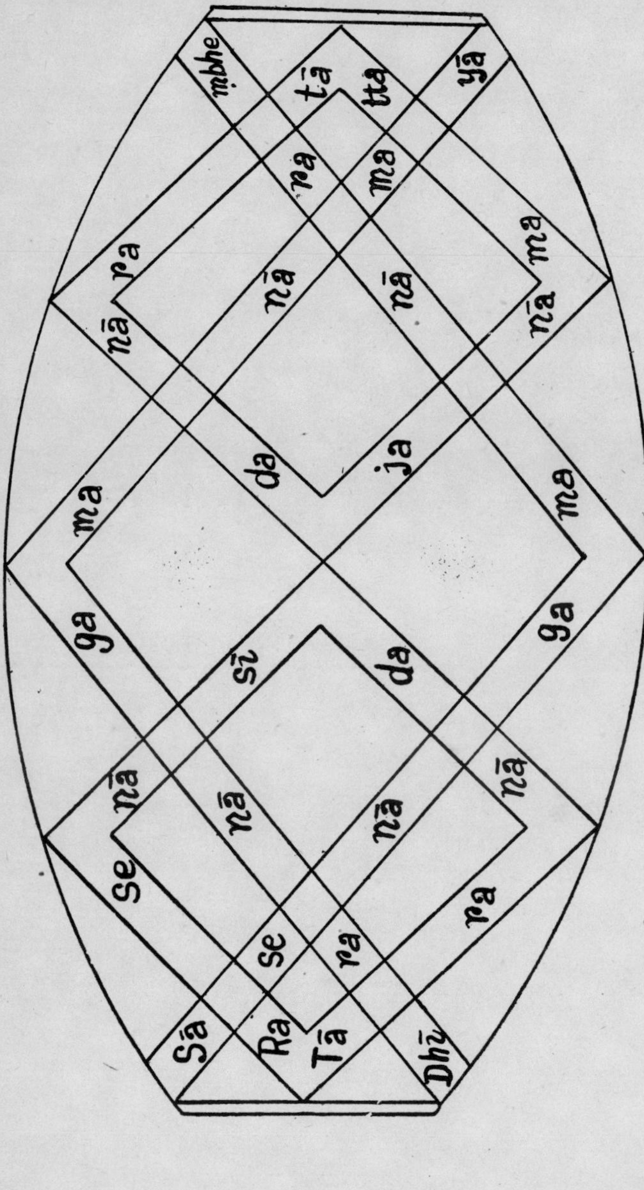
mbhe
tā
ttā
yā
ra
ra
ma
ma
ra
nā
nā
nā
nā
ma
da
ja
ma
ga
sī
da
ga
nā
nā
nā
nā
se
se
ra
ra
Sā
Ra
Tā
Dhī

Figure No.13.

INDEX

I VERSES QUOTED AS ILLUSTRATIONS

(Numbers refer to pages)

II. BOOKS REFERRED ON CITRAKĀVYA

III. NAMES AND TERMS OCCURRING IN THIS WORK

ERRATA

Page No.	*Para No.*	*F.N. No.*	*Line No.*	*Incorrect Form*	*Correct Form*
2	1	—	10	compiled the whole	compiled in the whole
5	2	—	7	decide which	decide as to which
8	—	1	2	Vāmaśchāyaṁ	Vāmaścāyaṁ
35	1	—	9	chekokticcāyā	chekokticchāyā
,,	—	11	—	Fn.No.11.p. 35	Fn. No. 9 above
39	1	—	6	dees	does
48	3	—	8	jewelery	jewellery
,,	,,	—	9	lips	hips
,,	—	2	1	mudāramaṇī-	mudāramaṇi-
,,		2	1	bhūṣaṇāḥ	bhūṣaṇāḥ
52	1	—	9	laboun	baboon
55	2	—	6	root	foot
57	—	1	2	Tārnikā	Tāmikā
59	—	4	2	-rayanchanapiditani	-rayāñcanapīḍitāni
86	2	—	16	A Viṣṇu	A=Viṣṇu
87	2	—	7	Bhavāniśa-karomeśaṁ	Bhavāniśaṁ-karomeśaṁ
96	—	6	1	RV.10, 17-8	RV.10,117.8
97	2	—	12	on	one
99	—	3	Last	nopakara e	nopakaraṇe
102	—	1	—	DL:	D-L:
112	—	—	30	equipolence	equipollence
,,	—	3	—	KPIX,	KP^1,X,
114	—	4	1 (last)	hanicandanena	haricandanena
119	—	3	—	KP,3X	KP^3, X
120	1	—	4	attributes Vastu-prativastu-relation	beautiful Vastu-prativastu-relation

Page No.	*Para No.*	*FN. No.*	*Line No.*	*Incorrect Form*	*Correct Form*
122	2	—8		prominenly	prominently
129	—	3	1	Saṁdhyārajot-thitai....	Saṁdhyārāgot-thitai...
132	—	1	1	Veṇūbhūta..i	Veṇībhūta...
151	—	2	1	parichhedaḥ	paricchedaḥ
154	2	—	2	Śl ṣa..	Śleṣa...
166	1	—	18	familiarity ; is	familiarity is
181	2	—	12	This, the	This,